Contents

DISRUPTING RAPE CULTURE

Public space, sexuality and revolt

Alexandra Fanghanel

BRISTOL
UNIVERSITY
PRESS

This paperback edition first published in Great Britain in 2020 by

Policy Press, an imprint of
Bristol University Press
University of Bristol
1-9 Old Park Hill
Bristol
BS2 8BB
UK
t: +44 (0)117 954 5940
e: bup-info@bristol.ac.uk

Details of international sales and distribution partners are available at
policy.bristoluniversitypress.co.uk

© Bristol University Press 2020

British Library Cataloguing in Publication Data

A catalogue record for this book is available from the British Library

978-1-5292-0258-8 paperback
978-1-5292-0252-6 hardback
978-1-5292-0255-7 ePdf
978-1-5292-0254-0 ePub
978-1-5292-0256-4 Mobi

The right of Alexandra Fanghanel to be identified as author of this work has been asserted by
her in accordance with the Copyright, Designs and Patents Act 1988.

Cover design by blu inc, Bristol
Front cover image: stocksy
Bristol University Press and Policy Press use environmentally responsible
print partners
Printed and bound in Great Britain by CPI Group (UK) Ltd, Croydon,
CR0 4YY

For Olympia and Bertolt, without whose
disruptive bodies this book would have been
finished sooner. And with less bloodshed.

Acknowledgements

Although I wrote this book quite quickly (by necessity, in the end, rather than because of any particular aptitude for writing books), this project has been almost a decade in the making. It could not have been completed without the personal and professional support of an array of different folk who have accompanied me for some, or all, of the journey.

Thanks to my thesis supervisors, David Bell and Robert Vanderbeck, who helped me to start out with these ideas in 2007. Thanks are also due to the Peter Harris Trust, whose financial support enabled me to spend a semester writing when I should have been teaching. Similarly, Sandra Clarke and Darrick Jolliffe, at the University of Greenwich, allowed me the professional leeway to pursue this project in ways that have been both hands-off and supportive (just how I like it). Thanks also to my colleagues at the University of Greenwich, especially Michael Fiddler, whose intellectual curiosity and wit kept me good company. Thanks also to the helpful anonymous reviews I received on earlier drafts of this text, and the support of everyone at Policy Press and at Bristol University Press, in particular, my editor, Rebecca Tomlinson.

For helping me to write this book, I thank Eleanor Wilkinson, whose notorious cynicism and steely brilliance continues to inspire me and whose warm friendship has kept me entertained. Similarly, I thank my sworn enemy, Jason Lim, who read some of this and whose intellectual prowess and searching questions continue to provoke me. Thanks also to Phil Hubbard for providing helpful comments on, and charming mockery of, this text when it was in its nascent stages. Stacy Banwell, with whom I share my office at Greenwich, continues to be a glorious interlocutor on questions of gender and of rape culture. Many of the ideas in this book emerged from our creative conversations and plans for revolution: Likewise, Emma Milne, helpfully always on hand with too many bottles of wine, has been great intellectual company (especially for Chapter Two).

From my dark years in room C422 emerged one of the best gang of pals – and WhatsApp group – that I could have found at work.

Combined, Debbie Allnock, Sarah Bunt, Paul Carré, Ash McCormack, Seamus Murphy and the pirate Ax de Klerk proved striking intellectual sparring partners. Along with the rest of our Wine and Theory group, the heteroglossia of their contributions introduced me to different theoretical ideas, different ways of thinking and different ways of being a person. Their influence runs throughout many of the debates of this book.

I want to thank my best gals Natasha Dhumma and Ruth Jacob who, constants throughout the crises, have at times figuratively pushed me through my life when I was writing this book and was too overwhelmed to do even the smallest things myself. Brilliant feminists, brilliant booze hounds, general bad asses, it is without hyperbole that I say I could not have written this book without their help.

Thanks also to my family. In particular, Ossiane and David Fanghanel-Powles, who quite simply helped me – organising my life, looking after my kids, armed with really strong liquor that no one wants to drink and over-sized bottles of champagne that everybody does drink, they provided safe harbour when writing this book got too hard. Similarly, the first feminist I knew, my Maman, Joelle Fanghanel, who set me on this path, and whose achievements continue to inspire me.

It is obvious that this book could not have been written without the kind and honest contributions of the participants in all of the fieldwork I conducted. I am also indebted to the students of my first course, 'Sex and Crime' (class of 2017/18) at the University of Greenwich, who gave me such good feedback on these ideas.

Always on hand with entertaining anecdotes, esoteric knowledge and extraordinary spirit, I could not have done any of this without the support and searing critiques of the inimitable Ludovic Coupaye. A fantastic ally along this journey, Ludovic's thoughts, our paradigmatic differences, his intellectual support, his pragmatic support, his rigour, his disdain for late 20th-century French philosophy, and his comments on drafts of this book helped me to transform my project from an idea into a praxis that might be okay.

ONE

Causing trouble

Given the array of ways in which feminist criminologists, geographers, philosophers, and social scientists have addressed the experiences and politics of women's bodies in public space over the past quarter of a century, we might ask what there is left to say about women's embodied experiences of public space. Yet issues of social and spatial gendered justice have never been more pertinent in contemporary post-industrialist societies. As the material in this book will demonstrate, despite the fact that sexualised and gendered experiences of public spaces continue to be taken seriously in contemporary discourse, injustices and misogynies also continue to thrive. It is imperative, therefore, that critical analyses of the way women's bodies appear in public spaces remain at the forefront of feminist criminological analysis of social and spatial justice. This book marks an intervention in existing debates about women's bodies, public space and rape culture in order to think through ways in which rape culture – the normalisation of violence against women – might be contested. Transforming rape culture is not easy; the problems outlined in this book cannot be fixed by policy changes or legal reform (alone). They necessitate an overhaul in the way in which bodies think and act in public spaces, including the exclusions that we are all – in part – complicit in enacting. In order to do so, we must consider how these bodies disrupt public space and what can they do to transform it.

Penetrated spaces

In 2012, one unremarkable April morning in London, the following scene unfolds: on his hands and knees, a white man in a white office shirt, dark suit trousers and black shoes and socks wears around his neck a collar that is attached to a pink dog lead. His companion,

1

a white woman, stands a little in front of him. She is also wearing formal-looking office work clothes. Her long dark hair is tied behind her in a plait. She carries what appears to be a cup of coffee in her right hand. The handle of her purple handbag rests on her forearm. In her left hand, she holds the end of the dog lead. Together they stroll, apparently leisurely, through the morning rush hour; the man crawls along the pavement on his hands and knees, and the woman walks upright, a few paces ahead of him. Farringdon, where this scene takes place, is a hub of creative industry, of office workspace, of lively nightlife, of gentrification, and at this time of day, of commuters travelling to the offices, shops, and cafes that saturate this area. But for their usual mode of perambulating, this couple, too, look like they might also be on their way to work.

The couple traversed some of the oldest parts of the capital: Fleet Street, historically the seat of the press in England, and still the site of different legal institutions (the Royal Courts of Justice, the Inns of Court, legal practices) to St Paul's Cathedral, a key London landmark and centre of the Anglican church in the City, up towards the ancient markets and trading areas of Farringdon, and past the seat of financial power in the country, the Bank of England. These places represent historic monoliths of state power. Part of the reason why this scene is so extraordinary was because of the way it disrupts the conventional ways in which public space – here, Farringdon in the centre of London – is understood, and how meanings and knowledges are created in these spaces.

Penetrating this time-space, in this fashion, the pair inevitably attracts the attention of passers-by. Pretty soon, several pictures of the pair appear online. Videos and tweets follow. In the hours and days after the event, at least 40 different newspaper articles will be written about the pair in publications from around the world. The scene is reported on as far away as India, Ireland, Saudi Arabia and the United States of America. Intrigue about this otherwise 'normal' looking couple is rife; people are not supposed to be walking about on their hands and knees on the asphalt. What these two are doing is disconcerting. It is funny. It is disgusting. So why are they doing it? Is this a dare? A kinky game? A publicity stunt? An 11-second video clip showing the two crossing Farringdon Road next to a building site was watched tens of thousands of times online.[1] Viewers across the globe looked on at this carnivalesque performance in horrified, bemused wonder.

In this book, I interrogate disruptions like this in order to better reveal the relationship between public space, disruptive bodies and social, spatial justice in the context of rape culture. The public spaces

I am talking about here are situated in the Global North and include streets, car parks, public transport services, green spaces, bars, clubs, shopping malls and online spaces. Not all of these sites are strictly public (from the Latin *publicus*, meaning 'pertaining to the people'); many are subject to formal and informal sanctions about who may or may not use them, when, how, and so on – but the focus on space that is outside the home, and thus subject to particular discourses, practices or regulations associated with the public sphere, helps us to understand how bodies that do not fit in, do not fit in.

Following Henri Lefebvre's (1996 [1968]) argument about the right to the city, here, the notion of social and spatial justice is understood as a forging of a mode of living outside of the constraints of exclusions and marginalisations that compose public space. The social and spatial forms of justice that I invoke in this book are inherently political categories. What counts as justice or as injustice is always partial, often problematic and, for Lefebvre (1996 [1968]), Edward Soja (2009) and others, rooted within the post-industrialist, liberal imaginary of democracy, of community, and of rights discourses. For Lefebvre (1996 [1968]), the right to the city involves the right to participate in, and the right to appropriate, public space. Fostering this form of justice would be made possible, in part, by restructuring dynamics of power from the State[2] to the people (Purcell, 2002: 102). Of course, as we will see, fostering social and spatial justice is not a simple case of understanding the 'bad State' against the 'benevolent People'. Discourses of belong, not-belong, being in- and out-of-place are enacted by individuals in public space as much as they are by larger-scale institutions (Beckett and Herbert, 2008). The boundaries between belonging and exclusion are premised on modes of regulating space that prefer certain forms of living over others, and that rely on this marginalisation for these preferences to cement, or to crystallise (Deleuze and Guattari, 2004a [1980]).

If social justice is forged through the institutions and apparatus of the State, and in intersubjective moments of connection between bodies, then spatial justice becomes an emplaced way in which this is manifest. Fostering spatial justice would entail 'equitable distribution of socially valuable resources' (Soja, 2009: 2). The valuable resources at stake here would be the right to occupy public space, and to not suffer from the politics of spatial exclusion which, as I have noted elsewhere, are laced with racist, classist, (hetero)sexist sentiments (Fanghanel, 2014). Whether implicit or explicit, exclusion and marginalisation from place marks the body as 'like' or 'other'. Despite the inherently capitalistic framing of Soja's proposition (what counts as valuable? What are the implications of justice being a 'resource'?), this framing invites us to begin to consider the hidden exclusions that compose how public space is composed and understood. In the context of rape culture, this shows us how certain time-spaces become places that normalise sexual violence against women in public.

Some of this is illustrated in an instructive text that examines 'race' and gender in the British capital. Nirmal Puwar's (2004) description of the coding of public space around the Houses of Parliament, Trafalgar Square, Whitehall, and other seats of State administrative power in the UK outlines how spatial justice emerges, how place acquires meaning and how bodies come to belong, or not, here. Her analysis illustrates how public spaces that might at first appear neutral are laced with masculinist, ethnocentric – we might add heterocentric and ableist – codes that casts the white, middle-class, cisgender, male body as the 'consecrated somatic norm' against which all bodies are measured (Puwar, 2004: 3).

Puwar's work examines how bodies that do not fit this somatic norm are cast as out-of-place – 'trespassers', 'space invaders' – whose out-of-place-ness marks that body as 'other'. She predominantly examines this in the context of sites of public politics and the public sphere, even if, as her analysis demonstrates, these are not places (bars, elevators, and the robing rooms of the House of Commons) that many members of the public ever have access to. Nonetheless, her analysis of these places helps us to understand similarly codified places, including, for instance, where this dog-walking scene took place. Codification suggests a system of signals that emerge at a socio-cultural level to designate ways in which, for instance, somatic norms are 'consecrated' and others are denigrated. A code is also the translation of a signal in order to facilitate the transmission of a message. Codes are thus organisational, ordering and normative. Here, the codes that compose public space, such as the streets of Farringdon or of Whitehall, are imbued with a historicity rooted within a colonial past, within a socio-cultural context that normalises heterosexuality, masculinity, able-bodiedness and whiteness. And it is these codes that striate space in order to attempt to produce precise, orderly subjectivities. This coding and subjectification has the effect of normalising certain modes of thought and of practice and of installing dominant modes of being and thinking in social life. The implications of this normalisation for the fostering of social injustice must not be underestimated.

If public space is coded in these ways, for Gilles Deleuze and Felix Guattari (2004a [1980]: 498), this is part of the practice of the State's attempts to transform uncoded flows into an organisation that produces subjectification. According to Deleuze and Guattari, part of the way in which this emerges is through the interplay between smooth and striated space. Striated space describes homogenised, ordered, territorialised space. As a capitalist tool, striated space is produced by the State to organise desire into productive practices in the service of itself. Smooth space is that which occurs beyond the State. Full of potentiality, of intensities, of eventfulness, smooth space is potentially limitless and harbours the capacity for all sorts of affects and events to emerge. Smooth space also has the potential to undo the organisation of striated space through deterritorialising lines of flight. The State, in turn, attempts to undo this deterritorialisation through reterritorialisations. The organisation of work, or of capital, is one way through which reterritorialisations emerge; the making-the-same – homogenising – of the meaning of space is another (2004a [1980]: 538-9). The city – like the one where this dog-walking scene occurred – is, according to Deleuze and Guattari, striated space *par excellence* (2004a, [1980]: 531). It is so tightly coded that it 'reimparts' or reappropriates smooth space against the potential counterattacks of deterritorialisations. Although often expressed oppositionally, striated and smooth spaces compose each other (2004a [1980]: 537). Smooth space, unlike striated space, is not absolute (2004a [1980]: 422) but is composed of haeccities and events. It cannot be measured, or plotted, or otherwise determined (2004a [1980]: 528). It is whence lines of flight – or of potentiality and transformation – emerge. Although the smooth and the striated are interconnected, they are also distinct. The intangible, affective, eventful deterritorialising capacity of the smooth has a potentiality to undo the organisation of the striated as much as it has the possibility to be recaptured by it.

Given this, what is going on in this dog-walking scene? Does this intervention in public space mark a deterritorialisation? Public speculation about this scene demonstrates how it took on a spectacular form. Most of the public who observed it thought that it was a publicity stunt rather than any other form of intervention (not performance art, not the consequence of a dare, not a game between friends). This notwithstanding, the fervent audience reactions to the pair demonstrated that this penetration did cause some trouble to neatly striated space. Part of the reason for this excitement was because of how burlesque and grotesque this seemed: a man crawling on the filthy concrete led on a leash by a woman. How very funny, and very abject!

One of the first things we note about the scene is the way in which it evokes a sexualised aesthetic. Kinky practices, which are associated with role-play scenes not unlike the dog-walking scene we witness here, are also associated with sexual practices that are, commonly, rooted within the private, personal realm (Rubin, 1984). Although in some contexts kinky practices have become more mainstream (Weiss, 2006), they are the expressions of private sexual desires and practices, occurring behind closed doors in the cloisters of people's homes, their bedrooms and their imaginations. They are not commonly associated with that which is public. So when a couple, such as this pair, penetrate public space in order to perform this walk – with its overtones of sexual power play – the intervention troubles the public/ private divide of this strictly coded and striated time-space.

Maintaining the distinction between the public and the private is also a well-recognised device used to control women's bodies and to striate and organise public space. Certainly, the distinction between the public and the private is absolutely a contingent one; one can only be understood through reference to its opposite (Puwar, 2004). The female body has historically been associated with that which is private, hidden from view, and unpolitical (Pateman, 1995). Sexual practice – which is also commonly cognate with the private sphere – can thus be situated with the feminine, the internal and the occluded. The association of the feminine with the private is part of what composes rape culture in contemporary social life; here, this association with the feminine serves to demonstrate how far the disruption of the public with the private can become political. If this dog-walking scene were taking place in a bedroom, a garden or even a particular club or cafe, it would not pose the same challenge to the way public space is coded and striated, if indeed, it posed any at all. The penetration of this dog-walking performance into public space evokes the trouble that disruptive bodies can cause for the way that public spaces are striated.

A second aspect of this scene that was widely noted in the press and in commentary on social media was the 'normal-ness' of the clothing and accoutrements that the couple were wearing, and its carnivalesque disjuncture with what they were doing. Dressed in their office clothes, occupying the office commuter space as they did, early in the morning, during people's commute to work, the decision to intervene in this space, in this way, at this time, becomes a deliberate act to trouble how space is striated. Indeed, a common observer reaction was to comment on how ordinary, or 'nonchalant' (Hooton, 2014), the couple seemed. Many press publications noted that the man-as-dog was 'smartly dressed' (Robson, 2014); others commented on how the pair seemed to be walking as if it was the most normal thing to do. The penetration of this extraordinary act, from otherwise ordinary-looking business people, perturbs the way in which this space is understood, the meaning it has, and the way it is coded. The very 'normal-ness' of their appearance suddenly becomes outrageous or profane (Douglas, 1992). Given the clothing they were wearing and their ethnocentrically normative mien, the surprise that was elicited about how 'normal' they otherwise seemed tangibly illustrates how this public space is striated along classed, 'raced', capitalistic lines.

How far does trouble transform what this public space actually comes to mean? A third aspect of this intervention worth considering is the laughter that it elicited. Some onlookers expressed disgust and malaise at the scene they were witnessing, but many more reacted to the scene with mirth. Mocking the couple, sarcastic comments about gender relations, about men's rights, about the streets of London, appeared alongside other speculation about which publicity company had organised this intervention. So, what are the implications of this mockery? Laughter, Mikhael Bakhtin (1984: 11-12) suggests in the context of the carnival, can be understood as 'festive', that is to say, shared – it is the 'laughter of all the people', it is universal, 'directed at all and everyone', and it is 'ambivalent', joyful. But it is also 'derisory'. The laughter joins people together. Those who are laughing, those at whom they are laughing, are all laughing as part of belonging to the same moment. Laughter is also an expression of the uncanny, uneasy grotesque or abject (Russo, 1995). In this scene we are not yet sure how far the 'dog walkers' are also laughing at those who are laughing at them, but the expression of laughter here, including the ambivalent laughter, highlights how the space in which this performance is taking place has been transformed by the intervention. Bakhtin's (1984: 10) better-known statement about the phenomenon of carnival is that it marks a temporary rendering asunder of inequalities, hierarchies and ranks. During a period of carnival, carnival is all that there is. Carnival is subject to its own laws, freedoms and 'spirit' (1984: 7). Most importantly, because carnival is a sensuous thing, it is inherently corporeal. Bakhtin's work on the carnivalesque is based on his analysis of 'grotesque realism' in renaissance European literature, in particular, the work of François Rabelais. The series of books by Rabelais that Bakhtin works from, about the giant Gargantua and his son Pantagruel, are so-named for the former's insatiable appetite and the latter's capacity to provoke insatiable thirst in others. Eating, drinking, defecating, copulating, 'fertility, growth and a brimming-over abundance' (1984: 19), are bodily practices. Bakhtin's analysis centralises the body as a locus around which transformation, however temporary, occurs, 'reinforc[ing] social order by allowing its temporary subversion' (Russo, 1995: 58; see also Jenks, 2003; Bruner, 2005: 138).

For our purposes, this dog-walking remains intertwined with the State apparatus that it grotesquely seems to subvert. The dog-walking is certainly supposed to degrade the male 'dog'; it is debasing to crawl along the ground and to make contact with the asphalt. But it is not *only* debasing, as the earth is also fruitful, it is whence new life emerges. Carnivalesque degradation generates new forms of living even as it reinforces old ones. We might understand carnivalesque practice like this as a forging of smooth space and an example of the way that smooth and striated space interact with each other. We might say that the dog and his walker are deterritorialising forces, that through them emerges a transformation. Here, the dog-walking inverts traditional gender roles by displaying a man in a position subservient to the woman who is leading him, and it brings sexualised practice into ostensibly non-sexualised space (the morning commute to work). Yet its capacity, or not, to cause trouble is also ethnically and economically marked. These disruptive bodies are white bodies that penetrate already white space. If the man on the end of the leash had not been white, if the woman walking him had not been, if they had swapped places, if they had not been wearing conventional office wear, would the carnivalesque laughter have been the same? Would they have been able to pass through this space, so noticed, and so easily? Would it have still looked 'normal'? Or would it have caused some different, more unsettling, uncanny sort of trouble? Trouble of this sort – when the private penetrates the public, when sexual practice saturates public spaces, when improper bodies and places collide, and the politics of this collision – are the concerns of this book in the context of rape culture.

Defining a rape culture

Rape culture describes a status quo in which sexual violence and exploitation (in all its forms) is normalised. Liz Kelly (1987) describes sexual violence as something that occurs along a continuum, with rape, sexual assault, intimate partner violence and other criminalised acts of sexual violence at one end, and violence that attracts less attention, for instance, stalking, harassment, cat-calling, flashing, unwanted sexual attention and objectification, at the other. The sexual violence that is sustained through rape culture includes all of these forms of abuse. Rape culture also sustains heteronormativity. It designates normative and idealised constructions of masculinity and femininity along heteropatriarchal lines. It constructs sexuality and sexual practice as antagonistic problems to be solved. It fosters contemporary anxieties about sexual ethics, sexual propriety, and sexual politics.

Yet the use of the word 'culture' within notions of what we call 'rape culture' can pose problems. Culture, from the Latin *cultura*, is associated with growing, nurture and cultivation. In the vernacular, culture is often opposed to nature (Lévi-Strauss, 1963) – something civilised and man-made, as opposed to an essential biological fact – even as it is, itself, reified into something immutable. Culture has become an alibi for some problematic acts of sexual violence (elective vaginal rejuvenation surgeries, for instance, or female genital cutting, or so-called 'honour killings'; see Okin 1999; Volpp, 2000). Thinking culture as a monolith in this way has the effect of precluding the possibility for change: it is this way because it has always been this way. Instead, in a book that is about transformation, this is a vernacular understanding of culture that will not do.

As Reed (2005: 79) suggests, culture as an analytical category is generative; it is a 'ceaseless process of unmaking old meanings and making new ones, of unmaking old ways of being, thinking and acting, and making newer ones.' Aimé Césaire (1983) describes 'culture' not as something rooted within a monolithic past, but rather as continually produced in dialogue with memory, with contemporary experience, with the circulation of knowledge, with technology, with politics. Rather than a rootedness, culture is dispersed through 'pollination' that forges hybrids, and that appears in unexpected ways and in unexpected places (Clifford, 1988: 15). I have argued elsewhere that rape culture is constructed and is non-essential, *and* it is a product of the socio-cultural context from which it emerges (Fanghanel, 2018). At the same time, as Paul Gilroy (1993) demonstrates, what we designate to be culture is fluid and contextual. There is no one culture in the UK or the USA, where many of the examples in this book are taken from. There is no one manifestation or experience of rape culture in these places. Yet, like capitalism, rape culture saturates all aspects of social life. Like capitalism, we are differently implicated in rape culture. In some contexts, you and I are oppressed, or aggressed, or violated by the manifestation of rape culture. In others, you and I benefit from the fact of rape culture. But how we benefit, how we are oppressed, will not be the same.

What is going on here is the interplay between culture – rape culture – as a vernacular category (as something that just *is*), and rape culture as an analytical category (how we come to understand the world). The transformation of rape culture from analytical to vernacular (common-sense, everyday) is what makes it hard to perceive and thus, hard to undo. What we need is to break away from this essentialist vernacular category into one that recognises rape culture as a mode of analysis. At the same time, some analytical modes of understanding rape culture offer incomplete critiques of it, as we shall see in some of the examples in this book. In this book, the work is to recognise the vernacular – the taken for granted – and to critique it analytically, without the analysis itself folding back into essentialism.

Because it sustains the heteronormative organisation of social life, rape culture also sustains (and is sustained by) other oppressions along ethnocentric, ableist, classist, speciesist lines. It is also why rape culture affects everyone, even if the important differences in the ways that it affects everyone make its impact hard to discern. Here, I posit that rape culture is the backdrop to social encounters and to how meaning is made in public space, and for this reason, it is an urgent and pertinent concern if we want to forge a more socially and spatially just contemporary life.

Calling out sexualised violence in public space *as rape culture* can be considered contentious. Because of the interplay between the vernacular and the analytical, what we call 'rape culture' has sometimes been misunderstood even among groups with expertise in dealing with sexual violence. In 2014, the Rape Abuse and Incest National Network (RAINN) in the USA participated in a consultation with the White House's Office on Violence Against Women's Task Force to Protect Students from Sexual Assault. In it, RAINN suggests that the 'unfortunate trend towards blaming "rape culture" for … "sexual violence"' distracts current anti-rape activist campaigns by obscuring the fact that it is 'a minority of individuals', not cultures, who rape. In their letter, RAINN posit that rapists, rather like 'bad apples', are individuals who choose to rape, rather than a product of culture more broadly:

> More than 90% of college-age males do not, and are unlikely to ever rape. In fact, we have found that they're ready and eager to be engaged on these issues. It's the other guys (and, sometimes, women) who are the problem. Rape is not caused by cultural factors but by the conscious decisions, of a small percentage of the community, to commit a violent crime…. While that may seem an obvious point, it has tended to get lost in recent debates. This has led to an inclination to focus on particular segments of

the student population (e.g. athletes), particular aspects of campus culture (e.g. the Greek system[3]), or traits that are common in many millions of law-abiding Americans (e.g. masculinity) rather than on the sub-population at fault; those who commit rape. (RAINN, 2014)

Arguing that 'rape culture' exists is, for RAINN, equivalent to suggesting that there are 'cultures who rape'. Of course this is an erroneous analysis of a false vernacular of what constitutes rape culture. It is a construction that has been mobilised to alienate, stigmatise and silence men and women of colour, who are already otherwise marginalised (Lorde, 1984; Staples, 1986). The notion of culture that is mobilised by RAINN is one that is particular, bounded and static. It does not recognise that rape culture saturates all these areas of life (athletic teams, the Greek [fraternities] system, masculinity) to normalise the sexual exploitation of, and violence against, women. Even if everyone on the football team agrees rape is wrong, and no one in the fraternity has ever raped anyone, how meaning is made about the world is still informed by rape culture. An analytical understanding of rape culture enables us to perceive this.

Take, for instance, the definition of 'rape culture' mobilised and contested by Luke Gittos (2015). He describes a case in which two male children (one depressed and with a low IQ) engage in sexual acts with each other, including an attempt to have anal sex, following which the child with the low IQ – the perpetrator – pleaded guilty to rape and was to be placed on the Sex Offenders' Register. According to Gittos, when the victim was asked why he did not speak up about the abuse before, he said he was scared that his brother (the friend of the offender) would 'call him gay'. The criminalisation of this boy marks, for Gittos (2015), an 'outrage', an 'appalling ... miscarriage of justice.' And Gittos (2015) lays the blame for this outrage at the foot of a poorly analysed vernacular 'rape culture' that is too ready to 'cry rape' where no rape existed. In his words, where 'people think they are raped, but are wrong' (what does it mean to be 'wrong' here? 'Wrong' according to whom/what? What is Gittos assuming when he makes this moral pronouncement?). Gittos manages to do this by completely overlooking the fact of rape culture that sustains a heterocentric dynamic in which it is still considered shameful to be 'called gay', for instance. One of the very arguments that he uses to demonstrate that what he calls rape culture has gone too far, or does not exist, is undone by the demonstration of rape culture thriving within it. It might be that this case – as Gittos describes it – is one of sexual experimentation as opposed to rape, and even if we allow this, it does not mean that rape culture does not exist. In the author's own words, the perpetrator had not 'used violence or physical force' in his sexual interactions with his friend's younger brother, but even the notion that violence or force might be expected in a case of rape or sexual assault is a rape myth borne of rape culture. Gittos' vernacular is so implicated in entrenched views of what 'counts' as rape that it is not surprising that he cannot see it emerge in his own language. An analytical understanding of rape culture enables us to perceive this, too.

Elsewhere, what might be called 'rape culture' has been blamed for 'victimising' women. Victim-blaming is a facet of rape culture, of course, but this form of 'victimising' describes labelling women as victims when they do not recognise that label for themselves. Some of the critics of #MeToo, and other forms of hashtag feminism that we explore in the last chapter, raise this complaint about calling out rape culture. Rape culture – with its emphasis on avoiding victim-blaming – has also been criticised for absolving victims of their own responsibility for their safety, which, as we shall see in Chapter Four, becomes a problematic assertion of intersectional privilege that entrenches the inequalities which enable rape culture to thrive. Yet even the notion of personal security, of things that you could do to make yourself safer in order to avoid rape and sexual harassment, are ingrained in vernacular rape culture that fetishises safety at any price, and casts public spaces where these attacks are imagined to take place as inherently dangerous, from which women as always-already victim, should be excluded (Fanghanel and Lim, 2017).

Indeed, one of the reasons why rape culture is able to thrive is because it manifests itself in so many places, and appears in so many guises, including vernacular guises that we take for granted. The sexual practices that are condoned or condemned in Rubin's (1984) representation of sexual hierarchies are informed by rape culture. The representation of female characters in many films or TV programmes, the use of certain types of women's bodies in advertising, sexist jokes, the normalisation of heteronormative romantic tropes, or dynamics of sexual encounter, even drawing the lines of nationhood and state sovereignty along lines of inclusion and exclusion and of designating who is with us and who is other, occurs, as we discuss in Chapter Two, through the lens of rape culture.

Part of the problem that this book seeks to address is the difficulty that we have in recognising what rape culture is (and is not), where it operates, and how. What, in this book, we call 'rape culture' describes not only incidences of rape. It is not about being too ready to 'cry rape' where there has been no rape. It is not about identifying and demonising 'cultures who rape'. It is not about criminalising sexual practices that are unusual, or non-normative, or 'just experimenting'. It is not about being 'politically correct'. It is not about disempowering women and needlessly criminalising men. It does not advocate 'witch hunts'. It is about recognising that rape culture is the thread with which the fabric of meaning about sexual and social life is woven. Rape culture cannot be solved by simply prosecuting more people. It requires an analytical shift in the way we think and act and imagine and speak. It is not about State interference; it cannot be, given that the State is also implicated in rape culture. It requires a new ethical praxis, some of which is outlined later, in Chapter Five.

Disruptive bodies

At the centre of this book about disrupting rape culture is the disruptive female body. The disruptive body, unlike, say, the 'invading' body (Puwar, 2004), the 'volatile' body (Grosz, 1994), or the body 'out-of-place' (Cresswell, 1997), alters that with which it comes into contact. A disruption marks a break in the present, the ongoing status quo. From the Latin *disrumpere* – breaking apart – a disruption 'renders asunder', splits, shatters where it occurs. When we dis-rupt something, we inter-rupt it, we cause it problems, we stir up trouble. Disruptions also describe a fundamental altering or destruction of the structure of an object. To be disruptive is, of course, to do damage, but this damage can also be creative. When public spaces are (over)coded as androcentric, heterocentric, ableist, transphobic, racist, classist, and so on, where striated space manifests particular affects, produces certain inclusions and exclusions, or forms of belonging, troublesome bodies harbour the capacity to disrupt these affects and to forge smooth spaces between these striates (Deleuze and Guattari, 2004a [1980]: 467-8).

Alongside the dog-walking with which we opened this chapter, consider a different sort of intervention in public space: in the early 11th century in England, Lady Godgyfu, wife of the Earl of Mercia, is said to have to have walked through the town of Coventry naked and on horse back in order to protest against her husband's taxation of the people. As the only woman landholder of this time, the Doomsday survey confirms that Lady Godgyfu – the Anglo-Saxon form of Godiva – was an important benefactress (Carr-Gomm, 2012: 93). That Godgyfu was an important historical figure appears to be beyond doubt. The myth of her naked protest, however, appeared only two centuries after her death. While it makes a compelling tale, it is doubtless apocryphal (Lunceford, 2012). This does not, of course, detract from the popularity of this famous legend that has inspired paintings, sculpture and popular culture over the last centuries. Part of the reason for this popularity is the titillation of the naked woman in public, which reminds us that the presence of a particular presentation of the female body in public space stirs up trouble. Or rather, has the potential to do so.

Of course, women's bodies in public spaces are not usually as inherently transgressive or troublesome as the myth of Godiva might suggest; much of the way that public space is used and understood occurs along these striated lines and within established codes of propriety and so-called common sense and how women should act (Kelly and Radford, 1990; Frug, 1992; Campbell, 2005). Indeed, one of the roles that rape culture plays is in controlling some of these codes. What is interesting, however, is what happens when women's bodies are disruptive, or are seen to be disruptive, and what happens when these disruptions, or resistances, are themselves met with resistance.

Some earlier works that consider the female body in public space are informed by feminist concerns about sexual harassment and discourses about the latent menace of sexual violence. Implicit in the analyses of Shirley Ardener (1981) and Carol Brooks Gardner (1995), among others, is the assumption that performances of appropriate femininity that conform to the consecrated somatic norms (Puwar, 2004) are central to avoiding sexual harassment. In this context, this coding of the female body as out-of-place forms part of a broader rape culture which, in part, is accompanied by other legal sanctions: sanctions against sex work, sanctions against abortion – even the privileges that are acquirable through marriage and family produce a female body that is disciplined and enfeebled – striated – by imperatives to rely on others when occupying public space (Frug, 1992).

Elizabeth Kissling (1991) argues that these low-level incivilities and interjections amount to a sexual terrorism acted on the female body. Indeed, sexual harassment in public space is a form of violence that affects women's bodies in a way that is particular to them *as women*. It is for this reason that sexual harassment of this form is a 'gender-specific injury' (Tuerkheimer, 1997). That is to say, as a mode of controlling the female body in public space, it accompanies a raft of systems of control, of exclusion, of sanctions that affect women's bodies in public spaces in ways that simply do not affect men's bodies (Kelly and Radford, 1990; Olney, 2015). Sexual harassment reminds the female body that she is open for male commentary, that she is a curiosity to be evaluated in public space, that she does not belong, and that she is, first and foremost, a sexual object within a heteropatriarchal striation of public space.[4] Not only is it the latent menace and objectification that accompanies this violence, but it is also chivalry in the form of the advice about safe-keeping, or about how to avoid rape and sexual violence, which nurtures (and is nurtured by) contemporary rape culture.

How did this body, in public space, come to be so out-of-place? In an elegant consideration of femininity and the city, Elizabeth Wilson (1991: 6) suggests that women 'live out their lives on sufferance in the metropolis.' Cast either as 'temptress, as whore, as fallen woman, as lesbian, but also as virtuous womanhood in danger, as heroic womanhood who triumphs over temptation' (1991: 8), women pose a problem to the ways in which space is coded and striated. According to David Sibley (1988), it is through the erection of boundaries around bodies and spaces that belong, and those that do not that these codes and striates might emerge. Not unlike the function that the carnivalesque plays in social life, Sibley (1988: 412) suggests that boundary maintenance is strategically invoked at societal levels to 'coerce' societies into order, and that it also operates at a more local level to literally clear up and 'sanitise' space. For this, Sibley, building on Mary Douglas' (1966) work about purity and danger, emphasises the importance of order and similitude within society. Douglas, whose work has been constructively developed by Julia Kristeva (1982 [1980]) and Elizabeth Grosz (1994), illustrates how similar sets can be understood as safe – in place – and disorder (which might manifest as dirt or pollution) is understood as unsafe, dangerous and out-of-place.

Dirt is not simply matter-of-place (although it is, of course, also matter-out-of-place; see Cresswell; 1997: 334); it is also ambiguous matter that cannot easily be put *into* place. Maybe it is indeterminate, vague, or unstable. Maybe it escapes order because it is fluid, contingent, and virtual. We might argue that dirt is of smooth space and that its designation as dirt, as unclean, as undesirable, is a reterritorialisation. Striated space renders abject that which menaces its organisation. We see this, too, in contemporary constructions of the disruptive female body. For Douglas, as for Kristeva, these bodies that will not be ordered become threatening or dangerous *because they are disordered*. Leaky, they defy classification and as such become abject, which means 'above all, ambiguity. Because, while releasing a hold, [the abject does] not radically cut off the subject from what threatens it – on the contrary, abjection acknowledges it to be in perpetual danger' (Kristeva, 1982 [1980]: 8). The abject – untidy, unpalatable, ugly – body is troublesome. It is also inherently gendered (Baker, 2010). This trouble is simultaneously one that reveals the body as outside of the 'somatic norm' and is also an effect of the presence of the body as out-of-place. On the one hand, the abject body troubles the striation of over-coded public space by being in the wrong place and by disrupting the ways in which space is striated. On the other hand, the very casting of a body as abject *is itself a form of striation* (see Russo, 1995). The smooth and the striated are intertwined, and the apparatus of capture, which reterritorialises, is never far away.

According to binarised imaginaries of social life, the hard, solid, self-contained masculine body is valorised over the fluid, soft, penetrable body of the female. It is the association of the female body with 'indeterminacy' and the subordinate cultural coding of the fluid to the solid that casts the female body as abject (Grosz, 1994: 203; see also Young, 1984). Thus, although certainly bodies that are not straight-forwardly female bodies (male bodies, non-binary bodies) can become abject in certain contexts, the female body that we are dealing with in this book is a body that is always-already striated with abjection.[5] The abject body out-of-place takes the wrong form, or occupies the wrong place, or does the wrong thing. It is 'what does not respect borders, positions, rules', it is that 'which disturbs identity, system, order' (Kristeva, 1982 [1980]: 4). In this unpredictable form, the abject body might become revolutionary.

One of the lines of argument that this book explores is that posited by Tim Cresswell (1997: 342), that the out-of-place body might be a 'liberating, dynamic entity that provides lines of escape from the confines of territorial power.' That is, by 'Becoming-minoritarian', by forging a *polis* out of exteriority, the out-of-place might also be a site from which to transform politics. It is certainly a tempting proposition. The politics of transformation are not usually so celebratory, however. The capacity of transgressive practices to undo social injustice such as rape culture, for instance, is uncertain (Foucault, 1998 [1976]). But, as we shall see, the potentiality of this position is a field rich for excavation.

Straying power

From Walter Benjamin's (1999 [1972]) exploration of Charles Baudelaire's (2010 [1863]) *Painter of modern life* and Edgar Allan Poe's (2017 [1840]) *Man of the crowd*, the *flâneur* has emerged as a figure of urban strolling potent with the capacity for transgression. According to Merlin Coverley (2010), the *flâneur* is emblematic of nostalgia for a way of being in the urban that is under threat. The near ubiquity of the motorcar (Thrift, 2004), the destruction of the arcades that *flâneurs* haunted, the disappearance of spaces in which to stroll, mean that walking in the city no longer takes the same form as walking in the city of Baudelaire. Coverley (2010) also points out that this stroller, much to his own dismay, no doubt, has been 'overworked' – commodified – in contemporary social and cultural commentary. Indeed, the *flâneur* appears in an array of discussions of public space, from the tourist as *flâneur* (Wearing and Wearing, 1996; Wood, 2005), to the *flâneurie* of lesbian desire (Munt, 1995), to the *flâneur* of digitally mediated environments (Atkinson and Willis, 2007; Dörk et al, 2011), to the *flâneur* as curious criminogenic Other (Werner, 2001; Lee, 2007). Even if, as Rebecca Solnit (2000), Coverley (2010) and Keith Tester (1994) suggest, the *flâneur* is no more, there is something political about the urban walker, and perhaps about what walking in public space can come to mean, especially when that walking is disobedient or disruptive.

That said, the *flâneur* that Baudelaire and Benjamin had in mind would not have approached walking as a particularly political act whatsoever. For walking to be considered to be transformative, we would have to turn to the Situationists and Guy Debord's (1994 [1967]) twin interventions in urban space: the transformation of public space through the creation of 'situations' and the development of psychogeography; and through critique of a society that is spectacular. For Debord (1994 [1967]), the spectacle is the ultimate of commodity fetishism. All culture is spectacle – a social life that is mediated by commodity – in which the relationship between things, images and labour is obfuscated by the hyper-real (where the commodity-object becomes a taken-for-real-object). One of the critiques that Debord (1994 [1967]) makes of the *flâneur* (aside from seeking to distinguish the Situationists' form of walking the urban from every prior concept of walking the urban) is that the *flâneur*, with his leisurely walk and his arcades, represents the spectacularisation of public space. Cast as a passive consumer of space, rather than a producer, or transformer, or preserver of space, the *flâneur* rests on the laurels of his apolitics.

As well as skirting the edges of the political by virtue of his class, the *flâneur* is also considered to be an inherently masculine figure (Pollock, 1988). And indeed, often, where women do appear in many considerations of the city, it is usually as sex workers (Mort, 1995), or as tragic muses (Coverley, 2010), or as virtuous Godivas (Lunceford, 2012). The female *flâneur*, or *flâneuse*, is much less prolific in discussions of the urban, and so her presence marks how spaces are striated (Solnit, 2000; Elkin, 2016). For Wilson (1991: 7), the *flâneuse*, where she does exist, is also much more troublesome. The *flâneuse* is a 'Sphinx', a monster with the head of a woman and the body of a lion. Fantastical and feral, the *flâneuse*-as-Sphinx is 'feminine sexuality, womanhood out of control'. She occupies a complex position in the city – in public space – she is unruly (we might say deterritorialising); the city is not for her, yet it is also an exciting place of possibility. In her discussions of cities across the world, Wilson describes the 'magic' of streetscapes (1991: 8), the 'spectacle' (1991: 158) and the 'vitality' (1991: 157) of cities. She takes pleasure in imagining cities as places of possibility for the wayward, straying-from-the-path feminine *flâneur* (1991: 11). Occupying place in this celebratory manner is, for Wilson, a way of transcending the polarised binary of women as 'angels' or 'victims' of space (1991: 46). The figure of the *flâneuse* here reminds us of how this enjoyment is rarely unproblematically accorded: the *flâneuse* must strive to stroll with ease.

What is bold or subversive or otherwise disruptive about occupying public space? When public space is over-coded as excluding some bodies and favouring others, or, more usually, excluding certain bodies in certain ways from certain practices, merely being *in place* becomes a protest, a resistance, a disruption (Staples, 1986; Munt, 1995). Brent Staples' (1986) seminal essay on the experience of walking as a black man illustrates exactly how political it can be to walk in public space. In her exploration of the practice of walking, Solnit (2000: xii) draws attention to walking as a tool to 'stand up to violence, fear and repression'. In the aftermath of disasters or of attacks, the image of throngs of people walking through the streets of London after 7/7, or walking away from bomb blasts in Aleppo, or from the site of earthquakes in Italy, or Japan, or New Zealand, are striking, not least because of how they contrast with those who cannot walk away. The practice of walking here is a practice of survival. It is the first and last means of perambulation when everything else is lost. Unlike driving a car that may, as Nigel Thrift (2004) suggests, have become a 'new mode of embodiment', the act of walking the city – particularly if walking in an unusual manner, as a horde, as a protest, as a naked woman on horseback, or as a man on a leash – is vulnerable, remarkable and political.

The *flâneuse* has the capacity to stray into spaces where she becomes trouble. This trouble can be resolved via a reigning-in of women's bodies in public space – a delimiting of how they should appear, when, and in what contexts – and a number of tools are used to do this.

Elsewhere I have outlined how safety campaigns and victim blaming have both been used to police the female body against a background of contemporary rape culture (Fanghanel, 2015, 2018; Fanghanel and Lim, 2017; see also Stanko, 1996; Pain, 1991; Brooks, 2011; Tyler, 2013). This book examines three different examples of how women's bodies are disruptive, how those disruptions are encountered, and how they transform or are transformed by a dominant heteropatriarchal politics of social, spatial justice. Taking three case studies in turn – women being pregnant, women participating in protest and women doing BDSM – and how they are performed in different public spaces, I consider the political relationship of these in relation to rape culture.

Like *flâneurie*, each of these embodied practices (being pregnant, participating in protest and doing BDSM) harbours the capacity to forge smooth spaces, and lines of flight, out of striated space. Each practice has the capacity to connect with different bodies, to forge different 'Becomings-'[6] and, at a molecular level, to express different affects: do different things to the way in which social, spatial justice works.

'Becoming- machinic'

If the female body – the *flâneuse* – is out-of-place in public space, she harbours the potentiality to dismantle the striated lines that determine what is in-place. If rape culture is one of the ways in which these spaces become striated, then we need a device to undo the conditions that enable rape culture to thrive, or to capture bodies, or to police and control them in public space. If State apparatus has over-coded the city of London as a site of work and capitalist production and consumption, then maybe the sight of a man being walked like a dog through this space becomes a device that troubles these codes which create smooth space, and opens up the potentiality that they may become other expressions, or become expressed otherly. Such a device has been described by Deleuze and Guattari as a 'war machine' (2004a [1980]).

The machine is a construct that appears over and again in Deleuzoguattarian thought. From the proto-Indo-European word *maghana*, the etymology of machine means 'that which enables' and 'to have power over', thus, the machine is dynamic. It acts. Machines are composed through flows of bodies that assemble together to do something. Of course, the body Deleuze and Guattari imagine is not simply the human body: celestial bodies, chemical bodies and political bodies can be incorporated into their framing of what is a *corps*. For them, the body is composed of flows, of intensities, of affects, of potentialities; it is neither inherently organic nor inherently human, but is non-determinate, non-essential and productive (Deleuze and Guattari, 2004a [1980]: 404). The composition of a body can be discerned only by what the body can do and what it is capable of (see Buchanan, 1997) (although, of course, what does it produce? The capacity for the machine to be captured by State apparatus is always latent and potential).

Defined between two poles – the line of destruction and the line of flight – the war machine is exterior to the State (to the striated, ordered politics of 'common-sense' thought), and emerges in smooth space (2004a [1980]: 466). The war machine contests the 'fundamental tasks' of the State, which are to striate space and to recapture lines of flight (2004a [1980]: 425). It therefore offers a multiplicity – a mode of 'Becoming-' – that causes trouble. It opens up smooth space and the potentiality of lines of flight for other ways of 'Becoming-' – other ways of acting – to emerge. This, of course, depends on what the Becoming- becomes, where the line of flight is flying. If it is simply to re-become a neoliberal subject, then we can try to flee as much as we want, but we may find that there is nowhere to hide from the spectacle (Debord, 1994 [1967]: thesis 13). We must deterritorialise – disrupt – as we make lines of flight.

Furthermore, war machines are not about actual 'war'. Wars form part of the economy of the State, and although a war machine can be captured by the State in the service of war, the war machine itself *is not able* to have war as its object. If it does so, it ceases to be a war machine. Instead, according to Andrew Robinson (2010), what we call a war machine might better be articulated as a 'difference engine', or 'metamorphosis machine', to more precisely articulate what it is that a war machine *can do*.

Let us not forget that totalitarian, fascistic conceptualisations of war machines have been mobilised, in military theory, for instance, with harrowing effects, most notably in the military tactics of the Israeli Defence Forces (IDF) against Palestinian citizens. Eyal Weizman (2006) reports that in the city of Nablus in 2002, the IDF 'applied' the concept of the war machine to tactics of terrorisation. Rather than arming spaces like alleys, roads, and pavements with bombs or booby traps, they would slash through existing buildings, dwellings and walls in sort-of 'overground tunnels' in order to 'walk through walls', to bring warfare into the homes of civilians and to exert 'profound … trauma and humiliation' through this 'unwalling of walls'. Inspired by a metaphysical philosophy where territories are in flux, where knowledge-production is de-centralised and the distinctions between 'private space' and 'borderless public surface' can be merged, the IDF mobilised a notional war machine for State-like war. Apparatus of capture, yes, but also devastating, destructive mobilisation of the war machine.

These critiques are compelling reasons why, when we talk about the war machine, how it emerges, and how it is identified, we must attend to the politics of location of how the war machine Becomes-, and how it acts (see Rich, 1984). The war machines that we are talking about mobilising in this discussion of rape culture are potent but precarious. Despite the potentiality that they harbour for recapture and annihilation, we need to uncover how we can harness their 'underlying transformative potential' (Robinson, 2010). For this, I suggest it is helpful to think about the type of machine we want to create as a 'guerrilla' war machine. Guerrilla, from the Old Spanish, is the diminutive of *guerra* (war) and describes irregular, unformalised, resistant fighting. In this context, a 'guerrilla' war machine might be about never being where we are expected to be, never acting as we are expected to, not consuming when we should, or only doing so when we should not: being agile, exterior and critical.

So how might we make a guerrilla war machine? Deleuze and Guattari (2004a [1980]: 419) suggest that the war machine is an 'invention of the nomads'. Nomadic thought is unchained from the striations of the state. Yet this is not a nomadic practice that finds its reflection in peoples who are actually nomadic, in Mali say, or Mongolia. This nomadism is not necessarily physical, according to Rosi Braidotti's (1994) well-known articulation of the nomadic subject. This nomad is rather a disembodied idea of rootless freedom to circulate, freedom to self-determine, freedom to flow and to Become-. New nomadism might describe the enticing lives of jet-set entrepreneurs working from anywhere, or it might mark the movement of exploited migrant domestic labour, for instance. Yet sustaining this distinction undermines, according to John Noyes (2004), the potentiality that nomadic thought suggests. Mobilising a romantic idea of nomadism while effacing the reality of nomads – even of exploited migrant labour – becomes a majoritarian manoeuvre of the State that silences subaltern voices. It has the effect of situating the intellectual nomad in the position of imperialist saviour of indigenous folk with their indigenous, local, grounded, immobile knowledges (Wuthnow, 2002). It also obscures the neoliberal imperatives cloaked within this burlesque of freedom. We see this in Julie Wuthnow's (2002) critique of Paul Patton's (2000) work about Australian indigenous rights. We see this in Paulo Freire's (2017 [1970/1968]) anti-capitalist critique of the oppressive colonial state.

Instead, Deleuze and Guattari suggest that the war machine might be the expression of the itinerant metallurgist, or smith. According to them, the sedent and the nomad are cast as opposites of each other; the sedent is of the striated city, the nomad is of the smooth steppe, or the desert, or the sea, but the smith is of neither and of both: 'their relation to others results from their internal itinerancy, from their vague essence' (2004a [1980]: 457). Thus smiths communicate with both smooth and striated space, through what Deleuze and Guattari suggests are 'holey spaces' that join the two. Certainly, the sedent, smith, and nomad about whom Deleuze and Guattari are writing must be thought as figurative iterations, despite Deleuze and Guattari's claim that they are not (Wuthnow, 2002). But for the purposes of this discussion, we can use these figures as a springboard into understanding how a war machine is composed, and what it can do.

If the nomad is completely deterritorialised in smooth space, and the striated sedent is completely territorialised, the smith presents a way to live in the striated city without being absolutely subjectified by it. She strides between the two. The smith, as Deleuze and Guattari note, was an ambiguous figure in non-modern and pre-modern societies, 'simultaneously honoured, feared and scorned' (2004a [1980]: 456); the smith has power over metal, who can, from the same material, create religious artefacts, swords, handcuffs, tools to tend the land and with which to dig for water. As an ambulant around smooth and striated space, it might be the smith who harbours the potential to forge lines of flight through the holey spaces she produces. With the power over life and death, the sacred and the profane, the smith also occupies a liminal space 'betwixt and between' (Turner, 1967). The liminal space becomes a holey space through which the war machine might emerge (2004a [1980]: 458-9). This liminal smith occupies transgressive, transformative positions. It will be by eschewing both the docility of the sedent or the abandon of the nomad that such deterritorialisations might start to emerge, even if only for a moment.

Deleuze and Guattari (2004a [1980: 321) tell us that the war machine forges a becoming-minoritarian. They oppose minor politics to majoritarian State-like, common-sense Becomings. In *A thousand plateaus*, they outline the sorts of things that become-potential through becoming-minoritarian (becoming-animal, becoming-woman, becoming-molecular). Becoming-minoritarian is not simply about adopting the positionality of a minoritised group (if this was even possible). Indeed, for Deleuze and Guattari, the naming a group as a minority to accord it specific rights or obligations is an axiomatic reterritorialising instrument of State thought, with its ordering, organising, homogenising affects. They suggest that 'becoming-minoritarian is a political affair and necessitates ... an active micropolitics' via molecularity (2004a [1980]: 322). The molar (static, staid) can become molecular (potential, eventful) through deterritorialisation.

Another way in which to think about this is as a 'molecular revolution'. For Guattari (1984), the molecular composition of bodies is what harbours the capacity for revolution or transformation. If, at a molecular level, revolution might occur – stirring, turning, rejecting – then transformation of State apparatus Becomes- potential. A molecular revolution, for Guattari, is moved by productive desire. Eager to connect the political sphere with the sphere of the individual, with the sphere of the personal, Guattari argues that we need to 'set up new theoretical and practical machines capable of sweeping away earlier stratifications and creating the conditions necessary for desire to function in a new way' (1984: 218). Mobilising these new theoretical frameworks and approaches through molecular revolutions offers, for Guattari, one way in which to forge a praxis to transform social life. And part of this transformation emerges through the expression of multiplicities: multiplicities that are guerrilla. It is not a question of making-the-same through fostering collectivity in the revolution, or of homogenising the different spheres that a molecular revolution might touch, but in harnessing desire as a basis of struggle, in all its difference.

But appropriation of the war machine by the State is a constant threat. Often this appropriation or 'capture' absorbs the war machine into its organised, striated apparatus. Whether as flight or as destruction, the war machine brings 'connections to bear against the great conjunction of the apparatus of capture of domination' (Deleuze and Guattari, 2004a [1980]: 467). The revolution is revolving; it assembles, it deterritorialises, it flows, and while it might transform, like the war machine, it always, always must avoid the apparatus of capture and reterritorialisation. Only thus will it 'lead to a desire to live and to change the world' (Deleuze and Guattari, 2004a [1980]: 229). Remembering that not all war machines or molecular revolutions (Guattari, 1984) are transgressive, it is also necessary to interrogate how they can become/might become/are recaptured and further commodified, spectacularised, or made tame (Debord, 1994 [1967]).

What remains important in this analysis is the capacity for transformation and difference. This helps us to critically interrogate the contemporary gendered social and spatial justice. Here, I achieve this by exploring different practices in turn, and excavating the commonalities across them. The three cases – pregnancy, protest and kink/BDSM – are chosen for their different insights into specifically gendered experiences of disrupting public space. Other case studies might also have done the job, but these three are closely entangled with rape culture, as both products and producers of rape culture. Although quite distinct practices or identities, there are threads of concern about rape culture that run through all of them. We weave these threads together in order to better understand how to tangibly make a war machine. And to explore whether it is possible to make a war machine – to bring about molecular revolution – that evades capture by the state. This is the story that will unfold over the following chapters.

Outline of the book

Chapter Two, organised in two parts, explores women's bodies in public space during pregnancy. Like the body of the *flâneuse*, the pregnant body is a public body (Longhurst, 1997; Lupton, 2012a, b). More than this, it is also a body that strides along the tension between sexuality and chastity or propriety (Musial, 2014). It is a body that is vulnerable while at the same time harbouring power over life itself. It is a body that is ambiguous, that is a leaky container, that is abject, and at the same time, that is revered, or honoured (Grosz, 1994). Liminal, it marks the unpredictable transition between life and non-life (Côté-Arsenault et al, 2009).

In this chapter, I do not focus on the many ways in which pregnancy in post-industrialist, capitalist contexts is heavily medicalised or subject to regulation by welfarist discourses (see Drglin, 2015). Instead, I examine what happens when the pregnant body in public space is perceived to be troublesome, or, because of its ambiguous position, disruptive. This chapter focuses, in particular, on the pregnant body in public space as a sexualised body (Huntley, 2000; Longhurst, 2006; Musial, 2014). Running through this chapter are snippets of sex advice given to women in specialist pregnancy magazines. I include these to demonstrate how far the pregnant body is fetishised as a sexualised/sexless body, and as a problem to be solved. Alongside this, the first part of the chapter examines the representation of sexualised pregnant bodies in mainstream discourses; notably, 'sexy' pregnancy photoshoots and advertising. The concept of herethical sexual ethics is analysed in dialogue with these representations of motherhood-to-come (Kristeva, 1985). This section argues that the valorisation of pregnancy as a beatific moment suspended in time serves to marginalise women from public life, to essentialise motherhood and, through chivalry, enshrine constructions of femininity and sexuality that sustain and are sustained by rape culture.

We see this come to the fore in the second part's discussion of sexual harassment. Drawing on data from women in the USA and UK, this part examines the (de)sexualisation of pregnancy and the sexual pregnancy as taboo. Sexual harassment is a mode of gender exclusion, in any case (Olney, 2015). When women who are pregnant experience sexual harassment in pregnancy, it becomes a further technique of control, fuelled by rape culture, which codes public spaces as places in which pregnant women do not belong. This striated space is troubled by the ambiguously sexualised pregnant body. It is perhaps in this ambivalent, liminal position that guerrilla war machines might be forged, that molecular revolutions might emerge, and that rape culture which sustains sexual harassment in public spaces – and harassment of pregnant women in particular – might be unwoven. I consider the politics of these possibilities in this chapter through analysis of the pregnant body out-of-place, as a disruption to the prevailing construction of public space.

Chapter Two establishes how norms of pregnancy are a form of striation that upholds heteropatriarchal performances of, and interactions with, gender and sexuality in public space. It argues that mobilising becoming-minoritarian politics established by Deleuze and Guattari and the herethical approaches of Kristeva, we start to set the scene for a guerrilla war machine to emerge.

In Chapter Three, the pregnant, disruptive body finds its resonance with the female body *as protest*. I have already demonstrated how the tale of Lady Godiva illustrates the extent to which the protesting female body (body-out-of-place) causes trouble. This chapter builds on themes established in Chapter Two and considers the naked or nearly naked protest as a carnivalesque disruption in public space. The first part of the chapter posits that these protests rely on spectacularisation (in the Debordian sense, 1994 [1967]) of the naked body to function. We explore this in the context of so-called feminist anti-rape protests, such as SlutWalk or Femen. The second part analyses these gendered dynamics in the context of non-human animal rights protests. Non-human animal rights groups have clearly understood the potential inherent in the relationship between female nakedness and disruption. People for the Ethical Treatment of Animals (PETA) and Lush cosmetics have fostered a reputation for sensational and *outré* animal rights campaigns that mobilise the naked female body (Pace, 2005;

Mika, 2006; Deckha, 2008; Glasser, 2011; Bongiorno et al, 2013; Wrenn, 2015). Here, I analyse one such campaign and draw on the auto-ethnographic experience of participating in naked protest to explore the potentialities of this as a mode of forging a war machine, although once again, we remain entangled in the complex ambiguity of the politics of these campaigns, and their relationship with rape culture.

Chapter Three demonstrates how the eroticisation of sexual violence is mobilised as part of these politics. The similarities between the non-human animal rights campaign performance and a kink scene (like the dog-walking scene) are remarkable. What does the penetration of this performance do to the public space in which it occurs? Does it forge a Becoming-animal (Deleuze and Guattari, 2004a [1980])? Does it make a war machine? Is it an *autre-mondialisation* (Haraway, 2008)? This chapter examines the interplay between smooth and striated space, rape culture, and the capacity that protest harbours for revolution.

In recent years, BDSM communities and sexual practices have received increasing attention in academic circles and in popular discourse (Weiss, 2006, 2011; Newmahr, 2011). What these interrogations of 'kink' communities tell us is that they form highly codified spaces, with their own sense of *communitas* forged through common norms, values, taboos, or hierarchies. Often inflected with neoliberal imaginations of freedom, autonomy, and choice, the kink community practices that I examine in Chapter Four take place in semi-public spaces (bars and clubs and online). These are, much like other public spaces, striated with politics of belonging and exclusion, of desire, of propriety and of sanction. In this chapter I examine the disruptive female body. The first part explores what happens at the threshold of kinky subculture and its penetration into the mainstream, within contemporary legal, cultural and commercial discourses. The second part explores the penetration of the disobedient body within the kink community, and interrogates how 'the community' responds to trouble or disruption. In this part, I draw on interview data with men and women in the USA and UK who talked about how, for instance, community is forged, consent violations are dealt with, the undesirable behaviour of members of the community are negotiated, and how sexualised relations emerge.

Examining how disruptions occur, how people respond to trouble and the politics of these practices, I argue that there exist agonistic sites of tension here, where disruptive bodies are simultaneously desired and reviled. The tensions between the public and the private, between freedom and regulation, between non-judgmental acceptance and hierarchies of desirability, between queerness and heteronormativity play out in the ways in which particular desires and practices are condoned, policed, punished or nurtured in these settings. According to Margot Weiss (2011), people who practice 'kink' believe it to be – and want it to be – a transgressive, revolutionary thing. Certainly, the capacity for revolutionary transformation is latent in kink's relationship with desire. This chapter explores the ways in which social and spatial (in)justice through disavowal, exclusion and the promotion of rape culture prevail in these encounters. Yet it is also hopeful, and considers how some interventions might become transformative and how molecular revolutions might emerge.

What does causing this trouble do? What might it do? How could these interventions open up new ways of politicising public space, or of transforming social life and spatial justice for a life outside of rape culture? Preceding chapters have outlined how the female body-out-of-space transforms public space within the context of contemporary rape culture. We have considered how the production of liminal, precarious life can become a position from which to forge smooth spaces that might transform what machines do and the affects they express, how they alter – even temporarily – the meaning of public space, and bodies that belong or do not belong there. Chapter Five builds on these themes by examining these potentialities in relation to the creation of war machines and establishment of a praxis (Freire, 2017 [1970/1968]). I return to a consideration of how the guerrilla war machine works in relation to State apparatus that produces codes in public space which, for instance, privilege certain types of body over others. I consider how we might create a war machine and imagine how this might foster the sort of molecular revolution that alters what dominant systems of exclusion, marginalisation and commodification might do. Certainly, this conclusion does not act as a diagnosis and prescription for contemporary crises that co-produce misogyny and rape culture, but, mobilising some politics of 'making the familiar strange' (Brecht, 1996 [1964/1935]), of critical exteriority (Kristeva, 1981; Lorde, 1984), and of disinvestment from power (Freire, 2017 [1970/1986]), it does offer some ways in which to conceive of different 'Becomings-' and alternative imaginations of social, spatial, gendered justice.

By marking how public spaces and the bodies that operate and interact within them are striated in concert with contemporary rape culture, this book ends by imagining creative possibilities – smooth spaces, lines of flight – outside these binds. The three case studies, in turn, provide different insights into how and why rape culture continues to thrive, despite ongoing work to counter misogyny in everyday life. The guerrilla war machine, the politics of alienation and the margin, and the significance of positionality are offered as ways to foster an alternative praxis to begin the work of dismantling rape culture.

Coda

Let us return to the dog-walking scene in Farringdon with which I started this introduction. In the week that followed the explosion of the story in the press and online, once the discussion on social media had cooled to a simmer, the female 'dog-walking' protagonist 'revealed' the 'truth' of the scene that took place (Morse, 2014). She was a performer, she said, and had been making a film that was directed by the male protagonist, the man on the leash. The purpose of the film was to record people's reactions to the pair. The path they chose through a busy commuter area, the clothes that they wore and the decision to 'walk' during the morning rush hour were all deliberate decisions taken to affect, engage and shock the members of the public around them; so they *were*, in fact, joining in with the laughter (Bakhtin, 1984). Recognising that they would be remarkably out of place walking around Farringdon at this time and in this manner, the pair's intervention is a conscious attempt to trouble the way this space was striated. Is it more contrived – more spectacular – because it is a knowing game that the pair was playing with the public?

What they were up to was curious, ambiguous and full of potentiality (despite onlookers' enthusiastic attempts to claim their intervention as a publicity stunt, the apparatus of capture is never far away). As a piece of performance art, the carnivalesque spectacle of a man being walked on a dog leash by a woman becomes even more spectacular. Indeed, it becomes entirely hyper-real. Neither commodified by industry for publicity or a kinky game, it nonetheless becomes a commodification of a particular representation of disrupting public space. The 'dog walkers' are not walking (only) for their own pleasure, or according to a game of their own devising; it is not a situational derive, as described by Debord (1994 [1967]), but a deliberate attempt to sensationalise through a simulacra of kinky play and of disrupting – deterritorialising – dominant codes of public space. It is to become deliberately out-of-place, which becomes misinterpreted and misappropriated – recaptured – by some onlookers as a marketing stunt. As a piece of art that was intended to shock, it is certainly less disruptive than if it had been a disruption for its own sake, but nonetheless, this pair did Become- a war machine and, even if only temporarily, caused a disruption, caused some trouble, which for a short time produced a small, smooth line of flight from the machine that produces public space. The rest of the book is an intervention into interventions like this. I examine what they do, what they can do, and what they might do.

TWO

Disruptive pregnancy

Years ago, as a college student, I spent a semester abroad in a beautiful, historic city where the two sentences I heard most in English, usually conjoined, were "You want to go for coffee?" and "You want to have sex with me, baby?" I lived near a huge public garden where I wished I could walk or study, but couldn't, without being followed, threatened and subjected to jarring revelations of some creep's penis among the foliage. One day in a fit of weird defiance I tied a sofa cushion to my belly under a loose dress and discovered this was the magic charm: I could walk anywhere, unmolested. I carried my after-class false pregnancy to the end of the term, happily ignored by predators. As a lissom 20-year-old I resented my waddly disguise, but came around to a riveting truth: being attractive was less useful to me than being free. (Kingsolver, 2018)

As we saw in Chapter One, the striation of public space fosters an ordering in which certain practices, people, or discourses, are normalised, and others are not. We saw that the intervention of a disruptive body harbours the capacity to trouble this striation. Woman – of the domestic, excluded from the public realm – is discursively out-of-place in public space (Wilson, 1991; Solnit, 2000; Elkin, 2016). As Rebecca Solnit (2000: 234) tells us, phrases such as 'public man', 'man about town', and 'man of the streets' mean something quite different when attached to a feminine noun.

Consider, then, the trouble posed by the pregnant body in public space. The penetration of the pregnant body into public space could be considered something quite banal – pregnancy is rather common, after all – but it is nonetheless a site of antagonism. Sex, which usually, although not always, is how pregnancies occur, is private, but

31

pregnancy itself is not.[1] Historically pregnancy, maternity, childbirth and childrearing have been discursively associated with the private realm of women. Confinement, also associated with the sequestering of a peri-natal woman in darkened and quiet rooms before and after the birth, takes its etymological origins from the Old French *confins*, and describes a boundary or border. The verb 'to confine' describes 'keeping in the limits of' a boundary or a territory. Indeed, in French, to be pregnant is to be *enceinte*, and *l'enceinte* is also the word used to describe the walls of a city, or of a fortress, so the removal of women from public space as restraint (confinement), and for protection, composes some of the discourses through which pregnancy is performed and constructed in public space.

Yet, despite its association with the domestic work of child birth and childrearing, pregnancy is, and always has been, a public problem, subject to public sanction and public scrutiny (Lupton, 2012a; Drglin, 2015). As Robyn Longhurst (1999, 2000, 2006) observes, the pregnant body is one that is regulated by discourses of appropriateness, of health and wellbeing, and of anticipation for a future. Discourses of nationhood and of sovereignty through which the public nature of pregnancy is made manifest also criss-cross and co-constitute the body of the pregnant woman as both in- and out-of-place (Mason, 2000; Tyler, 2013). That pregnancy is performative means that its manifestation in public space is constructed through its interaction with 'public and social discourse' (Butler, 1990: 136). What we treat as the pregnant body emerges through iteration and reiteration. Pregnancy, its appearance (or disappearance) in public, and its policing or control is thus an intrinsically spatialised performance.

In this chapter I examine the significance of the tensions between the sexual and sexless pregnancy in order to better understand how performances of pregnancy compose, and are composed by, contemporary rape culture. The quotation with which I opened this chapter illustrates how some of these tensions circulate; sexualised until she faked a visible pregnancy that enabled her to fade into the background, Kingsolver did not consider herself to be 'attractive' anymore, yet she was 'free'. However, as this chapter will show, it is not always as easy as this. Instead, I demonstrate how the embodiment – the fact of the body – of pregnancy contributes to the ambiguous sexualised position it occupies in public space, and to how this ambiguously sexualised body comes to be understood as disruptive. In the first part of the chapter, I critically interrogate how this ambiguity appears in the contemporary representation of sexy pregnancy in maternity photoshoots that form part of the performativity of contemporary pregnancy and in the marketing of 'sexy' products aimed at pregnant women. Interspersed with snippets of sex advice that appear in apparently pro-sex popular magazines aimed at pregnant women, this discussion illustrates the cacophony of voices that inscribe performative sexual/sexless pregnancy. The second part of the chapter then considers sexualisation from a different perspective: the violence of sexual harassment. At an analytical level, the de/sexualisation of pregnancy – as manifest in sex advice columns, pregnant photography poses and sexual harassment – composes a feminine ideal of who can be sexy, who can not be, and how this un/sexiness might emerge, which is inflected with rape culture. It is rape culture which, as we have seen in the previous chapter, normalises the erotic consumption and denigration of women within a heteropatriarchal economy. The warps and wefts of these texts (these images, these adverts, these stories and pieces of advice) will begin to show the involute ways in which sexual/sexless pregnancies become disruptive, and will explore what, if any, good can come of it.

> ...The cocktail of hormones coursing around your body means it might be time to tighten your seatbelt when it comes to your pregnancy sex drive....[2]

Essentialist discourses about the pregnant body as quintessentially feminine abound: fecund, of-nature, bountiful, beatific and also vulnerable, fragile, precarious, volatile, sex-crazed, leaky – pregnancy is a liminal state of Becoming-. When a woman is doing pregnancy – especially towards the end of a visible pregnancy – she occupies an ambiguous flow in the 'betwixt and between' of public space (Côté-Arsenault et al, 2009). The liminal is, according to Victor Turner (1967), the 'no-longer/not-yet' (Deflem, 1991: 13). That is, it marks a space of transition between two states. The liminal subject loses a state of being in order to become another thing before reintegrating, in a changed state, back into her new Becoming-. There is a moment within the liminal space where she walks the line (actually, figuratively) between life and death. Neither self nor selves, neither mother nor not-mother, desexualised yet marked by the presumed inevitability of sex, the pregnant body is disruptive because it eludes conventional orderings (Douglas, 1992; Musial, 2014).

Since actress Demi Moore's landmark naked appearance on the cover of *Vanity Fair* magazine when she was heavily pregnant, there has simply been an explosion of ways in which the pregnant body is 'celebrated' in public space (Oliver, 2010; Tyler, 2011; Musial, 2014).

Rather than feeling they ought to 'cover up' as women may have done decades earlier (Fox et al, 2009: 563), public images of distended pregnant bellies are much more visible. Moore's photoshoot was unusual in 1991. Now, the pregnant celebrity nude (or nearly nude) photoshoot is so common as to almost have become a new pregnancy norm rather than an impertinent interjection into public space. Yet, as Imogen Tyler (2011) highlights, the 'sexy' pregnancy is one that brings with it its own beauty norms. The permission to be sexy might be empowering, but it is a burden for some women, and an impossibility for others. Normative visions of pregnancy that are cut along lines of proper or improper pregnancy, or which cast the pregnant body as virtuous and demure, even as it is also cast as unruly and unreliable, are this way because of rape culture. It is rape culture that normalises certain ways to perform femininity, and which legitimates some bodies and denigrates others. This first section explores these tensions and then concludes by considering how we might mobilise an alternative imaginary of pregnancy in public – a Kristevian herethics – and via these alternative ethics, forge a war machine that contests the striations which compose rape culture.

Pregnancy as a feminist problem

I insist on the significance of pregnancy here simply to demonstrate that the social, cultural, historical and biological importance of the undeniability of pregnancy contributes to the way in which women's bodies are subjugated. There is no escaping the fact of the body in pregnancy. It is partly because of this that it poses such a problem in public space. There is an established history of philosophical writing on pregnancy and the questions that its embodiment provokes. Seminal feminist scholars, including Iris Marion Young (1984), Adrienne Rich (1980), Julia Kristeva (1977) and more recently, Imogen Tyler (2000) and Caroline Lundquist (2008), have explored phenomenological pregnant embodiment. Elsewhere, feminists, including Simone de Beauvoir (1953) and Shulamith Firestone (2015 [1970]), have denounced the 'tyranny of reproductive biology'. And pregnancy, childbirth and childrearing are denigrated tasks in contemporary socio-cultural contexts. Or rather, pregnant women are themselves cherished (women are sent away on their maternity leaves armed with flowers and baby grows; spa days, baby showers and massages for pregnant women abound), but they are also pushed out. Expected to focus on themselves and their pregnancies, they find themselves excluded from – or fighting to be included in – elements of their (professional, personal) lives that formally belonged to them, or that gave them pleasure. Public spaces offer public scrutiny of these performances of self-surveillance and maternal sacrifice.

From an anthropological perspective, because pregnancy occupies this 'sacred' position, it is also taboo (Hubert and Mauss, 1981 [1964]) and cannot be touched by anything that is not sacred (or profane). This is partly why there is such antagonism about pregnant bodies in public space; sacred things or people are kept in sacred places, set aside from everyone else. It is no wonder that pregnancy is accompanied by an imagination, in capitalist societies, of socially limited potentiality, even if, at the same time, pregnant women describe 'feeling valued' in their pregnant bodies (Bailey, 2001: 121). Pregnancy disrupts space in different ways – seats are ceded on public transport, help is offered with luggage, in some cases, arrangements in the workplace are altered to make the pregnant woman more comfortable – they are protected from the usual vicissitudes of being in public by a visible pregnancy. Nonetheless, as Longhurst (1997: 35) notes, pregnant women internalise the notion that the public is off-limits to them during later stages of pregnancy and exclude themselves from it. Given the dismissiveness with which some women who are peri-natal are treated, we might understand why some feminists decry the collocution of the maternal, the feminine and the woman as essentialist and harmful. That it has also been discursively constructed in this way in contemporary social life is an expression of structural sexism in public space, about who can be there and who cannot. It is precisely for these despisements that the presence of the pregnant body in public space needs our attention in this work on rape culture. Not least because this denigration has considerable implications for how social and spatial justice emerges, or not.

In Chapter One we examined an array of elegant and furious ways in which the gendering of public space had been articulated. From Elizabeth Wilson's (1991) exploration of the politics of occupying public space as a woman through to Carol Brooks Gardner's (1995) analysis of how public harassment alters women's experiences of public space, through to more recent stories told by Rebecca Solnit (2000) or Lauren Elkin (2016) of the power of walking, and being, in public space, the notion that women in public space are troublesome and that this troublesomeness needs, in some way, to be commented on, is well recognised. Given the ambivalent position that she occupies in contemporary public, and even feminist, discourses, it is perhaps not hugely surprising that the pregnant body in public space has not been more scrutinised by these spatial theorists. Banished to the private sphere, scorned for her preoccupation with the silliness of infants, suffering painfully, psychically, socially for her choice, what might a feminist politics recuperate from pregnancy?

Like Kristeva, I am not writing from a pro-natalist stance (McAfee, 2004). Not all pregnancies are chosen – many are not – and even those that are carried to term (and so, in some sense, chosen), are more usually than not experienced with some ambivalence from time to time (Ussher, 2006; Lundquist, 2008). This ambivalence must be recognised in order to de-reify pregnancy and in order to subject it to meaningful analyses. Even within the liberal post-industrialist context in which, along with Young and Kristeva, this discussion is situated, and where contraception and access to abortion are widely and freely available (with some notable and devastating exceptions), the notion of 'choice' is potentially problematic. Discourses of choice ignore the constraints that might compose those choices. When pregnancies are considered to be chosen, they accompany a host of neoliberal imperatives to take responsibility for that choice (Oliver, 2010). *Choice becomes part of the performativity of pregnancy.* Individualising, responsibilising – such choice in pregnancy is paid for with blame when, or even if, things might go wrong. In Deborah Lupton's (2012a: 330) words, the choice to be pregnant is also an imperative to engage in 'reproductive asceticism', to submit oneself to the scrutiny and interference of the public sphere, dominated by advice about diet, exercise, clothing, bath temperature, alcohol consumption, seat-belt wearing, supplement-taking, vaccines, sleeping positions and so on (Longhurst, 1999; Root and Browner, 2001; Fox et al, 2009). The abnegation of the maternal body to the 'precious cargo' can begin even before an ovum is fertilised (Kristeva, 1977; Lupton, 2012a, b). For Kristeva (1977), the pregnant body marks the threshold between nature and culture. It is composed of folds that trouble the ordering of things; it is abject, yet commodified; unruly yet tightly controlled; strong yet precarious; and, importantly for our purposes, of sex and simultaneously sexless. It is a beautiful body, it is a grotesque body, it is a 'polymorphic, orgasmic body' (Ainley, 1990: 58), it is a necessary body. It is also why there is nothing essential about pregnancy or about the ambiguous status that it occupies in social life.

Although, as suggested by the quotation that opens this chapter, pregnancy can be understood as a period of reprieve from the heteronormative grind of sexual objectification (Young, 1984; Bailey, 2001), it is also true that in recent decades the sexual pregnant body has become more visible in public space. Pregnancy, and in particular, the sexualised pregnancy, occupies an ambiguous position within the 'sex hierarchy'. Gayle Rubin (1984) developed the concept of the charmed circle that outlines how sexual practices are discursively situated along legitimate and sanctioned, or illegitimate and profane, lines. At first glance, pregnancy – necessarily procreative, usually heterosexual, usually monogamous, sometimes married and usually coupled – is situated within the 'charmed' middle of the circle. To sexualise this pregnancy – to talk about sexual practice in pregnancy – is to disrupt its construction as 'good, normal, natural' (Rubin, 1984: 153) towards the 'outer limits' of sexual legitimacy. Non-procreative, potentially promiscuous, potentially uncoupled (single), sometimes pornographic, sometimes in public space, the sexy pregnancy can cause trouble:

> ...Your breasts will be getting bigger and more sensitive, which isn't a bad thing – and certainly not for him. Most men will appreciate your fuller breasts, so get him to stroke your breasts and caress your nipples, so you can enjoy their heightened sensitivity. Let your new curves increase your sexual confidence, too....[3]

Young (1984: 53) suggests that visibly pregnant women become free from heteropatriarchal objectification; desexualised, away from the scrutiny and the 'instrumentalisation' of the leering gaze, women embody a form of 'innocent narcissism' in their new, temporary shape. Both Jane Ussher (2006) and Lucy Bailey (2001) describe how this ease with the body comes only once the body is recognisably pregnant and not ambiguously 'fat' as it might be in mid-pregnancy – once the curves can be established as 'new pregnant curves' and not the curves a woman might have anyway. The undesirability of fatness – especially feminine fatness – is a discourse that saturates many areas of contemporary social life in post-industrial socio-cultural contexts. Excessive fleshiness is denigrated as ugly (Baker, 2010). Rebecca Huntley (2000) and Jennifer Musial (2014) both talk about visual representations of sexualised pregnancy in various cultural texts including pornography and *Playboy* magazine. They demonstrate how sexual practice can intersect with pregnant performativity to resexualise pregnancy and to situate sexy pregnancy more visibly within the public sphere. Yet, that women who are pregnant are keen to avoid being mistaken for being fat illustrates how far pregnant bodies are nonetheless still haunted by heteronormative notions of desire and desirability. And as they demonstrate, *Playboy* magazine and pornography legitimate the sexualised pregnancy for the male gaze, even as they draw tight lines around how sexy a sexy pregnancy can be: the *Playboy* photoshoot remains the domain of the demure (Huntley, 2000). The advice above talks about women becoming more feminine, with more aesthetically pleasing, larger breasts that enable her to conform to heteropatriarchal performances of desirability. Sexual practice in this imaginary is situated within a heteronormative frame where women are pleasing to, and stimulated by, their 'men' – not by themselves, not by other women. All of this folds into, and emerges as an expression of, contemporary rape culture that instrumentalises, even as it sanctions, how the pregnant body should be represented in public. In this section I focus more on how this heterosexism emerges in visual representations of sexual pregnancy in public space; namely, in the nude pregnancy photoshoot and lingerie advertising targeting pregnant women.

In 2018, in order to better understand the rapid rise of the naked pregnant photoshoot ('doing a Demi'), I used Google Trends (which analyses internet searches from 2004 to the present) and the LexisNexis news reporting database (which only draws on newspaper articles within in the UK, but searches articles from the past 20 years), to get a sense of the frequency of online searches for pregnancy or maternity photoshoots, or a mention of them in the press. Google Trends demonstrates that online searches through the Google search engine started at a low level[4] in 2005, but picked up momentum in 2010/11, peaking in 2017, suggesting that interest in naked pregnant photoshoots is a relatively new development. Searches were based in countries as varied as Australia, Canada, India, the Philippines, Singapore, South Africa, the United Arab Emirates, the UK and USA, suggesting that this is also a widely occurring phenomenon. The newspaper database of LexisNexis also reflects that this is a contemporary trend. First mentions of pregnancy or maternity photoshoots in newspapers are recorded in 2011/12, and while there were some mentions in the years between 2012 and 2015, it is in 2016 and 2017 that most of the articles listed in the database date from. So, certainly the pregnancy photoshoot is a recent and increasingly widespread performance of pregnancy. The naked pregnancy photoshoot, as made famous by Moore in 1991, and repeated many times since, is a genre within these maternity photoshoots, and points to the possible acknowledgement of the sexual pregnancy, and simultaneously, the constitution of pregnancy through this potential-to-be-sexy gaze.

It is worth taking time to consider the representation of pregnancy, anticipated motherhood and sexuality in these photoshoots. In this discussion, I conduct a visual analysis of these pregnant photoshoots. I focus both on galleries of pregnancy photographs compiled by professional photographers to showcase their work, and on an instructional guide for professional photographers indicating how to pose and arrange these shoots. It is here that the typology of normative performances of naked pregnancy is rehearsed.[5] A search for naked pregnancy photoshoots returns images that are labelled as 'nude' pregnancy photoshoots or 'boudoir' shoots. According to Phillip Carr-Gomm (2012: 7–8), there is a distinction between 'naked' – 'the 'innocent' state of simply being uncovered' – and 'nude' – 'to be seen by others ... a naked body has to be seen as an object in order to become nude.' If nakedness is straightforward undressedness here, nudity is a conscious act of consumption. The photoshoots analysed here are therefore 'nude' photoshoots because the naked body appears in a deliberate, spectacular, stylised and objectified form of suggestive sexuality.

I limit my discussion to photographs where women appear alone in the picture and where they are naked or nearly naked, like the iconic Demi Moore photograph, rather than other common genres such as those where they appear dressed and with their partners or with their other children. These latter categories do not purport to present pregnancy as sexy in the way that solo and naked photoshoots might.

Framing the 'sexy' pregnancy

> It is important to not to over sexualise the image; you are trying to create portraits that she will want to hang on her wall or keep in a secret box somewhere. You are not creating pornography and nor do we want to create a situation whereby pregnancy itself within society becomes over sexualised. We aim to create portraits that are a celebration of her body and life, they may well include her sexuality but we want to avoid being overt with it. (Candyfields pregnancy posing guide, 2018[6])

A tutorial that sets out how photographers might frame their nude pregnancy photoshoots captures the anxiety of a pregnancy that might exceed the boundaries of the charmed circle (Rubin, 1984). According to these guidelines, a woman's sexuality ought only to be incidental to the photoshoot. Nude pregnancy shots are in an antagonistic relationship to pornography, and indeed, following these guidelines, the nude pregnancy photoshoot is implicated in a moral obligation to not over-sexualise pregnancy *itself*. In order to negotiate the oscillation of these ambiguous demands, the sorts of poses that are recommended are variations of standing, sitting and reclining postures, with the emphasis always on 'tasteful nudity'.

Common elements across these different photoshoots are the settings and compositional elements. These tend to take place in white bedrooms, on white sheets, or among white curtains or drapes, suggesting a symbolic purity and innocence. Otherwise they are in natural settings – forests, beaches, often fields – evoking the notion that pregnant women are bucolic and of nature. The proliferation of pastel or monochrome colours, of flowers in the hair, of women looking out of the window and of flowing sheets are common across all of these poses. A common iconographic pose for the nude pregnancy photograph is for the pregnant woman to be wrapped in a thin drape, usually in profile, so that the pregnant stomach is more obvious, looking into the distance, or looking at the stomach, and away from the camera. She is usually placed with her hand under or around the stomach. Other shots tend to feature faceless pregnant women's torsos – either their breasts are naked or covered by an open shirt – while they clasp their stomachs. Or they feature pregnant women reclining, so that the bump is clearly visible, looking away from the camera, into the distance, or at their stomachs. Finally, the woman standing with one hand on her stomach, the other across her body hiding her bare breasts and looking away from the camera, or in quiet contemplation of her stomach, is another frequently constructed image.

Here, the nude pregnancy may be more common, but it is not more sexual. The drapes, sheets, white palette and flowers in her hair construct an image of the pregnant woman as innocent, closer to nature, angelic perhaps, chaste: certainly. There are many poses with women laying their hands on their stomachs as if they are cradling the stomach, or cuddling it, visually emphasising the stomach and the future-baby in the photography. Similarly, when we do see her face, the gaze of the pregnant woman – at her stomach or into the distance – suggests modest anticipation of motherhood to come. These gazes are classically beatific (blissful), contemplative, and quite serious, as if in anticipatory abnegation. They express internal thoughts that are about her and her baby. The construction of these images centralises the pregnancy in the image by framing it with the hands, or effacing the head of the woman out of the image entirely. The gaze avoids the onlooker. By focusing on her stomach or at the middle distance, we have the impression that the camera is an interloper in a private moment between the woman, who she is and who she is becoming. Although these women are nude, or nearly nude, and these photographs are beautifully constructed, they are not performing sexy pregnancy. They are nude mothers-in-waiting. This is not to say that sexualised pregnancy photographs do not exist.

> ...If you don't feel like sex, take advantage of your heightened state of arousal by masturbating, or get your man to do it for you....[7]

Although they are in the minority, the difference between sexualised pregnancy photoshoots and the mainstream nude photoshoots bring into sharper relief how photographs about nude pregnancy, including the iconic photograph of Demi Moore, are rarely about sexual practice or desire. In contrast, a series of images by photographer Jennifer Williams[8] features a pregnant nude photoshoot where the client, dressed in her underwear, presents a performance of pregnancy that is certainly sexual. In these photographs, rather than wrapped up in drapes, the client is pulling them apart and looking fully and invitingly into the camera. In some shots, she poses with her arms above her head, bent at the elbow, holding up her hair, turning away from the camera with her eyes closed as if in ecstasy. In other shots, she is looking provocatively and deliberately at the camera and pulling the elastic of her underwear down over her hip. Elsewhere, she sits on the floor leaning against a bed, with her eyes shut, and her bra straps falling down from her shoulders, suggesting the conclusion of a satisfying sexual encounter. In another image, the woman appears to use her fingers, not to clasp her stomach, but to stroke the skin of her breasts and the inside of her thighs, her head is thrust back and her eyes are shut as if in erotic delight: images that are all the more transgressive when we consider this is a solo photoshoot and the suggestion of pleasure is that which she has brought herself. These images show a pregnant woman taking pleasure in her naked body on her own, and for herself. The gaze is sultry, it suggests orgasmic pleasure, and the viewer of the photographs is complicit in this sexualised moment. These photographs show a sexual pregnancy that is agentic, where the subject exudes sexual power that is not about subordination to the baby-to-come or the status-to-be.

Yet, as Tyler (2011) demonstrates, the increased *visibility* of sexualised pregnant bodies in public space should not be understood as a straightforward *acceptance* of their place in public space in general. HOTmilk (2018) is a luxury maternity underwear brand which promotes itself as selling lingerie that is 'empowering, feminine, practical and SEXY' (original emphasis).[9] The representation of femininity in their adverts echoes discourses of choice, autonomy and delight in the body that are manifest in Jennifer Williams' boudoir shoots, and masturbation advice from magazines. Yet, as Tyler highlights, only certain raced, classed, able and aged bodies appear here. And indeed, the very representation of sexy pregnancy itself in these adverts merits further scrutiny. The set of adverts called 'HOTmilk presents...' comprises series that are variously called 'Elegance and intrigue' from 2011, or 'Ever after' from 2010, or 'Take your time' from 2011/12. These feature heavily pregnant models in luxuriant poses, who, unlike in conventional images of nude pregnant bodies, gaze seductively or playfully, and directly at the camera, or concertedly and confidently – not reflectively – away from the camera, accompanied by text that conveys the theme of the collection:

> Her desire was dangerous, her playfulness was captivating, she blushes in delight, she craved a little decadence, she embraced the moment, midnight mystique, her radiance enchanted him. (HOTmilk, 2009)[10]

The settings in which these models pose are decadent. Even the ramshackle house, in which the 'Take your time' (2011) campaign is set, is bejewelled with crystal chandeliers and piles of fine china. These are aspirational settings for a consumer with money to spend. According to Johnstone and Longhurst (2009: 35), the manufacturers of this brand seek to remind pregnant women that they are 'beautiful, confident and sexy', which is why their models are shown in 'strong, powerful poses'. Indeed, these are not images of pregnant women clasping their stomachs, or wrapped in sheets, gazing at their stomachs; these are provocative, self-assured poses for the camera, intended to portray a sexually confident woman. And yet, although they are supposed to be empowered, these women represent a marginal and elite iteration of the pregnant female body. The models are able-bodied, taut, thin (but for the bump), predominantly white, young women. In the 'Elegance and intrigue' collection the reference to consumerism is explicit:

> Her tangled web tantalised, she was seemingly unaware, destruction followed her, mystery surrounded her, lost in a moment, she languished in luxury. (HOTmilk, 2011)[11]

Decadent, troubled, almost an aristocratic 'femme fatale', the construction of femininity here is one of mystique, allure: sorcery, perhaps. These are images we see again in the 'Ever after' collection that features women posing as female characters in fairy tales: Red Riding Hood, Snow White, Sleeping Beauty, Cinderella and Rapunzel. The text that accompanies this campaign reads:

> Tamed by her sensuality/her midnight charm was striking/ her enchanted dreams/awakened by her desire/radiant in her rescue/delighted with her victory. (HOTmilk, 2010)[12]

Some men do appear in these images, although they are faceless and objectified; Prince Charming has his back to the camera and kisses Cinderella's leg as she sits above him in a dominant position, smiling – not at him, but at the camera – draping a leg over his shoulder. In much the same faceless position, Prince Charming also attends a reclining Sleeping Beauty; while Rapunzel is saved by a faceless Prince with visibly muscular arms and shoulders. Again, she looks at the camera, not at him: the men are accessories in these images. Perhaps these are empowering twists on fairy tales that have conventionally often positioned women as submissive, in need of rescue, and always pristinely virginal. But they also reiterate the dominance of heteronormative desire, and the notion that the pregnant woman –'bewitching, beguiling' – is unknowable. Set apart in this way – taboo – sexualised pregnant women are once more presented as harbouring ambiguous and dangerous potentiality. Notwithstanding the empowering, erotic presentation of pregnancy here, it is also one that further entrenches some of the problems that pregnancy in public space poses. Rape culture composes women's bodies in public space as problems to be solved. The manifestation of uncanny sexuality that cannot be completely known or completely controlled and so is out-of-control reiterates this construction of women's bodies in public space as problems. This campaign is also an invitation for pregnant women to behave in a specific manner, to express certain desires, and to conform to a certain maternal aesthetic.

> …If he seems taken aback, it's not because he isn't interested – it's just because he might not be used to you being like this. But he's certainly not going to complain!….[13]

As this advice to pregnant women suggests, the hyper-sexuality exhibited (and desired) in representations like the HOTmilk advertisements is imagined to be unusual for women when they are not pregnant. These constructions of sexual desire position women as passive within a heteronormative encounter. Libidinous expressions are not part of the accoutrements of proper femininity. It is the men who are expected to be active pursuers of sex within the circuits of power made manifest through rape culture. This piece of advice imagines an *unusually* aroused female reader and her always-already ready-for-sex man who, in the performance of his own heteronormative masculinity, could not possibly complain about having a sexually interested partner. So, yes, pregnant and sexual women are more present in public space, but they are also more policed there (Fox et al, 2009).

Consider responses to a pregnant bikini contest analysed by Longhurst (2000) in New Zealand. The contest described was one of a series of competitions organised by a local radio station. On this occasion, the competition invited pregnant women to gather somewhere in downtown Auckland wearing only their bikinis. Other competitions organised by this radio show included 'driving to work naked, people pulling a bus, and several men ... wearing nothing but a fish bowl over their genitals' (Longhurst, 2000: 454); unusual practices – carnivalesque almost – which demonstrates the place that pregnant women in bikinis is thought to occupy in this imaginary. Some listeners of the radio station were angry, outraged and disgusted that a pregnant body should be exposed in public in such a way. Thus, even if women do not exclude themselves from public space, it is clear that public scrutiny certainly does so (Longhurst, 2000: 463-4). And even if the nude pregnancy photoshoot has become almost a rite of passage, and the appearance of the naked and sexy pregnant body in public more normalised, the form of sexuality that is portrayed and the type of body that portrays it is still tightly striated.

Against a background of contemporary rape culture, anxiety about the shift from the 'charmed circle' to the 'outer limits' is profound here for the way in which (in)appropriate performances of sexual desire in pregnancy are sanctioned (Rubin, 1984). This curtailment, control and delineation designates who can be sexy, and who cannot be, where sexiness is appropriate – necessary, even – where it is not, and what forms it might take. Legitimising certain bodies in certain places in certain ways in public space, and rejecting or excluding, or denigrating others, illustrates the tight grasp that contemporary rape culture has on the pregnant body in public along lines that are explicitly misogynistic.

Heretical ethics

Kristeva (2005: 1) is suspicious of a socio-cultural present that 'overvalues pregnancy' and erases the potentiality of what it can do, politically. For Kristeva, the pregnant body is politically creative. It can simultaneously occupy different sites, spaces and times. Through this, alternative feminist politics, which she calls herethics, or the 'heretical ethics of love', might be conceived. This is a philosophy that exceeds the space/time of the pregnancy to mobilise a politics of critical exteriority (McAfee, 2004: 81).

Herethics work by mobilising the idea of 'Women's Time', which Kristeva suggests emerges from the 'archaic mother' as bringer of life. Mother is universal, and all humans have a relationship of some sort with the mother. Pregnant women, in their not-yet-mother state, hold the memory of their own mothers and the anticipated memory of their child-to-come (Oliver, 2010). For instance, according to Kristeva (2005: 3), 'the child's language acquisition implies that the mother also re-learns the language'; she goes back in time even as she moves forward through it. Cyclical, recursive time is 'Women's Time'. It allows different subject positions to emerge simultaneously. It is a recognition of the porosity and indeterminacy of the pregnant body that mobilises this porosity as a political ethics of living, rather than trying to subsume the pregnant body into the striates of linear time (or of Men's Time).

For Kristeva (2005: 2), the power of herethics incorporates an ambiguous love that is narcissistic, but that is also, in the 'good enough mother', displaceable, or that could be sublimated. 'This motion of expulsion of detachment is essential', she explains, to create space for the love-object to thrive, to think, to take up space of its own. Part of how this is possible is through thinking herethics as a composition of flows. These are flows that enable the child to *live*, and also enable the child to *leave*; they resist the abnegation of the woman to the surrender of being-mother. They are muscular vacillations that are made possible through the heretical ethics of love.

Kristeva's philosophy is rooted in the distinction between the symbolic and semiotic, and this distinction helps us – especially those of us with an aversion to androcentric psychoanalytic universalisms – with this figure of the passionate mother. The symbolic is the written or linguistic way in which the indeterminate, expansive, eventful semiotic is articulated. Not unlike the relationship between the virtual and the actual, where the actual is the crystallised expression of the immanent and potential virtual plane, the relationship between semiotic and symbolic is not one of dichotomies (Deleuze, 2006 [1977]). Sure, the actual/the symbolic pierces the virtual/the semiotic so that meaning can be gleaned or shared or articulated, but the semiotic and virtual far exceed the points at which they are pinned into representation. Here, if 'the mother', 'Women's Time' and 'Men's Time' are all understood as semiotic mothers/women/men rather than actual women, or mothers, or men, we move away from universalising and heteronormative claims towards a mobilisation of herethical philosophy as Kristeva intended it; not inherently maternal, not inherently about mothering children, or even about women at all. The image-objects described here are symbolic representations of the semiotic of contemporary pregnancy. Whether contemplative, reflective, inward-looking and angelic as in pregnancy photoshoots, or mysterious, unknowable and excessive as they appear in pregnancy lingerie marketing, these representations pinpoint moments in which what is understood to be the performance of contemporary pregnancy is crystallised.

Two potential problems with this proposal must be addressed here: the charge that Kristeva is essentialist and reduces women to their maternal capacities, and the charge that Kristeva's psychoanalytically inclined framework is incompatible with the Deleuzoguattarian framework that mobilises the guerrilla war machine that we are looking for in this book. Certainly, the maternal, reproductive figure is important in Kristeva's articulation of Women's Time. Yet Kristeva herself rejects the notion that women *ought to be* mothers, or that the politics of Woman's Time should even be limited to individuals who identify as women (Kristeva, quoted in Guberman, 1996; Kristeva, 2005). The importance of the relationship between the symbolic and the semiotic cannot be overstated here. As we have seen, through Longhurst's analyses of pregnant women's use of public space, through Tyler's (2000) critiques of feminist philosophers' accounts of pregnancy, through the iconic poses of pregnancy photography, through Lupton's (2012a, b) and Carol Mason's (2000) debates around foetal citizenship, and through what Rebekah Fox et al (2009) and Robin Root and Carol Browner (2001) tell us about how far women comply with, or resist against, pregnancy 'norms' across generations, *pregnancy is performative*. What we recognise as pregnant practice is also *symbolic* pregnancy. How pregnancy is done, what it looks like and the place it occupies in contemporary socio-cultural contexts is defined by the iteration of 'doing pregnancy'. Even doing 'pregnancy trouble' through pregnant pornography (Huntley, 2000; Longhurst, 2006; Musial, 2014), pregnant bikini contests (Longhurst, 2000) or by rejecting pregnancy (Lundquist, 2008; Côté-Arsenault et al, 2009) reinscribes the performativity of pregnancy. Yet, what pregnancy might be like – has the potential to be like – is vast. This performative element marks it as something other than essential. And yet, the problem that pregnancy poses, and that we have seen, is, in part, its embodiment.

The period of gestation, the pain of labour, the separation of one body into two (or more), remain inescapable facts of pregnancy. So, while it is not accurate to say that Kristeva's accounts of pregnancy are essentialist, it is certainly not enough to say that pregnancy exists only through socio-cultural constructions, and this is an antagonism that casts pregnancy as a problem.

Part of the way in which we can discern that Kristeva does not intend for her construction of pregnancy to be construed as essentialist also helps us to address the seeming incoherence between her psychoanalytic approach and the vigorously anti-psychoanalytic writings of Deleuze and Guattari. As Noelle McAfee (2004) and Kelly Oliver (1993, 2010) note, Kristeva's writings are metaphysical, and about an eventful, rather than crystallised, body. The love that she imagines as transformative can be understood as semiotic rather than actualised romantic, emotional love. It has deterritorialising qualities; it 'embodies passion and dispassion, or passion and working through passion' (Oliver, 2008-10: 4).

By forging a subjectivity that is not fixed, not self, not other, in a flow of Becomings- across time and space, it resonates with the ideas that Deleuze and Guattari evoke in their philosophy. Woman's Time is a potential war machine forging smooth space through linear time, to disrupt orderings and open up metamorphic politics. Certainly, Kristeva's insistence on the psychoanalytical does not sit well with metaphysical approaches, and some of the logic she espouses is based on speciesist sentiments that distinguish between animal drives and human passions, but elements of her 'process' philosophy (with its focus on flow and eventfulness) can enter into a dialogue with elements of Deleuzoguattarian thought. Indeed, Kristeva's articulation of the dynamic between mother–child and separation – the herethics – is a way of transcending the dualisms that blight some of the ways that Deleuze and Guattari articulate their thought.

Kristeva argues that women are irreconcilably different because of this maternal power (whether real, actualised, or semiotic), which is why the maternal body – composed of flows – is subversive, and does not conform to dominant narratives of power. A feminist project should not seek to erase this difference, but rather ought to mobilise this 'permanent marginality', or this 'becoming-minoritarian', as 'vigilance that keeps groups from closing up, from being homogenous and so, oppressive' (Kristeva, quoted in Guberman, 1996: 45). Minoritarian politics are ethical responses to the aggression of State instruments (Deleuze and Guattari, 2004a [1980], 2004b [1972]). Becoming-minoritarian means avoiding the *dicta* of State thought. It is about thinking and acting otherways/wise. Making-the-same is a form of putting-in-place (Cresswell, 1997). Becoming-minoritarian is a form of resistance to, and disassembly of, this striated ordering. Proposing instead a position of 'outlaw', Kristeva's formulation is one that seeks to carve out of homogeneity, spaces of potentiality and of resistant Becomings– (Oliver, 1993).

Kristeva embraces the negative space of pregnancy, the ambivalence, the ambiguity, and through this, attempts to recuperate pregnancy from its potential construction as an essentially unfeminist act, or state, towards one that can be imagined as politically transformative. And it is this that we might begin to harness in order to undo the way that rape culture striates and is striated by pregnancy in public. Kristeva proposes that we build these herethics through disobedience of 'paternal law', or what we might think of as the State. Another way of thinking about this 'paternal law' is as a manifestation of rape culture. If, as McAfee (2004: 98) suggests, women are too 'entranced' by the image of 'woman as mother' to 'remain in the margins subverting or deriding the law', then this, in part, is what reifies and venerates or 'overvalues' pregnancy (Kristeva, 2005: 1). It is what is going on in debates about what a nude pregnancy photoshoot or a sexy pregnancy should look like, for instance. A discourse of pregnancy-as-sacred, or special, *is* 'entrancing', but it is a construction of sexuality as pure and sexless that finally excludes pregnant women from public space, or at least tries to. It reinscribes a culture that sustains, and is sustained by, contemporary rape culture, that women, their bodies, and their sexual desire cannot be ever fully theirs. Of course, sexlessness might be liberating for women, but must it be compulsory?

As Young (2005: 88) indicates, it is the separation of sexuality from pregnancy, or maternity, which is the fold along which patriarchy and, for our purposes, rape culture, is able to thrive. Elements of the sexual or sexy pregnancy have, without doubt, been recaptured by a heteronormative framing, such as this one:

> …nipple stimulation releases the hormone oxytocin, which can kick-start contractions, as can the prostaglandins in sperm. Just go gently. You can also give him oral sex. Prostaglandins are more easily absorbed in the gut than the cervix, so oral sex is likely to have a better effect than penetrative sex. Doctors think this is an old wives' tale, but there's no harm in trying and he'll sure thank you for it….[14]

The emphasis on having a pregnancy bump that is the right shape and size, emphasis on fashions that inscribe certain parts of the pregnant body as sexy – these do little to disrupt conventional notions of sexual practice. Here, the imaginary of the sexually enthusiastic pregnant woman who would fellate her way into labour, is one, once again, of heteronormative coupling, where here, sex is for the birth of the baby, or the pleasure of the man, but not explicitly the thrill of the woman. Dominant expressions of sexy pregnancy are also raced and classed, as we have seen in the context of marketing sexy pregnancy to pregnant women (Tyler, 2008; Fox et al, 2009). Nonetheless, we can perceive lines of flight from these inscriptions; Drglin (2015: 158) and Musial (2014) separately highlight how manifestations of sexual practice and desire can become subversive in the context of the sexual pregnancy. When not expressed as more chaste 'sensuality' or for the benefit of the foetus (Huntley, 2000: 355), the sexual practice of pregnant women crosses the taboo of pregnancy-as-sacred, particularly in childbirth.

> ...in the early stages (and in private, obvs), you may find that masturbating or using a vibrator really helps ease pain and move things on.... If you're intrigued enough to try it, keep Ann Summer's finest hidden from the hospital staff....[15]

Writing of Susie Bright's description of masturbating in labour as pain relief, Musial (2014: 402) demonstrates how transgressive sexual practice in pregnancy can be, particularly when it is framed as an agentic, sex-positive, and non-normative practice. Bright's approach to pain relief in childbirth is certainly a line of flight from dominant constructions of the performance of pregnancy. It might even be considered profane. But can this form of sexual agency be manifest outside of the delivery room and outside the space/time of childbirth? Dismantling constructions of pregnant women as demure, pure, nurturing, in need of protection or tainted by sex, and polluted, abject, dangerous, or otherwise out-of-place would also begin to dismantle rape culture. Interrogating these constructions would have the effect of challenging rape culture because they would begin to call into question the ease with which these narratives are able to circulate to inform all areas of social, cultural, and economic life. By analysing why it is that some sexualisation of pregnancy is appealing, why some is *outré*, why some is obscene, we come to understand better what composes our knowledge in the first place, and how far this knowledge is inflected by a rape culture that denigrates women's sexual subjectivity in public space more broadly.

These constructions of pregnancy do not emerge in a vacuum. They themselves compose how pregnancy is performed, which is a public manifestation of pregnancy norms and 'doing good pregnancy'. We see these in the discourses that compose pregnancy photoshoots, and that compose the sort of advice sex-positive publications give to pregnant women. If we take seriously Young's suggestion that 'patriarchy is founded on the border between motherhood and sexuality', and that this separation needs to be 'dissolved' for women to be free (2005: 87-8), then a herethical approach has some potential here, by mobilising a position that has the potential to politicise the borderline (Kristeva, 1981, 1995).

Certainly, pregnancy may cushion women from the 'sexually objectifying gaze which ... instrumentalises her when in her non-pregnant state' (Young, 1984: 53), and the desexualisation of pregnancy may actually be experienced as empowering for women who are otherwise subject to a scrutinising patriarchal gaze. Through this, women may move about in public space more freely, attending less to their movements or appearance or other things that may provoke comment from onlookers. But what if women do not want to be desexualised, despite their pregnancy? Agentic sexual expression is an important way for women to assert sexual autonomy. While sexy agency does emerge somewhat problematically from post-feminist discourses, as a classed, raced, ableist, youth-centric category, there are many women – queer women, fat women, poor women, Black women, old women, disabled women – whose sexual agency has been erased, ridiculed or ignored in contemporary discourse and who may want to contest this desexualisation. The desexualisation of pregnant women is part of a broader move to essentialise mothers as sacred, inviolable and pure. Such a construction sets these women apart from other un-sacred women and men: an exclusion that is bad for everyone (see also Young, 1980: 166; Oliver, 2010: 764). Women left behind – (hyper/hetero)sexualised women (which is itself a classed and ageist and raced category) – remain 'fair game' in the scrutiny of their bodies in public. This upholds a sacred/profane distinction that indelibly casts the sexual body of women and men as polluted, disgusting or abject, and this construction of sexual practice as pollution, or filth, as we have seen, sustains rape culture. Holding up this dichotomy denigrates women who do not conform to the sexless ascetic aesthetic, whether in pregnancy or not. Meanwhile, denied full sexual personhood, the chaste and venerated pregnant woman becomes excluded from other spheres, not least public spaces. This also sustains rape culture by consolidating constructions of idealised femininities as inherently out-of-place in public space (Hubert and Mauss, 1981 [1964]; Wilson, 1991; Solnit, 2000).

The agency that pregnant women manifest in their use of public space, and the manifestation of their sexuality therein, might forge a *polis* of pregnant space to subvert normative striations of public space that cast it as masculinised, patriarchal, heterosexist and exclusionary. Whether it is about reminding women that pregnancy is a public problem, and that their bodies are public property, even as their pregnancy discursively marks them as heterosexistly 'possessed', public space is striated with antagonistic exclusions. Through herethics, we might make a war machine that transcends a dichotomous notion of self/other, belonging/not belonging, public/private, sexual/sexless. We are able to do this, in part, because herethics are unfixed, eventful, and full of potential. But more than this, once we transcend these dichotomies, pregnancy need be neither vilified *nor* venerated. It is liminal, it is exceptional, but it does not need to be treated as 'in exception'. The next section of this chapter explores this question of exceptionalism in the context of pregnancy and sexual harassment in public space.

Sexual harassment and pregnancy: A public confinement?

In 2015, I was nearly seven months pregnant with my first child. It was an autumnal Sunday afternoon. I was on my way to meet my friend. The sun was shining brightly, but it was chilly. I was wearing a tight, black, velveteen mini-dress and knee-high Doc Marten boots. Like Young (1984) and others, I, too, was delighting in the sometimes ludicrous new shape I had acquired. It was the sort of frock that I would not normally ever have worn. I felt good. As I walked down the street − a street I had not long lived on − a man walking purposefully towards me, and holding out his hands, exclaimed "Beautiful!" and grasped my stomach just above my crotch, and looked me in the eyes, intently. I screwed up my face in exaggerated repulsion and made an 'urgh' sound as I skirted out of his grasp. Waiting at the bus stop, I remember feeling shocked that I had been touched so unexpectedly, and also a bit disgusted that my body − and my baby − had been touched in this intrusive and vulgar fashion. I said nothing. Then, two young men − maybe five or ten years younger than me − also approached the bus stop. "Hey baby", said the shorter one to me with a smile, "are you with anyone? Are you with anyone?" "Leave it!", rebuked his friend, "she's pregnant." I remember being angry, and frightened, and impatient for the bus, and also, and mostly, silent.

These two encounters, and my response to them, made me think about the role that sexual harassment plays in the ambiguous positioning of pregnancy. What does it mean to 'be with anyone?' Was this man asking me if I was actually alone? Unchaperoned? Does it mean, am I in a relationship with anyone? Am I 'spoken for'? In my visibly pregnant state, what would it have meant to not be 'with anyone'? And then, his friend, calling him back because I was pregnant: does this mean, in a world where pregnancy normatively suggests coupledom, 'of course she is with someone, don't waste your time'? Does it mean she should be exempt from your cat-calling because, in a state of pregnancy, she is not fair game? Does it mean she is not sexy enough to flirt with, because she is huge and pregnant, so stop it? And if I had not been pregnant at that time … would he have let his friend continue? Would it simply have just been okay? And the man who grabbed my stomach, which I experienced as groping, even though a stomach is not (usually) a sexualised part of the body.… He touched me because I was pregnant. Would I have been less horrified if he had touched me higher on my bump? Would I have been less horrified if he had touched my breasts? Certainly, I do know that what happened here in the space of 10 minutes was that I was both sexually harassed *and* protected from sexual harassment, *because I was visibly pregnant.*

Sexual harassment in public space is an expression of a latent, ubiquitous, striating and thriving rape culture. As Solnit (2000: 233) suggests, 'women have routinely been punished for that most simple of freedoms, taking a walk, because their walking, and indeed their very being, have been construed as sexual … in societies concerned with controlling women's sexuality.' Likewise, Gardner (1995), Elizabeth Kissling (1991), and Elizabeth Stanko (1990) have demonstrated that sexualised harassment is one form of this 'punishment'. Sexual harassment in public space by men towards women reinscribes heteropatriarchal, hierarchical power relations into the terrain of public space. It is a State instrument that striates public space and reminds women of the latent menace of sexual violence (Deleuze and Guattari, 2004a [1980]). Not simply a tactic of control, sexual harassment is also an expression of anxiety about bodies, about disorderly bodies, about bodies out-of-place. If contemporary rape culture constitutes public space as masculine, into which women's bodies are cast as interlopers, the spectre (and indeed the practice) of sexual violence becomes an attempt to deal with this trouble. Whether pregnant or not, women internalise sexual harassment in public spaces as something that must be navigated daily, usually without making a fuss. This is not to say that women are generally submissive to sexual harassment, or that they tolerate it even, or that they do not fight against it, but rather that the fact of sexual harassment is so banal – even as it cloaks something more sinister – that it rarely raises comment (Kelly and Radford, 1990). Reporting a look, a leer, a stare, a whistle, or an uncomfortable comment that is dressed up as a compliment, but that actually makes me/you/us/her feel awkward, is not easy. Even more obviously violent interactions – a grope, a flash, a threat, or lewd comment – although also frightening, are also difficult to draw attention to. Difficult, because they may not seem particularly noteworthy, or because the menace is hard to convey, or because the moment was fleeting, and to whom would you report your experience, anyway? These constraints form part of decentralised micro-aggressions that striate public space as a site of exclusion for women.

This gendered construction is rehearsed over and again through attempts to control women's entry into public space via the mobilisation of fear of crime discourses, women's historic exclusion from politics or from the workplace and their relegation to a denigrated private, domestic sphere. This sort of exclusion is one way in which spatial injustices are able to proliferate. Indeed, the very rape culture that is the subject of our scrutiny in this book sustains, and is sustained by, women's exclusion from public space, and their harassment when in public. In this section, I examine how the sexual/desexualised pregnant body discussed in the previous section becomes a site of antagonism and of violence in public space. I examine the ways in which women describe being sexually harassed – usually by strangers, as it turned out – in public spaces while visibly pregnant.

In 2016 I conducted a survey of women's experiences of sexual harassment in pregnancy. My intention was to hear of the different ways in which women experience sexual harassment while pregnant, and the extent to which this affected them in terms of their relationship to public space, their approach to other people and to their sense of self. The survey consisted of 35 questions, 20 of which sought qualitative responses, which is what I base most of my discussion on in this chapter. The survey included questions like 'How did this experience affect the way you felt about yourself/other people/public space?' and 'How much do you think about your safety in public space when you are pregnant/not pregnant?'

The survey was distributed via internet fora used by parents (usually women). Three websites were used to promote the survey – two based in the UK and one in the USA,[16] though the scope of these was worldwide – and over a period of four weeks, 318 women responded to the survey in full. Although this is a large number of respondents for qualitative enquiries, these results cannot be considered to be representative of women who have been pregnant in general, and indeed, this is not my intention. Although widely used in victimisation studies, the limitations of survey methods are also well recognised in feminist research (Smith, 1994; Koskela and Pain, 2000). Instead, I use this method in order to understand from other women what sexual harassment in public spaces, when pregnant, is like, what happens, and what the effects of it are. How is it similar to, or different from, sexual harassment when not pregnant? I decided to employ this method principally as a response to the fact that despite a wealth of research into sexual harassment and an emerging body of work about pregnancy in the public sphere, there remain no studies that examine the two together. The broader lens that this method afforded enabled me to put together a more expansive picture of how this manifests itself, and to better understand the tensions between sexual practice, public space, pregnancy and rape culture.

Researching sexual harassment in pregnancy

I base my definition of sexual harassment on that given in the UK Equality Act 2010 as 'unwanted behaviour of a sexual nature which violates dignity, makes women feel intimidated, degraded or humiliated, or creates a hostile or offensive environment.' Of the 318 respondents who participated fully in the survey, 200 were from the USA, 113 were from the UK and 5 from other countries in the world. Participants were aged between 18 and 64 (3% aged between 18-25, 23% aged between 26-34, 26% aged between 35-44, 31% aged between 45-54, 17% between 55-64). They were predominantly white (79% compared to Black 11%, South-East Asian 2%, Indian 3%, Other 5%). They were predominantly heterosexual (93%, 4% were bisexual, 3% Other). Eighty-seven per cent of participants answered that they had experienced some form of sexual harassment in public spaces during their lives; 18% ($n = 57$) of respondents reported experiencing sexual harassment while visibly pregnant. Although this is a smaller proportion than the number of women who had experienced sexual harassment ever in their lives, the later stages of pregnancy tend to represent a relatively short amount of time in a woman's life, and tend to only happen a handful of times in women's lives.[17] Other participants who did not fall into this category responded to questions in the survey about their experiences of sexual harassment in general, and their attitudes towards sexual harassment and fear of crime in pregnancy. Sexual harassment in pregnancy appears to affect fewer women than when not pregnant, but it still represents a significant number of women. It is the stories of these 57 women that I focus on predominantly for the rest of this chapter.

The most commonly occurring forms of sexual harassment reported were: unwanted sexual gestures (34%), being whistled at (56%), being called 'doll, babe, honey etc' (49%), being stared at (60%), unwanted sexual teasing, jokes or remarks and questions (39%), and sexual comments (40%).[18] Other forms of sexual harassment that women reported included being touched, pressured for sex, brushed up against, asked personal and intrusive questions, sexually assaulted, and raped. Most commonly occurring forms of sexual harassment, then, are those that are perhaps the least invasive. Unlike rape or sexual assault, it is not in itself a crime to stare at someone or to call them 'babe'. Instead, they form part of a cacophony of small-scale micro-aggressions that convey to women that they are fair game in public space, that they are consumable, and that discursively they could internalise the vulnerable position into which they are cast through these interactions.

Participants in the survey reported that their safety was very important to them in public space in general. During pregnancy the majority of women reported that they were no more or no less worried about their safety than when they were not pregnant (36%). However, a considerable number of them worried a lot more (26%) or a little more (22%) about their safety in public spaces during pregnancy; 6% said that they only worried about their safety during pregnancy, while only 1% worried a lot less or a little less than when they were not pregnant. Of course, worry about safety can mean more than worry about fear of crime or safety from sexual harassment in public space. As Longhurst (1997, 1999, 2001), Bailey (2001), and Lupton (2012a, b) have all demonstrated, concern for the unborn foetus – and the discursive necessity of this concern (Root and Browner, 2001) – are significant pressures on pregnant women and form part of the performativity of pregnancy. The notion that women are doing good pre-motherhood by worrying about their safety in a public space constructed to exclude them might contribute to some of these figures, and begins to paint a picture of the role that rape culture has in the performativity of pregnancy by emphasising this debilitating concern about safety. Beyond this, concern that the body might leak, or seep, or otherwise exceed its borders (Cresswell, 1996; Longhurst, 1999) might well lead women to worry more about their safety in public space when they are pregnant than when they are not, quite apart from specific worry about fear of crime or the threat of sexual harassment.

Women said that that they felt safer when they were with people they knew, when it was daylight, when they were in familiar areas, when they were near their home, or if they carried a weapon or something that could be used as a weapon. Conversely, factors that decreased feelings of safety included being in an isolated area, being near groups of men hanging around, when it was dusk, or night, or when they were lost. These are findings in line with dominant discourses about what is considered to be safe and not safe in public space. They confirm how safety in public space, which is highly prized by the women who participated in this survey, is discursively constructed through heteropatriarchal spatial limitations, through proximity to the home, the familiar, in a position of anticipated victimisation (carrying a weapon to use for defence, not offense). Being isolated, lost or obscured constructs public space as strange and unsafe. Being proximate to the menace of groups of men can be understood as an internalisation of a masculinist construction of public space. Echoing Solnit (2000: 241), these findings point to the 'conservative, gregarious' way in which these women imagine themselves in public. Not for them the dreadful delights of revelling in the city by night, of solitary walking as *flâneuse*, of the *dérive*, of losing one's way, of discovering others (Wilson, 1994; Solnit, 2000; Elkin, 2016). Not yet here the forging of smooth space.

Most women reported that they had been sexually harassed in pregnancy by men. Four respondents reported being sexually harassed by women or by both men and women, and 73% of women who were sexually harassed when they were pregnant did not know the perpetrator. The rest had been sexually harassed by colleagues, acquaintances, members of their family or friends. For the most part, the sexual harassment occurred in outdoor public space (streets, parks, the beach), but it also took place in shops, shopping malls, on public transport, at parties, at home, at work and online. Of the women who did tell someone about their experience, only one told the police. Most who did tell, told their families or friends. Those who did not tell anyone did not, because, in their words: 'it would just happen anyway so no need to mention [it]', or 'People are just like that, it's not a big deal.' These dismissive responses to sexual harassment certainly serve to diminish the significance of it on women's spatial subjectivities. They also illustrate some of the ways in which these small-scale harassments are considered to be casual yet ubiquitous. It is because of this banalisation of micro-aggressions that rape culture is able to thrive, by normalising these harassments as 'no big deal'.

The mundanity of sexual harassment

In order to further excavate what happened in these events, I asked the participants to tell me about the most recent instance of sexual harassment they had experienced during pregnancy. The examples drawn here concern women who are visibly pregnant and using public space in very ordinary ways. This is not to suggest that the women themselves are ordinary, but rather that their activities are unexceptional – going to the shops or going to work – and yet they become sites of antagonism in which women can be sexually harassed, in part because of the ambiguous sexual/sexless state that composes pregnancy and that has been critiqued in this chapter. The stories that they told demonstrate the trouble the pregnant body can pose when it interlopes into public space, and the attempts made to exclude or victimise it. This is because, within a heteropatriarchal framework, the irruption within the public space (dominated by men) of a private body out of place composes a series of micro-challenges to the consecrated somatic norm of public space (Puwar, 2004). Remarks about women's pregnant bodies, remarks which fetishised the stomach itself, remarks which transgressed norms of pregnant performativity and attempts to touch women's stomachs were all cited as examples of this form of harassment.

Given that unwanted staring, touching and comments were the most commonly occurring forms of sexual harassment they experienced, it is not surprising that many of the stories that the women told were about these sorts of events. Women wrote about being jeered at, being shouted at in the street, or being stared at. The examples I draw on here are specifically related to unwanted comments and remarks made to women about their pregnant bodies:

> 'I was getting out of my car and this guy was up the sidewalk, sitting on a bumper to the parking lot and he made obscene comments about "How fed up I was" and thought that was hilarious.'

> 'I was out on the beach fixing to go in the water and some people sitting nearby, both men and women, both said "Look, the whale has a suit on that blends with the water. Hope we don't hit her when we're surfing".'

These two women give examples of how their pregnant bodies were mocked by men, and in the latter case, by other women. The embodiment of pregnancy – that it is necessarily of the body –

inscribes the appearance of the body in public space as a public body. The particularity of the size of women's pregnant bodies – the 'whale', the play on words of being 'fed up' – reminds us of how, within the socio-cultural and geographical setting of the respondents, certain body shapes are valorised and others are stigmatised as fat, even in pregnancy. As we saw in the discussion of sexy pregnant photography, anxiety about not appearing 'fat' in pregnancy, having a pregnancy of a good shape and size, has become a way in which to 'do' pregnancy (Bailey, 2001; Tyler, 2011). Pregnant women are supposed to appear with a small-ish, tidy-shaped bump, a taut body, without visible stretch marks or unsightly swellings. Ridiculing women for the shape of their pregnancy is a way to remind women, discursively, that their bodies are to be consumed, and (*contra* suggestions by Young, 1984 and Bailey, 2001 that women in pregnancy are beyond the reach of sexist comments) that they remain within an sexist economy in which the evaluation of the body is a currency of control. Part of the reason why these comments about the size, shape or fact of the pregnant body are an attempt to striate or control or exclude women's bodies from public space is because women are not expected to take up too much space. Small bodies, small steps, timidity and trepidation are more usually how the female body is discursively imagined or desired. A body that is excessive takes up space. It is a more visible body, it is more demanding, and it causes more trouble:

> 'I was with my husband while he was talking to someone trying to sell his truck. This man that I did not know came out of the store and was staring at me. He asked me if I needed someone to rub my belly, and was acting like I should get on the back of his motorcycle with him. Very inappropriate.'

Not all comments about women's bodies were expressions that fetishised the pregnancy itself. Here, however, the comment that this participant reports describes precisely that. Like the participant above, who understood the comment about being 'fed up' as 'obscene', that this respondent describes this as 'very inappropriate', illustrates the taboo that such a comment transgresses. The construction of pregnancy as sacred, set apart, exceptional and in need of protecting, is part of what turns this into an 'inappropriate' comment (Hubert and Mauss, 1981 [1964]).

However, even if these interjections are expressions of sexual desire, they also emerge in a contemporary rape culture that casts them as acts of violence (and certainly why could expressions of desire not also be, simultaneously, expressions of violence?). Here, this is 'inappropriate' for the participant, in part because her pregnancy marks her as 'taken'. It is not clear whether this interjection happens in front of her husband, but given that pregnancies are usually a marker of an exclusive heteronormative coupling, the visible fact of her pregnancy means that this comment becomes a deliberate confrontation of this norm.

The ambiguously sexual pregnant body is mirrored by an ambiguously sexual remark about the stomach of the woman's body that is not usually considered to be a site of sexual desire or fetish. Focusing on the stomach, sexual harassment in pregnancy exposes women to aggression that is slightly different to harassment they might experience when not pregnant. This is also evidenced in ways that women reported being touched in pregnancy:

'Lady was insistent [on] wanting to touch my stomach. I told her to leave me alone but she kept coming to touch my stomach. I ran behind the counter and she ran after me. The store owner had to physically restrain the lady and call the police.'

'We were at a party, and also at work this happened, where people would touch my stomach without my permission or they would get into my space and I felt very awkward about it.'

'I don't know if you consider touching, but while pregnant, people in general always want to touch my stomach and I was not comfortable if they just did without asking and this is what happened; without asking.'

In each case, women reported the touching of the pregnant stomach as a form of sexual harassment. The contributors said that they felt 'awkward', that they were 'not comfortable' about being touched. One of them involved the police. Touching the stomach is an unusual form of sexual harassment, in part because the stomach is not, conventionally in the socio-cultural context from which we are speaking, a sexually objectified area in women in the way that breasts, legs or buttocks might be. In fact, the stomach is often constructed as a site of hate or of loathing if it is large, fat, or saggy or stretch-marked, especially if it is any of these things and it is not a pregnant stomach (Russo, 1995; Ussher,

2006). One of the participants was not sure it would even count as sexual harassment in this study, such is the unusual position it occupies.

What is stomach touching about? Touching without permission reminds us once again of how the pregnant body is a public body. Colleagues, friends and strangers touch pregnant women in a way that they would not if they were not pregnant, which also highlights how, in the words of Young (1984: 49), in pregnancy, we do not have a firm sense of 'where [one] body ends and the world begins.' For Young, it was her own ambiguity about the border between self and other that she described. Here, it could also be said to be an ambiguity shared with the 'world'. The body is public in part because it is neither one body nor more than one. This liminal neither/nor opens the body up to scrutiny, including unwanted touching of the stomach, and is one of the reasons why women report that people feel entitled to touch them in this way. It calls into question the discursive political integrity of the body. Echoing contemporary discourses of foetal citizenship (Lupton, 2012a, b), if this body is not fully mine, or not only mine, does it belong to the baby? Does it belong to everyone?

Certainly, the pregnant stomach holds a secret – a foetus that only the carrier can feel – and so touching might be a way to try to share this secret, to feel the foetus move, or to check that the pregnancy feels well, or to connect with power over life. But as an interaction, it is possessive. To 'lay your hands on' something is not only to find and seize it, but also to attack or brutalise someone. Within religious discourses, to lay hands on someone means to heal, or bless, or ordain them, which resonates with the notion that pregnancy is somehow sacred. Even here, the ambiguity of what it means to 'lay hands' reflects the different meanings associated with touching the pregnant stomach. These different ways of understanding stomach touching, including understanding it as sexual harassment, as a blessing, or as an aggression, demonstrate some of the problems posed by, and posed to, pregnant bodies in public.

Participants also reported sexual aggressions that were more explicitly expressions of heteropatriarchal possession of the pregnant female body as a chattel, and in some cases, the cuckholding of their partners:

> 'I was walking to a store and saw someone I recognised. I don't really know him well, but he was a friend of someone's. He came over to say "hi". Then he started making advances. Talking about how I looked good, and to forget my boyfriend, and saying other perverted things. Then he got closer and was rubbing up on me and trying

to touch me inappropriately. I felt horrible and weirded out. I moved as fast as I could to get away and went into the store so there was other people around, so he would leave me alone.... I was eight months pregnant and could only go so fast, but I did.'

Reading this participant's story, it becomes apparent that the 'perverted advances' that this acquaintance was making were when she was unmistakably pregnant. She describes moving to where there were other people and being hampered in her movement by her size. In wanting her to 'forget her boyfriend', this interlocutor suggests perhaps that he wants to take his place. He acknowledges that the boyfriend exists. As we have already suggested, women who are pregnant are usually in monogamous relationships with men (although this is certainly not always the case), and even if they are not, they are thus discursively composed, so this interjection is about possessing a 'taken' woman, as one might do a territory, reinforcing further the heteropatriarchy that is mobilised through this harassment that sustains, and is sustained by, rape culture.

'I was walking to work and I had to pass a crew of construction workers. The comment made was "I sure could love on you and not worry about getting you pregnant".'

Although usually associated with homosexual sexual practice, bare-backing – or penetrative or oral sex without a condom – is also associated with risky sexual practice that might be considered more intimate and more pleasurable than sex that is protected by a barrier method of contraception. Of course, once a woman is pregnant, she cannot get pregnant again during that pregnancy. This man affronts pregnancy norms with his comment by envisioning unprotected sex with this woman.

While there is no reason why women cannot have sex when they are pregnant, or indeed, why they might not have sex with someone who is not their partner when they are pregnant, there is a squeamishness about sexual activity with pregnant women in these contexts (Longhurst; 2006; Drglin, 2015). This is, in part, because the marker of pregnancy is also a marker of having been possessed by another man. The speaker transgresses two taboos – about non-reproductive and unprotected sex, and about sex with a woman who 'belongs' to someone else. This functions in an economy of rape culture where the pregnant woman, although publicly pregnant, is also of the private, domestic, personal, possessed realm. We can see the pernicious influence of rape culture here, in the heteronormative expression of desire about possession, and invading the body with semen that cannot make a woman pregnant, or in spite of her presumed commitment to another man (quite apart from whether or not there is a man).

In some cases, women reported being sexually harassed because they were pregnant, where the pregnant body was a fetish object or object of sexual desire in itself:

> 'I was on a social dating site I register[ed] for prior to getting pregnant. I went online due to boredom and just [to] conversate. A man suggested we meet to have fun. I advised I am pregnant. He insisted we go ahead and have sex, since his perception is [that] sex is better with a pregnant woman and he will pay me.'

> 'He was telling me how sexy pregnant women are and asking how sex was during pregnancy.'

> 'Dude stopped walking and came up and touched my stomach and said how sexy pregnant woman are and how it makes the pussy better.'

Unlike the previous case above, here the men are talking about pregnancy as sexy in itself, rather than just convenient for avoiding (further) pregnancy. In a socio-cultural context where pregnant women are constructed as sexless in public life – despite being marked, at least discursively, by sex – these comments trouble dominant constructions of the pregnant body in public space. Certainly, as Tyler (2011) and Longhurst's (2006) observations about sexual desirability in pregnancy demonstrate, contemporary attitudes are more accepting of – and in some cases, demanding of – the notion that a pregnant woman would also be a 'yummy mummy' or 'hot mama' (Tyler, 2011; Musial, 2014). These sexy pregnant subjectivities are usually manifest through consumption practices: photoshoots, fashion, celebrity magazines, work, exercise, these are all activities that pregnant women might engage in. They are not usually sexual pregnancies that have as their object expressions of sexual desire.

We are not talking about 'pussies being better' (for whom?) in pregnancy, or about pregnant sex-work in these manifestations of the autonomous, emancipated sexy pregnancy. As we saw in the discussion of naked pregnancy photoshoots, or in sex advice magazine columns, what we are talking about are curiously chaste, yet serenely sexy, women who have poise, who are self-assured, and who are looking forward to motherhood (Huntley, 2000; Tyler, 2011). Or we are talking about monogamously coupled, heterosexual, sexually confident young women. The anxiety around sexual practice in pregnancy means that despite this shift in attitude towards sexy pregnant bodies, the way in which this sexiness presents itself is saturated with a latent uneasiness about sex (Drglin, 2015). This squeamishness wants these women to be beautiful, to be enticing, but not sex-crazed, ejaculating, masturbating, sexually demanding women. Sexy pregnancy should be a manifestation of Rubin's (1984) inner charmed circle, not of the outer limits. The comments here, about 'pussies', or about how sex is when pregnant, or about paying for sex when pregnant, are of this latter order. And in a socio-cultural context – a rape culture – where women are still expected to occupy the inner limits of the circle despite the years that have passed since Rubin developed the concept of the charmed circle, these comments transgress a taboo about pregnant women's sexuality, and are all the more aggressive for it.

> 'A man had made a comment when passing him in the aisle about how pregnant women are beautiful, but he said it in a nasty way. Then while in line, I felt something behind me and it was the man pushing himself against my body. I moved forward, and after paying, hurried to my car quickly because it scared me.'

Here, even if what was *said* was less hostile, violence laced the way it was received. In rubbing up against her in the queue this participant experienced a sexual assault that 'scared' her, in part at least because of her 'beautiful' state of pregnancy. The event propelled her from the semi-public space of the shop to the security of her car.

Expressions of power are not simply top-down. The examples drawn on here demonstrate how sexual harassment in pregnancy can operate to shame and embarrass pregnant women for their bodies. They remind women of the public nature of the pregnant body, and are also an agonistic response to the ambivalent position a pregnant body in public space holds. Is it sacred and serene? Is it beautiful? Is it weak? Is it sexual or is it not? Is it frightening? Is it disgusting? Is it or is it not out of place? These aggressions might be understood as ways to reinscribe order in public space by trying to push pregnant women out of it, or they might more simply be expressions of anxiety about ambiguity and out-of-order-ness. One of the survey questions intended to excavate how far women felt they should be specially protected in public space asked:

> Most people agree that both men and women should be able to live without being sexually harassed in public space. On the one hand, some people think that women who are pregnant should be entitled to additional special protection from sexual harassment in public space. On the other hand, other people think that pregnant women should not be treated any differently in public space to non-pregnant women or men. What do you think?

Most women who answered this question agreed that pregnant women should not get special treatment. Claims for special treatment of women are based on a notion of pregnant exceptionalism. Some of the women, when asked about their experiences of sexual harassment, however, expressed this pregnant exceptionalism in the way in which they manage these interactions:

> 'He and his friend tried to lure me into their car and when that didn't work, he wanted a phone number. Even when I told him that I'm pregnant and married, he didn't care.'

> 'As I began to walk out of HEB [shop name] a man walked very close to me telling me I was the hottest thing he has seen and began to touch himself. I said to him "oh, okay" and walked faster he kept up. I then pretended to call my husband on my cell phone; he then backed off.'

Explaining how they reacted in the face of sexual harassment, some participants responded along the lines of saying, 'I ignore the call since I was married and pregnant.' Having internalised the fact that the pregnancy and married state meant that she was 'off limits' or sexless or 'spoken for', participants sometimes simply ignored that they were being cat-called. Ignoring sexual harassment can be a good strategy in order to diminish its impact. In the examples given here, this is something that was only available to these participants because of their status as married and expectant mothers.

Within a heteronormative and patriarchal economy, these participants used their status as 'another man's woman' for protection. One expected her interlocutor to leave her alone once she told him she was married and pregnant, but 'he didn't care'; the other pretended to contact her husband to protect herself. Discussions of women resisting attempts to make them fearful in public space are incredibly important. Although it has been decades since Hille Koskela's (1997) landmark paper on women's 'bold walk', there remain too few explorations of this in contemporary debates of fear of crime. These women do not say that they are scared or otherwise made uneasy by these interactions, which do seem unpleasant and dangerous, and so in some sense they were doing a 'bold walk' by moving away from, or trying to send away, their abusers (Koskela, 1997). When sexual harassment happens in public space as part of rape culture it is perhaps not surprising that these women employ tools that are also borne of heteropatriarchal strictures in order to avoid it or to undo it. It is the interplay between the vernacular and the analytical of rape culture that we can see at play here. At an everyday, vernacular level, women who respond to sexism in public space by themselves using the tools that rape culture produces – proximity to a known man, belonging to another – to defend themselves, help us to see how rape culture operates. It works by making safety contingent, in part, on adherence to heteropatriarchal constructs and expectations. Thus, women who refuse the suggestion that pregnancy merits special protection could, indeed, be said to be offering examples of resistant behaviour at an analytical level. If pregnancy is constructed as vulnerable, fragile, bearing precious cargo (Lupton, 2012b), and women refuse to allow this to exclude them from access to public space, then these resistant claims help us in the undoing of rape culture They are important because they contest the normalcy attributed to these constructions, in which women are cast as iterations of out-of-placedness, to be protected by their men. It is a taken-for-grantedness that dulls the critical praxis that we need to mobilise to undo rape culture and that we explore more in the final chapter. Tactics that exceptionalise pregnancy serve both as evidence of the trouble that the pregnant, sexualised body poses in public space and of the need for guerrilla war machines to trouble this trouble. So what might these war machines look like?

Pregnant potentialities

In Joel and Ethan Cohen's 1996 film *Fargo*, Frances McDormand's character is seven months pregnant. An officer of the law, she tracks down, confronts and apprehends violent professional killers hired by a used-car dealer to kidnap his wife in order to extract a ransom from her wealthy father. Throughout the film, her very visible pregnancy is mentioned only twice. This film is not about pregnancy. It is a film telling the story of a brave, competent, kind, funny – complex – female police officer as she successfully does her job, successfully supports her husband's modest achievements, and successfully encounters and refuses the sexual advances of an ex-lover. The pregnancy is not an encumbrance to the character, it does not cause her to retire from public space, it does not make her less physically, or cognitively, or emotionally competent. It appears to be offered to the audience to suggest a prosaicness or small-town-ness to the plot. In this sense, we are asked to consider this to be very normal and not exceptional, or even noteworthy. McDormand's character, Marge Gunderson, opens up the potentiality of a transformative pregnant imaginary. She is at ease with her self, with her work, with her body, with her sexuality, with her pregnancy. Other people are also at ease with it; in one of the final scenes, one of the perpetrators has no compunction about throwing a piece of wood at her head in an attempt to escape her. The pregnancy is only disruptive insofar as for the audience, it is such an unremarkable rendering of the pregnant body in public space it becomes, therefore, remarkable. This non-abject, untroubling pregnancy forges smooth space through the striates of what we know about pregnancy and desire, and this itself becomes disruptive against the background of rape culture that positions pregnancy antagonistically along de/sexualised lines.

The penetration of a pregnant body into many different spheres – at the gym, in the classroom, in a bar, driving a van, in the board room, at the ante-natal clinic, at the beach, at a gas station, in the supermarket, in the factory, in the airport – just some of the places mentioned by the women in this study – means that the public and private can never be distinct for these bodies. The pregnant body is thus private and public, and troublingly cannot be put in its place or easily designated as in-place or out-of-place. Contemporary rape culture constructs the pregnant body as sacred, as something that must be protected, yet because it is somatically tainted by sex, as something unruly, excessive, and which proliferates anxiety. This casts the pregnant body in public space as something that is troubling and disruptive. Tim Cresswell (1997: 334) notes that the placefulness of people, groups, things, and ideas informs current ideologies of right and wrong ('what is good, just, and appropriate'), so the ambiguity of the pregnant body troubles 'common-sense' ways of making sense of the world. 'Common-sense', striated, molar, arboreal thought is an anathema to the revolutionary imaginaries we are concerned with here. Instead, in order to draw these ideas together, it is helpful to think of different ways in which the placefulness of pregnancy in public space might become a war machine, and might move towards a transformative politics.

One way of approaching this conceptually is demonstrated by Lisa Baraitser's analysis of mothering practices and their capacity to transform public space, whether done by women or by mothers, or not. Baraitser (2009: 10) illustrates how the mundane and embodied practices of mothering interjects in public space to create what she calls a counter-public, which challenges the dominant 'bourgeois', exclusionary, striated construction of public space. Bringing the work of mothering – changing nappies, feeding, entertaining – into spaces where it ostensibly does not belong, produces a public which de-stigmatises, or which re-publics, the private and devalued and invisible work of mothering. By creating 'desire paths' of mothering, the texture of space is transformed, making place from spaces from which they might otherwise be excluded. At the same time, these practices of mothering are also capable of becoming especially commodified: cinema screenings, public lectures, yoga classes where parents (usually women) are invited to pay an entrance fee and bring their babies are increasingly common, especially in recent years. Yet these practices, when done deliberately and in the 'wrong' place, might, along with establishing herethical politics, be thought as guerrilla war machines that work to forge a *polis*, where women, looking after their children, reclaim public space and re-establish spatial justice (Baraitser, 2009: 21, Tyler, 2011).

To apply this concept to the problem of the pregnant body in public might enable us to imagine how it could transform the impact of rape culture on the way in which the pregnant body is evaluated. Understanding this performative element of pregnancy – that it is something that is done – means that the pregnant body already transforms public space. While the work of pregnancy lacks the visibility, or even the encumbrance, of parenting in public it is nonetheless a taking-up of space. The creation of this taking of space as a *polis* means that the positioning of the pregnant body in public space is politicised. The pregnant are already subject to a certain performance of pregnant citizenship in public: the politics of sitting or standing on public transport, of whether or not to wear pin badges requesting a seat on public transport, of whether or not to drink alcohol, or to drink coffee, or to eat sushi, these are all visible ways in which pregnancy is performed. They are also modes of subjectification that can be surveilled by others in public spaces.

What if this, like mothering in public, could be thought along women's own terms? Some women may enjoy the cherishing attention that they receive in public; they may not experience it as paternalistic or subjectifying. Others may be affronted by it and may struggle to be able to behave as they wish to in public space. Whatever it is, the particular *polis* that pregnant women create or take up might mobilise a different ethic, one that is not about surveillance and subjectification and appropriate beauty or sexuality, but one that emerges through a pregnant woman's own auto-poesies. This transformation might also be evidenced in the way in which women manifest their sexual subjectivity in public, as one that is not in crisis, and not in response to a particular expectation or manifestation of idealised femininity.

Attendant to this is the possibility that emerges through what Gilles Deleuze and Félix Guattari (2004a [1980]) understand as becoming-minoritarian: a political practice of subverting, troubling, sending into flight majoritarian ethics, the likes of which compose rape culture that also constitutes these antagonisms around the pregnant body. Alongside the 'irreducible, irreconcilable' woman who is on the critical outside of these discourses (Kristeva, quoted in Guberman, 1996), this position of deliberate, political outsiderness is one that fosters a different way to imagine what the politics of disruptive pregnancy might do. It is one that nurtures the potentiality of a herethical smooth space that disrupts what rape culture can do. More plainly, it is one that refuses the latent potential of pregnancy to be a subjectifying practice through its de/sexualisation:

> If maternity is to be guilt-free, this journey needs to be undertaken without masochism and without annihilating one's affective, intellectual and professional personality either. In this way, maternity becomes a true creative act. (Kristeva, 2005: 220)

Whether it is masochism through sacrifice for the unborn child, sequestered from public space and subjugated to pregnancy norms and performances, or the masochism of compulsory hetero-sexy pregnancy (one of consumption, of beauty practices, of commodified desire), the politics of disruptive pregnancy has much to contest. But this is what we need more of in order to dismantle the rape culture that denigrates women in public space. Liberated from the obscurity of stereotypes about the capacities, desires, or performances of pregnancy, we might dialectically open up to the creativity, to the smooth space of what the pregnant body can Become-. This, in negotiation with the tensions that compose pregnancy in public, might begin to compose the pregnant body as guerrilla war machine. Rather than folding in to the striates of how we might see the de/sexualised body emerge in public space, the pregnant body becomes, as we saw in Chapter One, smith-like – neither sexualised nor desexualised, the smith connects to smooth space outside these possibilities. She forges a way to live – to stride through – public space, and to forge new relationships with the encounters she has there. Encounters that trouble – that Become-war machine to – what we usually know about pregnancy in public space.

In this chapter we have seen how this body in public space poses a particular kind of problem, not only to feminist politics, but also to contemporary constructions of what the pregnant body looks like or can do. We looked at this in the context of sexualised pregnancy (through photoshoots, advertising, sex advice magazines, and sexual harassment) and also in the context of the desexualised pregnancy (also through different sorts of photoshoots and analyses of events of sexual harassment). I have argued that constructions of de/sexualised pregnant woman are based both on a representation of femininity that is simultaneously chaste, humble, renounced and hyper-sexualised, heterosexualised and consumerist. All of these manifestations of pregnant femininity are laced with classist, racist, ageist, sexist and ableist notions of desirability, propriety and maternal citizenship. These are all arcs along which contemporary rape culture is mobilised. The disruption that the pregnant body poses in public space – because she is ambiguous, liminal, disorderly, public and private – is mirrored by the potentiality of the disruptive pregnancy that emerges through the minoritarian herethical ethics. Yes, pregnancy in public discursively disrupts, but what pregnancy can do also disrupts this construction. The next chapter explores further the ways in which women's bodies, when they penetrate public space in different ways, are disruptive.

THREE

Disruptive protests

It was while readjusting my swiftly numbing legs and arms that, covered in fake blood, and lying on my back looking up at the cold, grey sky, I considered the spectacular quality of the naked female body in protest. All this is spectacle. That day, I was surrounded by other women; we were all wearing skin-coloured underwear and participating in an anti-fur protest in Trafalgar Square. It was late June in 2017, and it was raining hard, which could have been considered exceptional for the season. Although the protest was supposed to last for four hours, we called it a day after two. Fifteen 'underwear' participants had diminished to seven, which eventually became three. And yet, despite the rain, despite the disappearing size of the protest, I lost count of the number of photographs that were taken of us that day; the press, members of the non-human animal rights movements, members of the public.... We must have featured in the holiday snaps of many, many tourists. Despite the rain, I counted groups of 40 or 50 people around our protest space for the whole time (except for a lull to about 20 people, when a break-dancing group started their act next to us, although eventually they, too, ceded to the rain, leaving just us under the forbidding sky).

In this chapter, I examine this presentation of the female body in protests where the body is the canvas on which the protest is conveyed. I consider these protests as a disruption in the way in which public space is striated, and what this means for social and spatial justice against a background of contemporary rape culture. I examine how far these protests might be recuperated into a guerrilla war machine and towards a transformative politics. Drawing on debates within the non-human animal rights movement, the phenomenon of sexualised protest, analyses of human/non-human relationships and the spatialisation of these politics, I consider how these disruptions intersect with rape culture.

Corporeal, embodied protest is a striking thing. As we saw in the last chapter, in the context of pregnancy, the body 'represents humanity in its rawest form' (Eileraas, 2014: 41). A naked body in public space is disruptive. It disrupts normative codes of how a body should appear in public space and normative ways of using public space. It is a sign of vulnerability. It can be injured, abused, it can become ill; it is a conduit through which we feel pain. As Judith Butler (2011: 2) states, 'for politics to take place, the body must appear.' For Butler, as for Camilla Reestorff (2014), the protest emerges in the conjunction of the assemblage of bodies, of the 'material conditions' of space in which to protest, and of the visibility of the protest (the audience or witnesses to the protest) that connect with each other to form a political intervention. Once again, there is no escaping the fact of the body. It is in this oscillation between the body which is vulnerable and which, through this vulnerability is made strong, that the potency of naked protest becomes apparent. We see this in other forms of embodied protest – in lip sewing, eye sewing, dirty protests, menstrual blood protests, hunger strikes – when there is no more recourse to justice, when all possibilities have been explored and exhausted, or have failed.

A fundamental return to the body as a protesting tool, outside of formal legal, political, institutional structures – a line of flight perhaps – means that the body, in this abject violented state, becomes a forceful tool for protest (O'Keefe, 2006; Owens, 2009). This is not to confuse the naked protest of last resort with the politics of 'bare life', where individuals in a state of bare life are shunned by the State (Agamben, 1998). This is rather to recuperate this shunning as a *precarious* position from which to mobilise a politics of transformation from this position of exception (Butler, 2004). I return to these ideas in this chapter. In order to follow the complexity of the tensions within the debates across the anti-rape protest and the non-human animal rights protest, we must retain this idea of the protesting body as precarious. Thus will we be able to glean the ways in which these protests function (Stanescu, 2012; Wyckoff, 2014).

Protests: The spectacular and the cursed

A spectacle, from the Old French *spectacle*, is a specially prepared or arranged display, a public show: something to be seen. A spectacle needs a performer, a space in which to perform and importantly, an audience. The spectacle is an assemblage. Protest as spectacle needs this dialectical relationship with the place from which it emerges (see Butler, 2011; Reestorff, 2014). Yet spectacle is also a double-edged sword. The spectacle is an illusion, and, according to Guy Debord, accounts for the organisation of all social life in contemporary post-industrialist, capitalist societies. A form of hyper-reality, the spectacle describes 'a social relationship between people that is mediated by images' (Debord, 1994 [1967], thesis 4). Debord's notion of the spectacle is intimately tied to his critique of commodity fetishism that separates commodities from their mode of production; that distinguishes between 'the sign and the thing signified, the copy [and] the original, representation [and] reality' (Feuerbach, cited in Debord, 1994 [1967]). Commodification through this separation, leads, according to Debord (1994 [1967], thesis 24), to a 'fetishistic appearance of pure objectivity' that obscures the true labour, character or cost of a particular representation, event or object. It is this that leads to the 'proletarianisation of the world' (thesis 26). The to-be-looked-at-ness of the spectacle occludes how what is being looked-at emerges in the first place. Most insidiously for our purposes, the separation between the image and the object, the commodity and the labour, is that it has become, in Debord's (1994 [1967]) words, 'the sun that never sets of the empire of modern passivity' (thesis 13). This spectacle fosters benign acceptance of the *status quo*, or blithe apathy, which becomes an anathema to transformation, renewal, or a praxis of alternative politics of justice that might transform social life.

Part of how the spectacular works is that it is so beguiling. Indeed, part of what makes the protests analysed here beguiling is the mobilisation of the naked or nearly naked body. It was the embodied experience of these politics that I wanted to explore during the anti-fur protest that I describe here. What is it like to use the undressed human female body in a protest for non-human animal rights? What does this performance of semi-nakedness in public do to the politics of the space? What is lost, or found, through this performance?

According to Bruce Lunceford (2012: 1-2), naked protest dates back to ancient Greece and the Cynics, for whom the presentation of the body in public (here Diogenes' male body) was an embodied manifestation of the 'norms he wished to create'. For Lunceford (2012: 3), it is the vulnerability of the naked body that renders it political. Nudity becomes a position of last resort after all other avenues for attention, or for change, are exhausted. This emerges potently in Imogen Tyler's (2013) analysis of naked protest conducted by female detainees at Yarl's Wood Immigration Removal Centre in Bedfordshire, UK in 2008. Here, women – mothers – undressed in protest against the treatment of a fellow pregnant detainee who was forcibly restrained and separated from her six-year-old son (Tyler, 2013: 211). Detainees explained that their undressing was a deliberate tactic to create a spectacle; to draw attention to the degrading treatment they were receiving (being treated like animals) in a manner that would attract the attention of the media. And indeed, they were successful. The protest was widely reported, in particular because as Tyler (2013: 212) highlights, the naked presentation of the maternal body, the aged body, the Black body, or the pregnant body challenges taboos about the sorts of naked bodies that we might see.

The other taboo that this form of protest transgresses is said to be rooted in African[1] symbolism about the relationship between life and death. Here, what is known as 'the naked curse' or 'genital power' – the exposure of the genitals to men, particularly of menopausal women – causes social death, which is believed to lead to the actual death of those who look on the naked body (Turner and Brownhill, 2004: 67; Stevens, 2006; Tyler, 2013: 214). The naked curse is never threatened lightly and is invoked only in extreme circumstances, once all other avenues for action have been exhausted (Ekine, 2001; Turner and Brownhill, 2004; Stevens, 2006). In 2002–03 Nigerian women protesting against the oil company Chevron's abuse of the land and people of the Niger Delta exposed their bodies in order to shame or 'infect' the men who would look on their nakedness (Ekine, 2001). The functioning of the taboo is that by showing men the naked genitals of women who may have birthed them, those women are 'taking back' the life those bodies have given them (Turner and Brownhill, 2004: 71; Stevens, 2006: 59; Tyler, 2013: 214).

As we saw in the context of pregnancy in public space, this maternal power is extraordinarily liminal; the naked body is itself shamed, vulnerable, desperate and yet, at its most debased, it is the naked body that does the shaming, that attacks those to whom it is shown, that makes people mad or commits them to a 'lifetime of misfortune' (Oriola, 2012: 545). In the post-industrial societies where the debates of this book are played out, the meaning of what it is to be liminal has become more and more diluted, and less and less tied to the compulsory, ritualistic or coming-of-age process that Victor Turner intended.[2] However, in this context, the Medea-like maternal body which gives life, and which can take it away, retains this quality of life-changing transformation. Powerless and powerful in the self-same moment, the protesting, naked maternal body transforms her position of subalterity – of liminal, precarious life – into a position from which to challenge the power of the sovereign/the State, whether that State power manifests itself through Chevron/Texaco Oil in the Niger Delta, unfair taxation in Nigeria, unlawful interrogation of tribe leaders in Cameroon, or the private security company that manages Yarl's Wood Immigration Removal Centre in the UK (Stevens, 2006; Oriola, 2012; Tyler, 2013).

Phillips Stevens (2006: 597) suggests that the naked protests of the sort enacted by the women of the Niger Delta 'inspired protesting women elsewhere in the world to use nakedness as a weapon'. It might certainly be the case that naked protests are becoming more prolific – in this chapter we consider quite a few examples of them – but what is the relationship between these naked protests and the social death or ostracisation that *this* naked curse deploys? It is presumably impossible to transliterate this African naked curse into non-African protests. To begin to think Stevens' (2006) suggestion through, this section considers cursing, spectacular, protesting nakedness in the context of the anti-rape politics of the SlutWalk and Femen protests.

SlutWalk is a specific form of feminist protest that contests the proliferation of rape culture and of victim-blaming in safe-keeping discourses. Originating in 2011 in response to a sexist and victim-blaming piece of advice given to female students at the University of Toronto in Canada by a police officer about how to stay safe on campus, protest marches known as 'SlutWalks' spread around the globe with energetic alacrity. The officer's advice to women was to not 'dress like sluts' in order not to get raped. A slut, in this context, describes a sexualised slur on women – it is inherently gendered – and connotes sexual promiscuity, slovenliness and low levels of morality. According to the *Oxford English Dictionary*, 'slut' is a derogatory term used to describe a woman 'who has had many sexual partners' or 'with low standards of cleanliness'[3] (see O'Keefe, 2011). In response to his statement, female students at the University of Toronto organised a march in which women and men were invited to dress in a stereotypically sexy or 'slutty' manner in order to draw attention to the falseness of the claim that women provoke rape in the way that they dress. The appeal of the protest was extraordinarily popular, and satellite groups established themselves in urban centres in countries all over the world.[4]

Tens of thousands of newspaper articles have been written about SlutWalk in the years since its inception. The protests have received academic attention from a number of different disciplinary directions (see Kapur, 2012; Miriam, 2012; Mendes, 2015). In 2011 and 2012, I, along with a colleague, conducted participant observations of SlutWalks in London, UK, and spoke to people participating in the protest about its politics and their motivations for being there. It is clear that as a form of feminist protest, men and women marching in public spaces in their miniskirts and stockings (sometimes less) has been absolutely compelling. But the politics of SlutWalk are perhaps as contested as they are appealing. I have discussed some of these contestations elsewhere (see Fanghanel and Lim, 2017). SlutWalk is certainly marred by accusations of racism, of pro-capitalism, spectacularisation and of reinforcing rape myths, even as it seeks to dismantle these myths (O'Keefe, 2011, 2014; Lim and Fanghanel, 2013).

Femen, on the other hand, rather than a form of protest *per se*, is a feminist protest group which, as O'Keefe (2014: 107) scathingly suggests, 'grab headlines for their protest tactics more than the issues they seek to address'. Founded in 2008 in the Ukraine, the group is notorious for its preference for bare-breasted political intervention. Borne out of a liberal imaginary of democracy post the Orange Revolution, Femen mobilises a call for gender equality that opposes the prevailing patriarchy of the Ukraine, through performances of essential, innocent femininity (Zychowicz, 2011, 2015: 87). The flower garlands, or *vinoks*, that protesters wear in their hair and the bare breasts that are a symbol of maternal nurture, evoke a specific vision of post-revolutionary Ukrainian femininity that positions itself against patriarchy. According to Femen:

> Our Mission is Protest! Our Weapon are [sic] bare breasts!
> And so Femen is born and sextremism is set off.[5]

The women who organise politically as part of Femen participate in noisy protests with political slogans written on their naked torsos. Relatively few in number compared to the thousands who participate in SlutWalk, Femen define themselves much more by their shared ideology and 'world view': a feminist organisation rather than an organised feminist protest.[6]

SlutWalk is ostensibly about challenging rape myths, although in practice a number of allied causes tag along to protests (for instance, protesting against rape jokes in stand-up comedy and budget cuts for women's services). Femen's work promotes, according to them, 'global women's mob law over patriarchy as the historically first, and last, existing form of slavery', and manifests itself at political summits, anti-war protests, LGBT Pride events, protests against the Euro Football tournament, protest against the Pope, or against the wearing of the hijab, and so on. Both Femen and SlutWalk target rape culture in their work. Both mobilise the naked or undressed female body in public space to do this.

What happens at the intersect of this unclothed body and the space that it occupies? How far is this action indebted to the notion of the naked curse, as Stevens (2006: 697) suggests? What does this tell us about the spectacular contestation of contemporary rape culture?

Erotic violence I

One of the issues to highlight is the representation of the politics of these groups. Both rely on the sensational and titillating mediated images of their protest to draw attention to their work. One of the ways in which they appear to achieve this is through the public mobilisation of a heterosexually desirable female body (Reestorff, 2014).

SlutWalk invites participants to make a stand against rape culture by 're-appropriating' the word 'slut' and to wear ostensibly sexy clothing in order to highlight that 'being assaulted isn't about what you wear; it's not even about sex; but using a pejorative term to rationalise inexcusable behaviour creates an environment in which it's okay to blame the victim'.[7]

Women (and some men) who participate in the SlutWalk march topless, wearing just their underwear, fishnet tights, basques, often with the word 'slut' scrawled on their exposed skin. In short, they embody an aesthetic of the young, desirable hetero-sexy, and submissive body.[8] As a political tool, the body is exceptionally powerful (Butler, 2011). Presenting it as a site of protest in itself can be very affecting. In the current case, the spectacular quality of the SlutWalk protest certainly attracts media attention, in part because this presentation of the body is easy to consume. It echoes sexualised advertising, representations of female celebrities in the media, and so on. It does little to challenge stereotypical constructions of women's bodies as commodities to be consumed.

Similar charges can be levelled at the way that Femen organises its protests. As Theresa O'Keefe (2014) highlights, the group appears to deliberately select young, conventionally attractive, white, feminine, thin, able-bodied women for its interventions. These bodies are also not challenging to look at (Reestorff, 2014). Indeed, an image taken of an 'anti-dictatorial attack on [Russian president] Putin' in 2013 by two Femen protesters shows him giving them a thumbs up sign in apparent approval at their actions, which he later explained he enjoyed (Vasagar and Parfitt, 2013). Reflecting on the protest subsequently, Putin reported that he 'didn't make out whether they were blondes, chestnut-haired, or brunettes' – presumably because he was looking parts of their bodies that were not their faces – which, in the context of a protest against his leadership, reduces the protesters to no more than their appearance, instead of their political message (Vasagar and Parfitt, 2013).[9]

In 2013, Kitty Green directed a documentary film about the Femen group. Called *Ukraine is not a brothel*, this film revealed several interesting devices and techniques used by the group to convey their politics. In the film, Femen talk about building a 'brand' of people who conform to a certain aesthetic. The film features 'sex bomb': one of their campaigns that protested against the Euro 2012 football tournament taking place in Ukraine. The influx of football fans who would solicit Ukrainian sex workers and brothels were the target of this protest. In this protest, a Femen supporter who was somewhat older, and somewhat larger, and who conformed less to the conventional aesthetic of Femen women, positioned herself in the entrance of the metro station in Kiev. Smoking a cigarette from a long cigarette holder, wearing a bright yellow wig, knee-high socks, a bright pink thong, red PVC elbow-length gloves, a black garter over her knee, red sunglasses in the shape of hearts, and zebra-print high heels, the performer had the words 'sex bomb' written on her naked torso. Other members of Femen surrounded her, but these were fully clothed in bright pink boiler suits (playing the bomb disposal squad, perhaps) and ran around her with loudspeakers shouting, 'Danger! Danger! Sex bomb!', 'Please keep back!', 'Run, people, run!' The 'sex bomb', meanwhile, smiled and blew kisses at the surrounding onlookers, and adopted sexually provocative poses. She appeared amused and delighted in the 'panic' she was causing. The message of the protest seemed to be that if men came to Ukraine during the Euro 2012 tournament to visit its brothels, this monstrous feminine is what will be waiting for them. It is worth pausing to consider what this protest conveys about the Femen brand and about this naked protest as a disruption.

The 'sex bomb' performer was dressed in deliberately gaudy colourful clothes. The high heels, the thong, the elbow-length gloves all mimic the imagined sexy attire of a sex worker, the heart-shaped sunglasses recall those that were made famous by the actress Sue Lyon in the poster for Stanley Kubrick's 1962 film of the Nabokov novel, *Lolita*. Yet, her body was presented as grotesque, a parody of a sexually attractive woman or sex bomb (see Russo, 1995). Her stomach hung heavily over the top and sides of the thong, her legs dimpled with visible cellulite contrasted with the smooth skin of the other protesters in other Femen campaigns, her breasts hung low on her body. These are not the pert and round full breasts that confronted Putin and

Merkel. Yet, this non-conforming body in the Femen protest ought not to be taken as evidence that Femen is corporeally inclusive. Instead, the participation of this performer works to enshrine norms of beauty, of aesthetic femininity and heteronormative desire (Baker, 2010).

The display of the unconventional body of this performer, and the parodic clothes that she is wearing, casts the 'sex bomb' as a grotesque (meaning wildly formed, boldly odd, the grotesque body is at the heart of the carnivalesque). The presentation of this body amidst the cacophony of warnings to onlookers to be careful, to stay away, that this sex bomb is dangerous, cedes acknowledgement that many onlookers would not find the sex bomb conventionally attractive, that she is, in fact, more challenging to look at than Femen's usual protesters. Ugly, even. A 'sex bomb' is conventionally understood to mean a very sexually attractive woman. So, with this play on words, Femen are deliberately designating this woman as unattractive. The discursive message appears to be that men should stay away from brothels, otherwise unattractive women like this performer will not hesitate to approach them or attack them or perhaps explode onto them, like a bomb. This is not a body-positive or inclusive moment. It relies on the discursive, accepted ugliness of the performer for the political message to resonate.

Femen protests also attract a lot of hostility (Zychowicz, 2015: 84). At the 'sex bomb' protest, one of the accompanying protesters in a boiler suit appeared to be struck violently in the stomach by a man whose path to the entrance she was blocking. Green's film also shows other incidences of protesters incurring violence. There is a particularly sinister passage of the film where the women are describing some terrifying violence that they suffered in Belarus when they went there to protest. They show their bruises to the camera, they described being forced to strip, being covered in petrol, and being abandoned kilometres from the border that they had to cross on foot. This story is distressing, and the women look distressed when they are talking. Then, almost from nowhere, a man's voice is heard instructing the women to move the camera between them as they talk: "make sure it looks handheld". Not only is this the first indication in the film that Femen was organised in part by a man at this time (Eileraas, 2014: 48), but it demonstrates how curated the Femen relationship with violence is, in their protests.

Indeed, elsewhere in the film, we see many instances in many different protests where protestors enter into direct physical conflict with the police or other security forces and members of the public (for more examples, see Reestorff, 2014: 487). The sight of a naked or nearly naked woman dragged around the street by her arms or carried over their shoulders (like a piece of meat?) is remarkable and disturbing. In Istanbul, Turkey, in a protest against domestic violence, the protesters run around topless holding their heads and wail 'Why?' over and over again, *as if* they are being beaten and are in pain. The women resist, are dragged around by their arms, their bodies limp, they scream and cry, and sometimes it looks like they do get injured.

This violence heightens the visual impact of their protest. It plays on the vulnerable yet strong image of the naked body that we see also in the naked curse. Yet naked women screaming and being dragged around is also presented because it is titillating, it is evocative of sexual violence. It resituates sexual violence against women as erotic, even as Femen claim to fight against this. Their protests are, to a certain extent, disruptive, in that they are noticeable and violent; they mark a potential line of flight from the conventional striated ordering of space, but their reliance on normative conventions of beauty, and normative attitudes to the eroticisation of violence, and also to liberal Western feminist visions of equality and justice, implicate them more in maintaining the *status quo* rather than subverting and contesting rape culture.

Naked, but not bare

While Femen may deliberately seek to present only women who conform to a 'narrow yet hegemonic category of idea woman' (O'Keefe, 2014: 9), SlutWalk at least purports to be an inclusive movement, even if its claims for intersectional inclusivity has been questioned and is problematised (O'Keefe, 2011, 2014; Lim and Fanghanel, 2013). The Toronto march invites as follows:

> We are asking you to join us for SlutWalk, to make a unified statement about sexual assault and victims' rights and to demand respect for all. You needn't claim the word slut for yourself; whether a fellow slut or simply an ally, you don't have to wear your sexual proclivities on your sleeve, we just ask that you come. Any gender-identification, any age. Singles, couples, parents, sisters, brothers, children, friends. Come walk or roll or strut or holler or stomp with us.

While in London:

Everyone is welcome – all genders, races, religions, ages and sexualities. Bring friends, family and banners, and come along feeling beautiful, ready to show the world that we are proud of our sexuality and that there is never any excuse for rape.

While we were conducting fieldwork in London, it was clear that there was a broad range of people participating in the march. Not everyone was dressed in the 'slutty' uniform. As I have discussed elsewhere, the discourse about reclaiming the word 'slut' was controversial and contested by some of the women and men to whom we spoke (O'Keefe, 2011; Fanghanel and Lim, 2017). Certainly, the SlutWalk ethic is imbued with neoliberal notions of choice, autonomy and self-determination, which reflects a certain classed and raced privilege that cannot extend to everyone who is affected by rape culture such as poor women or women marginalised by disability and racism, for instance (see Lim and Fanghanel, 2013). Indeed, in satellite marches in other parts of the globe, such as India, Israel and Singapore, the focus of the marches is not so explicitly on the state of undress of the participants, and more about fighting for gendered justice, against rape culture (see, for instance, Rosenberg, 2012). These marches explicitly intersect with the political, cultural and social context in which they take place. The same is true for SlutWalks in Toronto or in London: they are a product of the context from which they emerge, which all the more pertinently demonstrates their complicity with rape culture.

Despite its apparent openness to diversity, there is an established narrative within the SlutWalk movement that the undressed protest does little to deviate from. Discursively, the protest is situated around young bodies, moreover, young bodies that are at risk from stranger-rape as opposed to any other form of (more common) sexual violence such as intimate partner violence, acquaintance rape, incest, and so on. It is also modelled on a heteronormative sexual encounter where women respond 'yes' or 'no' to a supposed offer of sex, rather than being about having sexual agency and, for instance, pre-emptively refusing or pursuing sex as opposed to waiting to be asked (Fanghanel and Lim, 2017). So far, so striated.

Within this framework, women in their underwear in Trafalgar Square are not rewriting sexual scripts, but rather perpetuating existing, if different, rape myths to the ones they seek to contest. When I was speaking to young participants in the 2011 London protest, some mentioned to me that they saw an older woman bearing the placard 'Pensioner Slut' – who, it later transpired, was the noted feminist Selma James – and that they thought the placard was fantastic. Certainly, James' experience of the SlutWalk was that it was inclusive, and that people remarked positively on her placard might also suggest this (James, 2011). Yet what the placard does is simply draw attention to the discursive impossibility of an older women being a 'slut' within these striations. The adjective of 'pensioner' serves only to highlight how unlikely a woman of her age would be to be considered sexually active, much less sexually desirable, which is a construction of sexuality that emerges straight out of contemporary rape culture. Naked protest here, as with the Femen group, is (supposed to be) a young woman's game.

Although there are topless protests that take place that are not allied with Femen or SlutWalk,[10] the militant, slogan-daubed, bare-breasted protest of Femen has become iconic within the genre (Reestorff, 2014). On their website, Femen explain that their topless protests are driven by the following ethic:

> We live in the world of male economic, cultural and ideological occupation. In this world, a woman is a slave, she is stripped of the right to any property but above all she is stripped of ownership of her own body. All functions of the female body are harshly controlled and regulated by patriarchy.... Manifestation of the right to her body by the woman is the first and the most important step to her liberation. Female nudity, free of patriarchal system, is a grave-digger of the system, militant manifesto and sacral symbol of women's liberation. Femen's naked attacks is a naked nerve of the historic woman-system conflict, its most visual and appropriate illustration. Activist's naked body is the undisguised hatred toward the patriarchal order and new aesthetics of women's revolution.[11]

The naked female body as gravedigger of patriarchy is an evocative image. Femen's rhetoric mobilises the imagery of an essential feminine power. The garlands of flowers in their hair, and reference to nudity as the 'sacral symbol' of womanhood recall an imaginary of essential feminine power/mother earth. Femen describe their naked protests as the most appropriate 'visual' illustration of the 'historic woman-system conflict'. Nakedness is 'undisguised hatred' of patriarchy. The naked or topless protest, is, for Femen, following their argument here, an expression of the recuperation of the female body that is otherwise subjectified through pornography, capitalism, and sexual reproduction.

This violent refusal of traditional modes of exploiting women dovetails, in part, with the notion of 'precarious life' (Butler, 2004). In pitching 'woman' against the 'system', their discourse recalls the relationship of the State to that which is excluded from the protection of the State (which is in the state of exception, to borrow from Giorgio Agamben, 1998). The State, as I am talking about it in this text, reflects institutions, discourses, instruments, or technologies of power that have an ordering, dulling effect and that foster apathy. It is striating. For Femen, woman is a 'slave'. The slave – with no rights, no freedom and no agency – is a figure in the state of 'bare life', for Agamben (1998). In this sense, this nakedness might evoke the potency of the naked curse (Stevens, 2006).

The naked curse is so dangerous both to the women performing it (who can be killed or raped), and for those at whom it is targeted, that women who enter into such a protest are essentially saying that they are prepared to kill or be killed in the pursuit of their justice. Driven by a desperation to be recognised or to transform the *status quo*, this naked curse is an act of last resort. *But it is not an act of bare life.* Certainly, where traditional appeals to justice have failed (to governments, courts, or regulators), actors who enter into such a naked protest have no other avenues to pursue; they are out of the conventional sanction of the State and therefore beyond traditional notions of *bios* or of political life.

But they are not simply in a state of *zoê*. *Zoê*, the 'natural' and unembellished animalistic life, is the form of life that Agamben (1998) ascribes to refugees, concentration camp prisoners, or patients in persistent vegetative states in his exploration of governmentality and how the power of the State (the sovereign) emerges. These are people whose rights *as humans* have been voided in some way.

The distinction that Agamben makes between *zoê* and *bios* and humans and non-human animals is problematic. James Stanescu (2012) and Patricia Owens (2009) both suggest that Agamben's notion of bare life is not only anthropocentric in its privileging of human over non-human life, but also precludes the possibility that there may be *bios* within an excluded life, that might otherwise be considered *zoê*. While Agamben may not have anticipated that the position of bare life might become a political position from which to act, the impossibility of this, is, for our purposes here, troublesome. As Owens (2009) demonstrates in examples of refugees in detention camps who engage in lip and eye sewing as a form of life/death protest, these are detainees who might be in a state of exception (without the protection of or recourse to standard socio-legal liberal understandings of rights), but the lip and eye sewing is itself an act of *bios*. For Butler (2011), the organising of everyday life (of tents, of food, of sanitation) in the protest spaces of Tahrir Square in Egypt, for instance, is a form of fostering political life – of *bios*. Better, then, to articulate these political manoeuvres in terms of precarious life: a status that is contingent, temporary maybe, which is political life nonetheless.

Femen's protests are often violent. There could be something of the naked curse in their approach. Certainly, the rhetoric they espouse suggests that their nakedness is an act of final resort. The interplay between the naked and vulnerable yet powerful body evokes this political precarity (Reestorff, 2014: 487). And yet, if recalling the desperate power of the naked curse is Femen's intention, this is not how the message of their protest is received. As we have seen, a protest operates in an assemblage. The connection between the protest, the bodies, the space, the audience, is, in part, what makes a protest effective. The performance does not need to be big, or to last a long time to be considered a success (think, for instance, of the Putin protest described earlier). Here, as in SlutWalk, it is able-bodied, young white women (usually), with aesthetically appealing bodies, wearing conventionally titillating clothing, performing 'sexy' femininity, in collusion with those who see the protest, and who mediatise it. They together make the protest into a spectacle where the work that the protest seeks to achieve is occluded.

Attention-grabbing and enticing, naked bodies in public spaces are not threatening here: they are not dangerous. They are fun to look at; they make a good story in the papers (Reestorff, 2014). This is not to be trite. Certainly, drawing attention to an overlooked area of social or spatial injustice is worthwhile. The question remains; how transformative is this, really? What does it do to public space? How far does it challenge the rape culture that it purports to contest? How far does this 'dig the grave of the system'?

What might have been the greatest disruption that these women's bodies can make in public space is neutered by the spectacularisation of the protest. Detached from any ontological kinship with the African naked curse, these protests become mired in the promotion of rape culture rather than the promotion of social and spatial justice. Spectacles to be consumed and to be evaluated against a background of contemporary rape culture, these disruptive bodies become complicit in a broader assemblage that commodifies women's bodies and normalises sexual violence. Participants in Femen and SlutWalk could be said to trouble the spaces in which we see them because they are naked and because of the parody that they themselves make of the female body; exaggerated performances of 'slutty' femininity, or of bucolic, fecund, mother-of-the-nation femininity. Arguably, however, these are carnivalesque parodies, which, as we know, mean only temporary, ritualistic, 'conservative', subversion of the power dynamics that construct public space (Turner, 1967; Russo, 1995: 58; Bruner, 2005). All this is spectacle. The body – the protest itself – is commodified, and it is there to be consumed. This takes on a more sinister turn when naked protests are commercialised, as is the case with the non-human animal rights protests that I discuss in the next section. In those protests, the playfulness of the carnivalesque is somewhat usurped by the problem of the woman as absent referent (Adams, 2016 [1990]), and although they are not committed to the eradication of rape culture in the same way as are the naked protests of Femen and SlutWalk, these protests also further entrench rape culture through their actions. In the next section, I consider these protests as a disruption in the way in which public space is striated, and what this means for social and spatial justice. I examine how far these protests can be recuperated into a war machine towards a transformative politics. Interspersed throughout is an auto-ethnographic account of participating in these protests as a semi-naked protester. Drawing on debates within the non-human animal rights movement, the phenomenon of sexualised protest, analyses of human/non-human relationships and the spatialisation of these politics, I consider how these disruptions interact with rape culture.

Becoming-Godiva?

Mobilising the naked female body in protest is a device used, controversially, by the non-human animal right movement. The People for the Ethical Treatment of Animals (PETA) have an established and notorious reputation for their use of naked women in their political campaigns (for a discussion, see Pace, 2005; Mika, 2006; Deckha, 2008; Bongiorno et al, 2013; Wrenn, 2015). It is interesting to hear how PETA account for their decision to showcase the naked female body-as-commodity in their campaigns. Faced with considerable criticism in popular and academic discourse about the extent to which PETA exploit the female body in order to convey their politics, they respond that:

> ... women – and men – should be able to use their own bodies as political statements. Like Lady Godiva, who

rode naked on a horse to protest taxes on the poor in the 11th Century, PETA knows that provocative, attention-grabbing actions are sometimes necessary to get people talking about issues that they would otherwise prefer not to think about.[12]

The Lady Godiva motif appears again and again in PETA's accounts of why they centre so much of their work on the naked female body (Glasser, 2011). In commentary to the press, in campaign literature and in communications to donors and potential donors, the story of Lady Godiva acts as an emancipatory alibi for this presentation of the female body.

The story of Lady Godiva, as we began to explore in Chapter One, is a myth dating from the 11th century in which the wealthy landowner entreated her husband, Leofric of Mercia, to reduce the taxes he was imposing on the people of Coventry in England. Tired of her protestations, Leofric apparently agreed to lower taxes if Godiva agreed to ride naked through the streets of the town, which she decided to do as long as all citizens 'remain[ed] behind closed doors and did not look out of their windows, while she rode her horse with nothing but her long tresses of hair to hide her nakedness' (Carr-Gomm, 2012: 92). This 13th-century version of 11th-century events is embellished in the 17th century with the addition of the 'Peeping Tom' character. In this later version, Peeping Tom is the only citizen of the settlement who violates Godiva's request and who is blinded, either by God, or by the townspeople themselves, as punishment for this infraction. Certainly, historians have demonstrated that the story of Lady Godiva and Peeping Tom is no more than a myth (Carr-Gomm, 2012: 92-5). Although the events are unlikely to have taken place, the conjunction of the nudity, protest and public space has proved beguiling. Over the centuries, festivals, films, sculptures, and paintings have evoked the presentation of virtuous female nudity astride her horse in the humble service of social justice. Are PETA protests indebted to this apocryphal tale in the way that they think they are?

The legend of Lady Godiva holds enduring appeal as a story because of her nakedness *per se*, rather than what her nakedness might be mobilised to mean politically. Godiva is compelled to ride naked through the town at the demand of her husband. This is not the expression of feminist autonomy or sexual agency, but rather a submissive, obedient response to Leofric's attempt to publically humiliate Godiva. Her nudity – supposed to bring her shame – is the price he asks her to pay for the pecuniary reprieve of the people of

Coventry. Many organisations that specialise in nude feminist protest have men at their helm, or directing the action (for example, Femen), and therefore entail an element of this dynamic whereby men decide that women shall go unclothed for their politics (Green, 2013; Eileraas, 2014: 48; Wrenn, 2015: 135).

This is not, presumably, the legacy that organisations like PETA wish to recuperate from the Godiva myth. Instead, it is probably the dignity with which Godiva appears to bear her humiliation, the fact that as a result of her unclothed entry through public space she succeeded in ending the extortion of the people of Coventry. It would not be impossible to envisage a scenario where Godiva (or indeed, any of the townspeople) unclothes in order to protest at the way in which their treatment is dehumanising as an expression of precarious life, of anguish, and of last resort, like the embodied protests described by Owens (2009) and O'Keefe (2006). Yet as PETA state themselves, these tactics are intended to be 'attention-grabbing actions'; they are never presented expressions of desperation or of last resort. The gendered dynamic of women who undress at the behest of men was completely normalised in the anti-fur protest that I describe at the outset of this chapter. The tone and content of online discussions about non-human animal rights protests take female nakedness as a given. Even the casual and unselfconscious way in which, at this protest, my co-protesters and I undressed in the rain, in Trafalgar Square, on a busy Saturday afternoon, illustrates how unexceptional the naked female body is in these campaigns.

If the popularity of the figure of Godiva emerges because she is naked, then this image is rendered even more titillating with the addition of Peeping Tom. The only one to watch the naked Godiva make her way through the streets – to violate the taboo that Godiva had tried to invoke around her nakedness – Tom comes to stand in for the observers of these protests in general. As part of the assemblage of protest, the character of Tom is added to the tale, we could say, to draw attention to just how out-of-place, yet compelling, female nudity in public is. He watches the spectacle unfold and figuratively consumes the body of Godiva on her protest. Tom – and his eventual blindness – reminds us of the (im)morality of nudity in public space. When PETA – and other similar organisations – embark on protests that mobilise the naked female body, they need a 'Tom' figure in order for the message of their protest to be received. During the anti-fur protest that I participated in, we revelled at being watched by the crowd. Yet Tom, like Leofric, uses his male privilege to exploit and objectify Godiva, so that rather than being the feminist icon that

PETA would like her to be, Godiva is always-already subject in this encounter (even if eventually Tom is punished for his transgression by divine intervention).

Indeed, these reactions to the protest are what make the protest. At SlutWalk protests that I have observed, and non-human animal rights protests that I have participated in, it is the audience response to the spectacle that in many ways indicates whether the protest has an impact. At SlutWalk, onlookers took photographs and made films and laughed and shouted at the protesters in a jovial manner. Tourists joined the march; women and men working in the shops of Oxford Street came out on to the pavements and balconies; road labourers stopped what they were doing and watched. At the anti-fur protests, the women with whom I was performing and I talked among ourselves – almost vainly and with palpable pride – about the size of the crowd around us. We talked about how exhilarating it was for us to be watched by so many. Photographers had travelled from across the country to take our picture. The photographs, their shareability, the provocativeness of the image that we created, stretched the scope and reach of the protest well beyond the short time/space during which we occupied that place in central London, sandwiched in between the National Gallery and a political protest about Venezuela. Although we did not interact with the onlookers verbally, and although we were only seven people, we did have the impression in the response of the crowd that the protest had in some way been effective. The encounter with the crowd in this assemblage made this so.

Carol Adams (2016 [1990]) has written most prolifically about human and non-human animal politics. Adams' principal thesis in *The sexual politics of meat* is that the relationship between meat (dead non-human animal to be consumed) and women is maintained by patriarchy in contemporary society that devalues human women and non-human animals in particular. The subordination of women and of non-human animals is enabled, in part, through the mobilisation of what she calls the absent referent. A parallel concept to the spectacle – in which that which is occluded has a potent significance – the absent referent recalls the concept of lacunae. The lacuna speaks to the concept of an absence, or a lack that has presence and meaning; meaning that is possible *because of the absence* of the object to which it refers (Fanghanel, 2014).

Here, according to Adams, both human women and non-human animals are absented through language. In the preface to the 20th anniversary edition of her text, Adams (2016 [1990]: xxvii) gives the 'Hooters'[13] restaurant logo as an example of an absent referent.

'Hooters', ostensibly, are owls, and the double 'o' of 'Hooters' are owl's eyes in the logo, yet 'Hooters' is also a slang term for women's breasts. Women are the absent referent here. Elsewhere, in the realm of butchery, referring to pig animals as 'pork' makes an absent referent of the non-human animal. Describing industrial development of agriculture, for instance, as 'the rape of the land', makes an absent referent of women within conservational discourses. Adams traces the parallel ways in which women and non-human animals have been oppressed (2016 [1990]: 27) through objectification (being considered an object rather than a sentient human); fragmentation (animals cut into meat parts, such as chicken thighs or pork belly, parts of women's bodies especially breasts, lips or legs, objectified in advertising); and consumption (being eaten, or the consumption of objectified women in images). Adams' thesis is particularly scathing of advertising or other media that either present women as is they are non-human animals (Playboy bunnies, for instance) and meat as if it were a sexy human woman in order to entice eaters (see, for examples, Adams, 2016 [1990]: 199-204).

Critics of Adams' work have objected to its apparent reliance on essentialist and generalist observations about who eats meat, what eating meat means cross-culturally, and the relationship between eating meat, masculinity, and sexual violence. Meat, Adams argues, has historically been associated with men's diets, with men 'needing' to eat meat and women socially or culturally excluded from meat-eating (see Adams, 2016 [1990]: 4-7, 20-6). Vegetarianism is effeminate; concerns about non-human animal welfare, soft. The relationship between sex and meat could indeed be said to be cross-cultural (Tuzin, 1978), but what Adams neglects is the cultural specificity of the context in which meat-eating occurs (in particular, the capitalism that is embroiled with her analysis of contemporary meat-eating). And while certainly Adams' contention that non-human animal exploitation and the exploitation of women are rooted in capitalist patriarchy is convincing, she neglects to consider the specificity of the case that she is, in fact, talking about. Adams (2016 [1990]: 24) makes the link between animals oppressed in the fur trade and 'the oppression of blacks as slaves'. Elsewhere (2016 [1990]: 34) she draws equivalences between rape and the consumption of animals: 'you are held down by a male body as the fork holds a piece of meat so that the knife may cut into it'. Critics may, and do, argue that not only can these not be equivalent cases, but to suggest that they are is offensive and dehumanising. Moreover, this is a capitalist and occidental understanding of the relationship between human and non-human animals. This understanding of non-human animal consumption describes contemporary capitalistic understandings of hunting where not only is the labour that produces the animal as meat occluded, but also the speciesist imaginary of power relations remains intact. This forgets the ways in which meat-eating can be considered a matter of reciprocal exchange, or a form of gift giving with the non-human animal, in which the non-human animal is revered (Tuzin, 1978; Bird-David, 1990).

But to venture this rebuke is to reckon without the epistemological basis from which Adams speaks. For Adams (2016 [1990]: xxxvii), the oppression of non-human animals and women is intrinsically linked. Concern for non-human animals is another manifestation of social justice for minoritised groups. In an argument that resembles an intersectional defence of why activists interested in social justice should also attend to non-human animals' lives, Adams (2016 [1990]: xxxiv-xl) contends that to ask why we should care about what we eat when there are women in the world who 'needed any food whatsoever' is to reinforce the 'script of meat' that silences this minoritised perspective. Indeed, this race to the bottom argument is the sort of arboreal logic that forever returns on itself and obviates any kind of line of flight from contemporary oppressions.

In the foreword to the 10th anniversary edition of her text, Adams (2016 [1990]: xxv-xxvi) levels a charge of defensiveness at her critics; those who think she has 'gone too far', or that she has 'no sense of humour', or who have been made to feel uncomfortable by her analyses. In trying to regain ground, they espouse patriarchal and majoritarian discourses of oppression. In the original of her text, Adams (2016 [1990]: xxxix) points out that 'holding a minority opinion in a dominant culture is very illuminating' in terms of identifying what informs resistance to these politics. Minoritarian perspectives and minoritarian politics, like Julia Kristeva's (1977) herethics that we explored in the previous chapter, are outsider politics. They are critical positions from which to bring about socio-cultural change and to promote social and spatial justice. Becoming-minoritarian enables analyses of the structures that sustain an oppressive regime of power (like rape culture) because it brings to light that which we have taken for granted. Adams writes of the moment where she saw from this minoritarian perspective. Eating a beef burger on the evening of the day her pony was shot and killed by a neighbour, she describes the moment of what we might think of as Brechtian alienation from the meal she was consuming. This moment of 'seeing things differently' – seeing things from a minoritarian perspective – nurtured Adams' activist vegetarianism. Therefore, notwithstanding the sometimes swift and somewhat vulgar way in which she unveils her demonstration, those who find Adams' argumentation distasteful, would, in her mind, simply be reiterating a normative and majoritarian speciesist world view where women and non-human animals are oppressed, but where women are considered to be more important than non-human animals, even as they are subordinated within rape culture. Notwithstanding these reservations, Adams remains an influential voice in the work to promote social justice and eradicate patriarchy through this twin project of feminist and anti-speciesist emancipation.

Adams' observations about the tensions between feminism and non-human animal rights activism demonstrate complexities that help us to understand what is going on (and not going on) in naked protest. Speciesism – the concept that by virtue of *being* human we are intrinsically more important than, and are superior to, other species – forms part of the objections against her work. Speciesism also informs feminist rhetoric, including some of the rhetoric discussed in this chapter. When protesters say 'They were treating us like animals', or at SlutWalk, 'I am not a piece of meat', they invoke the speciesist sentiment that to be like-animal is degrading or dehumanising. When animal rights protesters cover themselves in fake blood and roll around on the ground in their underwear next to photographs of maimed animals, they invite a human exceptionalist or anthropocentric response – the concept that the human species is the most significant species on the planet – to how treating female humans' bodies as if they are non-human bodies is an outrage. To have no truck with anti-speciesism, as Adams' critics sometimes do not, is to not see from her epistemological perspective how this injustice is manifest. Instead, in order to understand as far as possible how these politics might transform social and spatial justice, I approach this text here with curiosity, and with what Lugones (1987) would describe as 'world-travelling loving perception', even if its argumentations are sometimes unsatisfying.

Protest as commodity

I want to explore the dynamics of these contested politics further. One way in which to examine this is by looking at the commercialisation of non-human animal rights protests. Lush is a British cosmetics company that demonstrates one example of this. Founded in 1995, it manufactures handmade toiletries and cosmetics. Lush espouses brand values about reduced packaging, anti-animal testing, producing vegetarian products, ethical trading, and charity work.[14]

In 2007, as part of its campaigning and charitable work, Lush campaigned against packaging by inviting its staff to work in the stores wearing nothing but aprons emblazoned with the words 'Ask me why I am naked'. Staff have participated in hunger strikes, petitions, and awareness-raising in support of the incarcerated of Guantanamo Bay (2008). In 2008, in order to protest against the use of shark fins in cosmetics and medicines, a performance artist painted in silver (like a shark) suspended herself by her back, piercing her skin with two shark fishing hooks in the front window of Lush's Regent Street store (see Aronczyk, 2013; Wrenn, 2015). In 2010, Lush, along with the Rainforest Action Network in the USA, campaigned against the degradation of areas of tar sands in Alberta, Canada (Aronczyk, 2013). They lobbied the USA and Canadian government and tried to draw attention to the damage that the exploitation of these lands causes by dressing some of their employees in their underwear and in 'oil barrels', and by performing a montage that depicted protesters dressed as oil pipeline executives pouring a liquid resembling oil over a semi-naked woman sitting on the Canadian flag (Aronczyk, 2013: 12).

Lush protests are often about environmental issues and are often conducted in collaboration with charities and non-governmental organisations (NGOs). Usually Lush creates a product — a soap or a shampoo — part of the sales of which are donated to the cause in question. As Melissa Aroncyk recognises, this form of corporation-led activism can be viewed with suspicion. Corporate activism is 'a condition of contemporary capitalism' (2013: 2), and, as a State instrument, is the manifestation of an apparatus of capture through which anti-establishment, so-called progressive or social justice-orientated ethics, are captured, tamed, commodified and sold back to the consumer to further entrench capitalism within a system of organising everyday life. The reality of these campaigns, the politics behind them and the position of corporations is complex, but there is little doubt that corporate activism must inherently be tied to the desires of the State when protest is mobilised as commodity.

In 2012, Lush, along with the Humane Society ('a leading force for animal protection') and a couple of artists staged a 10-hour 'endurance' performance in the shop front of its largest store in the UK. The performance was intended to raise awareness about, and to protest against, cosmetic testing on animals, and was part of a simultaneous campaign in 800 of Lush's stores across 49 different countries. The performance was enacted by a man (who was the director of the piece), who played the 'scientist', and a woman, who played the 'animal'. Both performers appeared to be white, able-bodied and young. The man was wearing a white lab coat, a blue medical cap and a mask. We could only see his eyes and his hands as he worked on his subject for the day. She, in contrast, was barefooted, wearing a full-body leotard that matched the colour of her skin, giving the appearance that she was naked. Her long hair was tied away from her face for much of the performance. Unlike the 'scientist', this 'animal' was almost completely exposed: every expression on her face, every impression that the scientist's experimentations made on her body was visible (all the more so because of her positioning in this shop window in this busy shopping area). Already the differential power dynamics between the man/woman, subject/object, scientist/animal emerged through this visibility. A video of the event, filmed and narrated by Lush, made explicit the purpose of this performance (Lush, 2012).

In it, we see the 'animal' being led roughly into the performance space, through the Lush shop, on a leash (the shop window looks out on to one of the busiest shopping streets in London). The leash is yanked around her neck; her facial expressions convey that she is in pain. The scientist then attaches a lip spreader to her face – hooks that strap around the back of her head and hook into her mouth in order to force it open – and she is force-fed. As what appears to be pureed food is spooned into her mouth, the 'animal' appears to be crying. She already has marks on her face from where she has been manhandled. The 'scientist' then spreads various creams on to her face, and roughly scrapes them off using a spatula-like implement. The 'animal' is then blindfolded with bandages and forced to lie down by being pushed in the throat by the 'scientist'. In contrast to her expressive face, which suggests the distress and pain that the 'animal' is feeling, the 'scientist' betrays nothing in the way he looks at the 'animal' or the gathering audience outside. His gaze is impassive – it could be called cold – he appears unmoved by what he is doing or the effect he has on his 'animal' subject. Later in the performance, the 'scientist' uses hair clippers to shave the front of the head of the 'animal'. He then applies a cream to her eyebrows and proceeds to pluck one of her eyebrows entirely off her face using tweezers. He applies cream to the areas that he has shaved. The audience who witness these acts watch the performance, mouths agape, seemingly horrified by what they are watching. The 'scientist' 'drugs' his subject by roughly forcing what appears to be a tablet into her mouth. She is lain down in the shop window, to rest, we imagine. Later, the lip spreader is back in her mouth, the 'animal' appears to be hooked to electrodes and simulates receiving electric shocks, receiving injections, receiving solution sprayed into her open eyes. She appears, once more, to be crying. She has a label tied to her wrist reading 'Specimen No. 3652C'. The 'animal' is force-fed more tablets and appears to fall asleep (we learn that the 'animal' has, in fact, 'died'), whereupon a female 'nurse' enters the shop window space, places a bin liner over the head of the 'animal' and, together with the 'scientist', they carry the 'animal carcass' out into the street, and lay her down among the rubbish bags on the pavement.

All the while that this performance unfolded, members of the public were walking past the window. In the words of Lush's campaign manager, Tamsin Omond, 'people are watching and looking with complete shock in their eyes' (Lush, 2012: 2.36). They took photos with their phones, the press reported the story, and promotional pictures were taken for Lush's own campaign materials. People were entreated to sign petitions and to visit stores to find out how they can get involved with the campaign.

Erotic violence II

Certainly, there are aspects of this performance that recall the approaches adopted by PETA: the performance of violence and humiliation; the absent referent of the non-human woman-as-animal; the equivalence of the body of the woman and the body of the non-human animal; the near-nudity, the performance of pain, the violence.

Like the work of PETA, this performance piece was criticised for its eroticised representation of gender violence. It is telling that this campaign was mistaken by some onlookers for one highlighting domestic violence (Rosario, 2015: 98). Organisers of the performance, including Nicole Cataldo-Davies who played the 'animal' herself, countered the accusation that the male 'scientist' and the female 'animal' represent gender violence through their performance. According to the head of Lush campaigns:

> Our aim was most certainly not to titillate. The bodysuit was not attractive (regardless of how the mainstream media may have presented or written about it). The costume made her an anonymous test subject and stripped her of the accoutrements of sexuality or eroticism. (Omond, April 2012)

A view that is confirmed by the 'animal' herself, who:

... described how they attempted to keep the costumes as androgynous as possible, both in the design of her body suit and with [the 'scientist'] in loose-fitting white overalls and a mask obscuring much of his face. (Rosario, 2015: 98)

Of course, these claims are somewhat disingenuous. If the intention of the performance was not to draw parallels with gendered violence (violence against women because they are women), then the performers could just as easily have swapped places; the man playing the animal, the woman the scientist. Instead, the presentation of the man-as-scientist (active, aggressive, clothed, composed, of-science) compared to the woman-as-animal (naked, victim, passive, objectified, dehumanised, emotional, of-nature) not only reinforces traditional gender hierarchies, but also, in a resounding echo of rape culture, institutionalised violence between the State and subaltern subjects of the State.

At the anti-fur protest in which I took part, campaigners displayed a poster that showed a woman screaming while having her skin pulled off her back. Intended to discourage the wearing of fur, this poster employed the non-human animal as absent referent to show the human female model in pain and in a position of submission. This poster accompanied a gendered dynamic within this anti-fur protest where all but one of the 'naked' protesters were female, white, under the age of 35, apparently able-bodied, for the most part conventionally attractive to look at, and for the most part fashionably covered in tattoos (the one other 'naked' protester was a good-looking, able-bodied, non-British white male in his twenties). Other protesters speaking to the crowd, and to the media, handing out leaflets, and holding placards, were mostly older, clothed men and women from a range of ethnic backgrounds. There was no question that they would join the 'naked' part of the protest: the very suggestion of it was treated as a joke by everyone. This dynamic reinforces oppressive power relations that saturate these protests where men decide what women protesters will do, and the women obey. Such a dynamic eroticises feminine submission in these protests (Wyckoff, 2014; Wrenn, 2015: 132).

The aim of Lush's intervention into public space may not have been to titillate – Catherine Rosario (2015: 101) explains that the 'animal' performer, Cataldo-Davies, was very keen to distance herself from any suggestion that what she experienced brought her any pleasure whatsoever – but it nonetheless evoked key tropes of BDSM/kinky sexual practice (Weiss, 2006). The public, performative element of the scene in the window echoes the 'scenes' that practitioners of BDSM might perform in a club or other semi-public area dedicated to the purpose of enabling practitioners of BDSM to 'play'. This practice is not usually abusive, but it is a practice that has violent themes, and if we look at the Lush protest through the lens of BDSM practice, these become apparent in this protest. The efforts that Cataldo-Davies and Omond make to distance themselves from consensual sexualised violence further confirm, rather than rebut, the more problematic aspects of the protest.

From the contrast between the clothed male 'scientist' and the apparently naked female 'animal', to the violent way in which she is manhandled, this performance has the look and feel of a scene between a male dominant actor and his female submissive (not least because the actor playing the 'scientist' was also the director of the scene; in a conventional BDSM scene, it would usually be the dominant actor who would decide on the intricacies of the action, even if the broader details are negotiated with the participating submissive before the scene commences). The photographers and filmmakers at the anti-fur protest that I participated in were also all older men, which is a dynamic that is found again and again in BDSM communities – older men establishing themselves as photographers to pay younger female models to pose for them – and in this protest we responded to photographic requests to hold positions for them, to pose in certain ways together, so they could capture a certain aesthetic of the protest quite outside of any decisions about the form of the protest that we may have organically and independently decided on, as the key, and central, performers.

We know that both the 'scientist' and the 'animal' had consented to participating in the Lush performance. We see the 'animal' appearing to cry, to grimace, and to look downcast and distressed during the performance. These expressions of affect help to contribute to the narrative of the scene that non-human animals are exploited in cosmetics testing. They are also suggestive of 'consensual non-consent': a particular type of edgework that involves 'play with forcing themes' that we explore more of in Chapter Four (Weiss, 2011: 21). Torture scenes might be considered to be forms of consensual non-consent play. According to Rosario's (2015: 98) interview with the female performer, details of what the performance would entail were deliberately kept from her by the 'scientist' so that she 'could reach closer to the state of a powerless animal passively reacting to whatever he did'. She had consented to participating in the performance in general, without necessarily consenting to each component part, and had consented to this ambiguity around what would happen, how, when, and so on. It should be noted that consensual non-consent is still consensual, and the organisers of the performance make it clear that the 'animal' could have stopped the performance whenever she wanted to, if she wanted to, as with conventional BDSM play.

The dehumanisation of the 'animal' also evokes traditional power exchange in BDSM play. Not only is she 'naked' and exposed to the on-looking public, she has her hair shaved off the front of her head, one eyebrow painfully removed, and is force-fed food and tablets by use of a lip-spreader that is a recognisable piece of BDSM dungeon play equipment. The label that is tied to her wrist, identifying her specimen number, suggests to the audience that she had no subjectivity, no name, and no agency in these events. Numbering people is sinisterly dehumanising and is a device used to demoralise and degrade. Within a Marxian vulgate, and in parallel with rape culture, this objectification renders the female human-as-animal into a commodity. Accompanying this is the obscured and commodified labour of the 'scientist' who is also easily implicated in the exploitation of the 'animal'. The obfuscation of this relationship is why these protests remain in the sphere of the spectacular. The crescendo of the scene, at the end of the 10-hour performance, sees the 'animal' carried into the street and cast out with the rubbish. This final humiliation for the 'animal' reminds the audience of the way in which non-human animals used for testing are commodified, consumed, and discarded.

Within the context of the Lush protest, this dehumanisation and degradation of the 'animal' serves a twin political purpose. On the one hand we are asked to see the woman-as-'animal' and to be horrified by the way she is treated as an animal. On the other hand, we are asked to see non-human animals as equally worthy of life and justice as human animals. We would not accept this, this protest argues, if it were done to a woman, so why do we accept it for a non-human whose life is as important? Yet the protest only works if we simultaneously hold that 'being treated like an animal' is unacceptable, inhumane, and will not pass. Holding these two somewhat paradoxical positions in tension with each other illustrates some of the problematic aspects of naked protest in public space, and demonstrates, as with the critiques of Femen and SlutWalk above, some of the ways in which these protests, like those of, for instance, PETA, rely on the fact of rape culture to mobilise their politics (Wyckoff, 2014; Adams, 2016 [1990]).

If the Lush protest was not about mobilising the abhorrence of violence against women in order to elicit horror in the audience at the way in which non-human animals are treated, why centralise the figure of the female body as the subject of the violence and humiliation? Protests against exploitation of oil sands in Canada or against unnecessary packaging also disproportionately feature undressed female Lush employees as part of the protest. In the oil sands protest, it was a female protester who received tarry molasses poured over her head: something that was repeated at European Lush stores, also with female models. The image of a woman covered in black molasses recalls the ancient 'tar and feather' punishments that were used to humiliate women for sexual misdemeanours, even into the last century (Wallace, 2007). Indeed, at the anti-fur protest that I participated in, when we were lying on the concrete covered in fake, but realistic-looking, blood, I heard children discussing among themselves whether or not we were alive. Reassured that they could see us breathing, they moved on with their families. More than PETA's 'I would rather go naked than wear fur' campaigns, this image/performance of seven women lying on the ground, nearly naked and covered in blood, in no small way evokes gendered violence. In their defence of the dynamic that they had established, Omond from Lush stated that:

> It was a performance of violence (not violence against women) where – unsurprisingly – the oppressor was male and the abused was vulnerable and scared. We felt it was important, strong, well and thoroughly considered that the test subject was a woman…. This is important within the context of Lush's wider Fighting Animal Testing campaign, which challenges consumers of cosmetics (a female market) to … demand that the cosmetics industry is animal-cruelty free…. It would have been disingenuous at best to pretend that a male subject could represent such systemic abuse. (Omond, April 2012)

Certainly, this does reflect in part that women more than men work in the cosmetics industry and are more engaged with non-human animal rights movements (Wrenn, 2015; Adams, 2016 [1990]). It also capitalises on the fact that in socio-cultural contexts where these protests take place, violence against women, and the sexualisation of this violence, is normalised by rape culture. In her claim that this protest was a 'performance of violence (not violence against women)', Omond betrays the complexity of the politics of the animal rights movement that I have pointed to. When Omond is asking the audience to acrobatically accept that a performance in which a woman experiences violence is not a performance of violence against women, she is asking them to efface the presence of the woman in the scene of violence (indeed, she does so herself in the first sentence). This is an effacement that echoes the systemic silencing of women's experiences of gendered violence in all realms of life, due to rape culture.

Making an appeal to the absent referent, Omond also relies on audience outrage and political action *because* the individual receiving the violence is a woman. To then claim that because women predominantly buy cosmetics and male subjects cannot 'represent such systemic abuse', both serve to blame women for cosmetics testing because of their consumption practices (which is also a form of systemic abuse) and rely on the fact of systemic abuse (male violence against women) to evoke emotive responses in the audience. Omond (2012) answers critics of this aspect of the Lush animal testing performance, saying, 'it is a horrible compromise that a performance of animal testing and abuse could conjure up such distressing lived memories for real women'. This 'compromise' captures what is troubling in this sort of naked protest; it relies on the power of rape culture 'to challenge public apathy', which always encourages powerful forces to oppress the less powerful, regardless of gender, sexuality, ethnicity, or species, rather than challenging the social relations that allows rape culture to thrive.

Similarly, PETA (in Glasser, 2011: 63) may claim that their campaigns 'aren't driven by patriarchal power structures', but they rely on these structures in order to work. It is an argument that suggests that the ends of a political protest justify the means. Rather than 'questioning the *status quo*', these campaigns utilise the *status quo* to mobilise reactionary campaigns. Here, as with some of the other protests undertaken by other animal rights groups, the means of protest are to use rape culture to mobilise a message (Pace, 2005: 37). Certainly, neither Lush nor PETA claim to work towards the eradication of rape culture (unlike, say, SlutWalk or Femen); however, their protests actually instil the commodification of violence against women as sexy in the pursuit of affecting their audience (Glasser, 2011). They make a spectacle of their politics by mobilising this anti-speciesist ideology as a commodity that is sold through sexual violence. Sex sells, of course, but the sex that seems to sell the most is that of the beaten, victimised female body within a hegemonic construction of heterosexual gender relations, masculinity and femininity. Lush capitalises on this to convey its message as powerfully as possible. The degraded female body is the price of this power. Of course, animal rights activists are not protesting against rape culture, which might excuse them from the charge of promoting rape culture. They are, however, promoting a political message that seeks to promote inter-species equality and justice. It would seem difficult to achieve this in a context where the exploitation of female human bodies was the price to pay.

Animal politics

This message – the relationship between the human–non-human, the woman, the animal and the woman-as-animal – is rendered more complex by the other politics that these organisations rely on. The naked protest that Tyler (2013: 211-12) describes in Yarl's Wood Immigration Removal Centre in 2008 occurred because, in the words of one of the protesting women from Nigeria:

> 'I took my clothes off because they treat us like animals. We are claiming asylum, we're not animals. They treat us as if we've done something terrible.' (quoted in Dugan, 2008)

Here, the positioning of non-human animals as of lower status than human animals works to highlight the abuse that women interred at this detention centre suffered. As a rhetorical device, being treated as an animal is vernacular for being treated as less-than-human, within a post-industrialist capitalist and speciesist ontology where non-human animals are commodified. Treating women in detention as if they are animals, leaving them with no recourse but the naked protest, draws attention to how the naked protest is potent as an expression of precarious life, even as it relies on notions of human exceptionalism (see Owens, 2009). As I have demonstrated above in discussions of PETA and Lush, non-human animal rights campaigns position themselves paradoxically on the lines between anti-speciesism and anthropocentrism; these campaigners would argue that human and non-human animals are not, and should not be, thought to be in a hierarchical relationship of importance with each other, yet they rely on speciesist sentiment of mainstream discourses to draw attention to their campaigns that shock and outrage and titillate onlookers precisely because of the hierarchical relationship they attribute to human and non-human animal relationships. This section explores the political possibilities of protest outside of this bind. There are, therefore, a number of ontological strands that trickle through these arguments about the female body and how far it disrupts public space.

Gilles Deleuze and Félix Guattari (2004a [1980]) have famously (and notoriously) written about the politics of 'becoming' and the capacity that 'becoming' harbours for transformation. Indeed, the notion of Becoming- goes right to the heart of the transformative politics that this book expounds. Deleuzoguattarian notions of 'becoming' rely on an understanding of a world that is composed through flow, through smooth and striated space, through multiplicity, through rhizomes, through molecularity, and through desire.

Many of these ideas we encountered in the first chapter, and these work in parallel with the politics of Kristeva's herethical maternal politics that we encountered in the previous chapter on pregnancy. Here, together, they accompany each other to describe the 'becoming-animal'. The 'Becoming-' described by Deleuze and Guattari is imminent. The state of Becoming- is the means through which the molar ontology of the subject is challenged. Subjectification is an ordering tool of the State. That which is molar is static; is stuck. It cannot be nomadic and disobedient to the dominant ways in which life is striated. As we saw in Chapter One, Becoming-animal does some of this work towards nomadism, via, perhaps, the figure of the smith who weaves a life through and between smooth and striated space. Here, Becoming-animal does not mean to imitate or copy or evolve into an animal (Deleuze and Guattari, 2004a [1980]: 262-3). It means to form a 'band', or a 'pack', or a 'multiplicity', and to forge alliances that are not propagated by institutions of the family, for instance, or by the sanction of the State (Deleuze and Guattari, 2004a [1980]: 264).

Multiplicities harbour the potentiality to emerge in infinite ways, including in infinite ways that have not been imagined, or thought, or lived. Although it seems, in their articulation, that the non-human animal might be pitched against the non-animal human as a different and lesser form of life, the animal that Deleuze and Guattari identify is characterised by its awesome potency. Packs of vampires, wolves, even dogs or cats who are treated as swarms are the Becoming-animals we are looking for. Within these packs, anomal animals – exceptional individuals – are with whom alliances might be sought. Deleuze and Guattari give the example of Herman Melville's *Moby Dick* as an anomal, exceptional creature among whales. Disinvested from subjectification, order, or hierarchy, Becoming-animal is, for Deleuze and Guattari, the way in which their twin enemies, capitalism and psychoanalysis, might be combated, by exceeding the striates of the State.

Animals as a political possibility also appear in Donna Haraway's (2008) elegant text on human-dog interspecies relationships that reads like a love letter to her dog, and to dogs in general, in all their forms. Haraway offers a vision of the world that takes seriously the meaning of relationships between companion animals and their humans. Taking place at the junctional interstice of technical devices, nationhood, bioethics, heritage, colonialism, and microbes, Haraway (2008: 3) politicises human and non-human animal relationships by advancing what she refers to as a move towards *autre-mondialisation*, or 'just and peaceful other-globalisation' that she seeks to achieve by 're-tying some of the knots of ordinary multi-species living on earth'. It is here that she notices parallels in her project for different, and more just way of living, and Deleuze and Guattari's anti-capitalist project of becoming-animal (Haraway, 2008: 27). The authors both talk about animals, but here the similarity ends.

Haraway's assessment of Deleuze and Guattari's politics of the animal is as scathing as Deleuze and Guattari are about the sorts of companion animals that interest Haraway. '"My" cat, "my" dog', they say, 'invite us to regress … into narcissistic contemplation … *anyone who likes cats or dogs is a fool*' (Deleuze and Guattari, 2004a [1980]: 265; original emphasis). Pets, or companion animals, are scorned in the grand anomal project of becoming-animal, not for the form they take – not for being a cat, or a budgerigar, or a gerbil – but because of the way they are created, the way they are thought, and the affects that they express: the way they are individualised, owned and sentimentalised. For Haraway (2008: 28), 'no earthly animal would look twice at these authors', whose emphasis on 'sublime wolf packs', for instance, has no time for the everyday, mundane, prosaic of human and non-human animal relationships that Haraway explores. Deleuze and Guattari (2004a [1980]: 269) have no patience with the 'little cat or dog who is owned by an elderly woman who cherishes it', which, as Haraway (2008: 30) explains, betrays a certain ageism and sexism and speciesism that might be unexpected in scholars of revolutionary thought. Indeed, their scorn for the woman (who must, of course, be 'elderly') has something of the striated about it. At the same time, let us be clear that this scorn emerges because of the *commodified relationship* between a domestic animal and its owner.

Notwithstanding the ageist stereotyping that Deleuze and Guattari expose here, there may be something that we might recuperate from this form of animal politics for our work against rape culture. Transforming the self, in a social sense, in connection with other beings, human and non-human, is part of the transformation of a social world. Similarly, *autre-mondialisation* is a focus on making another world – another way of living that is more attentive to the human non-human symbiosis. Certainly, neither Deleuze and Guattari nor Haraway discuss explicitly the way in which these animal politics might counter rape culture. This is not the intention of their works.[15] Nonetheless, the conjunction of thinking about non-human animals in a state of precarity (as in the Yarl's Wood protest), of thinking about non-human animals as a relational connection through which to do the world differently (*autre-mondialisation*), or of thinking about non-human animals as transformative forces (Becoming-animal), sets the scene both for taking the non-human animal seriously as a political problem and as a political vehicle for developing a praxis that transforms contemporary rape culture.

Becoming-animal?

Placing these ideas about justice, anti-racism, anti-misogyny, the non-priority of humans, the immanence of meaning and of affect alongside the work of Adams (2016 [1990]) and the absent referent, there are explicit links to be made between these approaches and our concern here about rape culture. How far are PETA protests, or Lush protests, or Femen protests, or SlutWalk protests, forms of *autre-mondialisation*, precarious life, or becoming-animal in the context of rape culture? Were we, lying in the rain, evoking animals skinned for their fur, becoming the guerrilla war machine this book is looking for?

Although I was lying on the ground, appearing to be naked and covered in blood, it was not until I heard the little voices of children in the crowd wondering whether we were alive that I realised how we were supposed to be being animal carcasses. It was cold that afternoon, and while I moved my arms and legs and readjusted my position to keep warm and to make myself more comfortable, some of the other participants worried that we were talking and moving too much, that we should be still, much more like carcasses. Yet, 'becoming-animal' for Deleuze and Guattari would not simply have meant mimicking, or drawing analogy with, animals. To 'become-animal' we must 'endow the parts of [our] body with relations of speed and slowness that will make it become-[animal]' (Deleuze and Guattari, 2004a [1980]: 285). Speed is a Spinozist idea that is articulated by Deleuze and Guattari (1994 [1991]) to describe a present infinity that is molecularly composed of bodies that connect to form other bodies. The form a body takes, the affects it expresses, depends on the speed of its components. Speed describes the chaos and instability of the world, but also how that world is made sense of. Here the speed/slowness of the anti-fur protest might have helped us to become-animal. To think this through, I draw on my field notes:

Afterward I feel exhausted, like I have done an exam, or like I have swum some great distance, which is appropriate given how damp I am. The kind of euphoric tiredness you feel after you have achieved something challenging. I am soaking wet. Sticky, sugary, homemade fake blood is covering me. My hands are covered in red dye. My makeup is running. People look at me strangely on the bus home. I am pleased with what I did. I felt happy while I was doing it. I felt a sense of belonging with the people with whom I did the protest, even though I did not know them, and actually was sad to leave. The rain was huge though. How important is it that I am not vegan? And that even if I sympathise with their ideas, I do not really support what we were protesting about? I am a bit worried about these questions. But mostly, I want to do it again. I felt a happy thrill lying in my underwear covered in fake blood, covered in rain, in the middle of London, the heat of the bodies of strangers to warm me. It was cold though. While I didn't at any point think I would give up, it was certainly an endurance test. Some of the others were violently shivering from the cold at the end. I admired their commitment. The nihilist in me took strange pleasure from the despair of it. At first, it was not uncomfortable lying on the concrete. At first, I was enjoying the rest, but later it became painful to stay there. At the end of the protest, I was so cold, so wet, so euphoric about what I was doing that I was gripping onto the sheet beneath me as if I might fall off the ground, even though I was lying on flat concrete. The tension in my clenched fist became the focus for my strength, my endurance, and became what would keep me warm, what would keep me there, in the rain. While I did not think about what it would be like to be a non-human animal in this state, my mind did drift to thoughts about what it would be like to be homeless, or to be interred in a concentration camp, or in Guantanamo Bay in similar conditions, and I shamefully became aware of my privilege in participating in this comparatively trivial act by choice. I suppose my anti-speciesism still needs some work.

Becoming-animal is an affect in itself (Deleuze and Guattari, 2004a [1980]: 284). As these notes demonstrate, a cacophony of affect emerged through my body, in conjunction with the other women and men who were protesting, in conjunction with the onlookers, the photographers, the rain, the political message that I did not quite agree with, the cold and then warm concrete, the police who were protecting us (or protecting the onlookers from the violence of the message? I never made it out). Euphoria, shame, despair, hubris, pain and delight emerge and converge through the assemblage of these various bodies, coming together at different speeds and slownesses. Did I manage, through this shifting attachment to the protest, within this assemblage, to 'endow [my] elements with the relations of movement and rest, the affects, that would make [me] become-[animal]' (Deleuze and Guattari, 2004a [1980]: 284)? I am wary of making too many grand claims, so it is tentatively that I posit that there was, in some way, some becoming-animal going on here.

What emboldens me to make this claim is the very obvious way that my becoming-animal sometimes failed, and I was pulled back into an individuated subject position, with filiations, crystallised affect, and thoughts (Deleuze and Guattari, 2004a [1980]: 286). There was a moment when an attractive and fashionably dressed woman with a broad London accent came up to the edge of the sheet on which we were lying. I could not see her face well, but I remember her asking what was going on, "Feminist, innit?", she answered her own question. The protester handing out flyers corrected her and explained that this protest was "to show what happens" to animals in the fur trade, to which she responded, "But why are you using women? We are not animals." I could not hear his response. "But we are not animals. It's different", was her response, as she sped off. Her anger angered my protesting colleagues and brought me rudely back to the original reason why I was doing this protest in the first place; to consider precisely the gendered politics of these sorts of protests. Suddenly I became a researching, observing subject again, and had lost my sense of abandon and of deterritorialisation.

On another occasion a drunk, and I thought homeless, man also stepped up close to the sheet on the ground and started calling to his friend to come and have a look at us. He was holding a bottle of whisky in his hand and was peering over us. Then he said to his friend, "Watch out. Old Bill[16] mate!", indicating police officers, and swiftly disappeared. I felt, for the first and only time, vulnerable and stupidly grateful for the two police offers who were guarding the protest. The latent menace of sexual violence from stranger men, a fear of the 'other', the sense of being objectified, a reminder that I was a woman lying in my underwear in Trafalgar Square, all converged to reterritorialise how I felt about my self and what I was doing. At the same time, I felt shame about my feelings towards the man in the pursuance of my perceived safety. If he was homeless, he was already marginalised by the State instruments that I relied on to protect me. It was not my fear, or my embarrassment, or the expression of my privilege that he needed....

Yet, outside of these two events, I was subsumed into the speed of moment. I was simultaneously aware and unaware of what I was doing or thinking or feeling. Not committed to the politics of animal protest themselves, my motivation for being there was quite outside of filial obligation. I was there for the sensation itself, in part. In part, I was there to see what my body could do. These moments reflect a savage multiplicity of affect. It was in these moments that becoming-animal might have happened. Not because it was a non-human animal rights protest *per se*, but because it was a protest that was so corporeally demanding and, for me, alien.

The despair and hopeless abandon that I felt, and shared with some of the other protesters is worth revisiting in the context of occupying a position of precarious life (Butler, 2004). It is clear that I, even in the rain in my underwear, in Trafalgar Square, was not precarious. I was, and remain, privileged by class and by 'race', and education, and nationality, and by agency. I am not disabled, I am not poor, I am not fleeing war, or any other kind of violence. Yes, I felt vulnerable at points, but this naked protest was not one that came from a place of bare life, or out of necessity, or because I was outside of the legitimate protection of the law (the presence of the two police officers is evidence that we were very much within the protection of the *polis*, even if their presence did irritate me and my co-protesters).

It may have been a protest of last resort only in the sense that other more conventional and more clothed protests against non-human animal abuse attract less attention than the sight of naked protests, which have become ubiquitously synonymous with the movement do, and so these have *become* necessary. The bloodied corpse images of us in Trafalgar Square and the test subject in the Lush window and the brutal image of women having their skin ripped off in PETA posters are *spectacles* of precarious life. The representation of violence is a masquerade – a pastiche – of violence that obscures the more fundamental gender violence which has been commodified and put into service of these politics. The onlooker is asked to see a woman in peril, in misery, and to believe that her plight is an expression of desperation and of last resort. Precarious life is a necessary part of how these protests are impressive, but is quite apart from the actual precarity of the participants. Precarious life, as a discursive idea, however, relies in part on the notion of human exceptionalism – we cannot tolerate seeing humans suffer in the way that non-human animals do – which highlights one of the internal contradictions of these forms of protest within the animal rights movement.

Do these protests offer some form of *autre-mondialisation*? It is the case that they seek to promote justice for non-human animals. Would this form of justice call for a 'retying of the knots of ordinary multispecies living on earth' (Haraway, 2008:3)? It is possible that in the search for another world, or for another way of living, that *autre-mondialisation* is going on in these protests. *Mondialisation* (in English, 'globalisation', or more literally, 'worldification'/'worldilisation') is something that happens in the continuous present tense, which means that these protests might be the making of small worlds. Humble lines of flight, attempts to smooth striated space, the penetration of these politics into public space might attempt this. Of course, *autre-mondialisation* suggests an *a priori* notion of what that world might be, it certainly suggests knowing what it is not. Haraway might be relieved that *autre-mondialisation* is therefore not total deterritorialisation, becoming-animal or a war machine. Instead, language like this maintains 'other worlds' within existing logics of the *polis*. It is a shame, within these non-human animal rights protests, that within these existing logics of the *polis*, gender violence and exploitation is not expelled, as animal cruelty might have been. Indeed, this will not be possible as long as these protests remain within the sphere of the spectacular (Debord, 1994 [1967]). They will not get to the radical roots of power relations as long as spectacle *par excellence* is mobilised to eschew or obviate relations with women, and with non-human animals, and with commodification. Indeed, capitalist modes of production that are concealed here, also conceal the inherent violence with which they are embroiled.

Can naked protests in public space transform rape culture?

Protesting bodies form a multitude. Naked protesting bodies can be 'awe-inspiring' and troubling (Lunceford, 2012: 5). Intimately complicit in the construction of the spaces in which they take place, protests can cause rupture. Naked protests do this in a number of ways. Nirmal Puwar (2004: 2) illustrates how the space of Trafalgar Square is a formal place 'from where the British nation is celebrated' and also where protests take place. Named after a naval victory against Napoleon in 1805, its central column and three of the four plinths venerate 19th-century military figures. The famous lions at the base of Admiral Horatio Nelson's Column remind us of the imperial era in which these people were celebrated, and finds its echo in the Commonwealth embassies around the Square: Uganda House, Canada House and South Africa House. These public buildings are monumental, reminding us of an era when buildings representing political power were grand structures to be impressed by, as opposed to the more humble and discrete buildings of more contemporary times (think, for instance, of the transparent UK Home Office building). To the north of the Square is the equally grand gallery of the nation. To the west of it, the portrait gallery of the nation. Although also, often, the end gathering point for rallies at the end of marches and protests, Trafalgar Square is a formal and grand space, emphatically imbued with colonialist, white masculinity.

As we saw in Chapter One, Puwar (2004: 3) describes the bodies of trenchant, colonialist, white, male bodies in this space as the 'consecrated somatic norm', meaning that bodies which do not adhere to this norm are Other, are outsiders, are space invaders. We could also add that this space is highly coded and striated, both as a representation of power, prowess, and nationhood, and also as the correct place in which to protest. Thus, a protest in Trafalgar Square is not, in and of itself, necessarily transformative. It is the nakedness of SlutWalk or of anti-fur protests that might be considered to transform the politics and construction of this public space. The naked body elicits a response from those to whom it is shown. Whether it is the naked body of the naked curse that has the power to take life, which shames the onlooker (Turner and Brownhill, 2004), the naked body that angers or amuses (the protests of Femen), the naked body that embarrasses or titillates (SlutWalk), or the naked body that eroticises violence (the protests of Femen, PETA, or Lush), this a body that confronts and elicits affect differently to when it is clothed.

Whether in the service of anti-speciesism or of anti-rape campaigns, these naked protests propose different worlds (*autre-mondes*) to that in which we currently exist. They suggest, respectively, one that does not discriminate between species, one that does not tolerate sexual violence. In this respect there is a glimpse of a war machine, a glimpse of a becoming-animal that we might create. Yet, for Femen, for SlutWalk, and for these non-human animal rights groups, nudity is normative. Bare breasts, dressed in underwear, naked and covered in blood are performances of the body that are synonymous with these forms of protest. Protesters know what they are going to do, and onlookers know what they are going to see. The somatic norm, then, of these protests is (usually) one of young, thin, white, able-bodied women undressed and proximate to violent imagery or slogans. Of course, this is not to say that these norms are not still disruptive in a broader sense. To witness the violence of the Femen protests is to be aware of how disruptive and offensive, and thus effective, these protests might be, if they were not so spectacular. At the same time, within this UK context, the spectacularisation of these protests means that these protests mobilise female nakedness to eroticise their political content, which is altogether a much more outrageous commodification because it purports to critique, rather than compound, the *status quo*.

These protests entrench their positions within rape culture and rely on rape culture to mobilise their politics (Wrenn, 2015: 135). One exception might be that of the 'sex bomb' protest I described in the context of Femen. We may object to the objectification of the performer in this protest. We may dislike that she appears in a Femen protest only in so far as she can appear as grotesque femininity, but this performer may also, beyond the discursive narrative constructed by Femen, be causing the most disruption to public space. She may be making a guerrilla war machine, forging a smooth space in this intricately striated norm. Femen's decision to centre the protest around the undressed body of a woman whose body does not conform to *their* usual somatic norms foregrounds a body that is more confrontational and less easy for onlookers to consume. Within the context of this protest, this activist's lascivious, fat, and old body was presented as something to be frightened of, to run away from, so its transgressive potential is curtailed by Femen themselves.

But presenting a non-traditional body in a naked protest enables the politics of the protest to operate, somewhat, outside of rape culture. It does not require the body of the woman to be young and thin and conventionally beautiful for it to make a mark. It thus harbours the potentiality to be a line of flight, to form a war machine that breaks prevailing norms and values even if, as we have seen, it is always at risk of recapture by apparatuses of normative desire, vulnerability, and beauty around which bodies we want to see, which bodies will be seen, and which bodies can speak.

Using the examples of feminist anti-rape protest and those of the non-human animal rights movements, this chapter has demonstrated how the naked female body might disrupt public space in protest. Building on the discussions we started in the first chapter in the context of 'walking' a man on a leash in public, and on the debates about the political possibilities of this nakedness to Become- a war machine, we have seen how the transgressive appearance of this body troubles how public spaces in which these protests appear are striated. At the same time this critical analysis has uncovered some of the ways in which these protests are complicit in the proliferation of contemporary rape culture. This discussion illustrates the difficulties faced by political movements that seek to change how things are done, and to promote social and spatial justice. The apparatus of capture, and the vernacular spectacularisation of rape culture for political ends here, will always render this a difficult project.

In the next chapter we examine the ways in which these tangled politics trickle through the negotiations of intimate sexual politics between members of a kink community. Here, the sexual practices that these participants adopt troubles normative sexual imaginaries and striations even as they are themselves composed of tightly striated dynamics. As with what we have seen in the context of public protests, this chapter explores how kink both disrupts the mainstream and sustains the mainstream of contemporary rape culture.

FOUR

Disruptive play

During a rope performance at a kink[1] conference in Las Vegas, Star,[2] a renowned and highly esteemed female rope performer, is non-consensually fingered by XY before their audience as she is suspended in elaborate rope arrangements.

During a club night in London, Melody, a female 'sub', is non-consensually punched in the vagina by Orpheus, a well-known club night organiser and prolific member of the UK kink scene.

Both women swallow the violence acted against them which, for over a year, remains private and unspoken. Then both, separately, are provoked by a further act of violence by their abuser. XY contacts Star to ask her to help clear his name as he was struggling to get work now (a request that provokes her distress again); Melody is non-consensually pushed to the ground by Orpheus in the consensual non-consent room of the club night he organises. They both, again separately, tell their stories, and denounce their abusers on social media. From that moment, the treatment that they both receive at the hands of the community that encounters their complaints could not be more different: people are quick to rally around Star, while Melody is reprimanded and shunned.

Disruptive sexual stories

In previous chapters we have explored the body as a container, an image, a protest, and a spectacle. In this chapter we move towards analysis of the political relations that emerge out of specific bodily sexual practices, which have been considered deviant, but which are implicated within mainstream discourses around sexuality, desire and rape culture. In this chapter, I explore the potentiality of kink as a disruptive practice that is bound up with, and implicated in, a majoritarian capitalist commodification of sexual desire in which desire is objectified and spectacularised. I do this first, by interrogating how far kink disrupts the mainstream of sexual practice by exploring the tension between kink and the so-called 'vanilla' or non-kinky world. Second, I explore disruptions occurring in kink itself and how those disruptions are dealt with. Analyses of kink and other non-normative sexual practices provide us with a crucible, or a lens, through which to glean how sexual practices that occur within public spaces compose, or contest, contemporary rape culture. Within kink, sexualised practice is explicit, it is foregrounded, it is ritualised, and it emerges in a communicative and enthusiastic manner within the community. It is what happens at the intersect of kink with non-kink, and of 'bad' kink within 'good' kink, that will show us the role that this explicit sexualised practice plays in the pursuit of gendered social and spatial justice.

The stories of Star and XY and Melody and Orpheus help us to perceive these disruptions. The two stories came to light at the same time as each other in the community in which I was conducting my fieldwork in 2016. I encountered neither Star, nor Melody, nor XY, nor Orpheus during my research, but I did encounter many, many participants who knew them or knew of them, and I was told these stories over and again. The similarities and differences of the tales illustrate the crux of what I explore in this chapter: how 'bad behaviour'[3] is dealt with in the kink community, how far kink can be conceived of as a transformative political practice, and what role rape culture plays here.

Between 2015-16 I conducted research with 40 individuals who responded to a request made online to participate in a project about the ways in which norms are established and maintained within BDSM culture in the UK and the USA. Recruited using a non-probability snowball method, the 40 interviewees comprised 22 women and 18 men aged between 19 and 63. Twenty were from the USA (interviews via email and online conference platforms) and 20 were in the UK (interviews were face-to-face). Of those who agreed to reply to demographic questions about themselves (24: 10 women and 14 men), most, although not all, said that they were white, all but two (who were working class), identified as middle class (one described himself as 'middle class but willing to get his hands dirty'); all were cisgender. Experience of kink in the community varied from 1 year to over 30 (but this should not be taken to mean that identification as a kink practitioner did not pre-date identification as a member of the community; in many cases it did).

All but one of the men was heterosexual. Of the women, only three identified as heterosexual, with the rest identifying along the queer spectrum, or refusing to identify their sexuality. Two participants had a disability. Twelve were in relationships (monogamous or non-monogamous) and 12 were single. The sample reflects the profile of people who know each other within certain parts of the community. The majority of the sample identified as being 'in' a BDSM community (and would go to clubs and 'munches'[4] and would meet each other socially). Six were BDSM practitioners but did not identify as being part of the 'community'. Four men identified as submissive or bottoms, two were switches, the rest identified as Dominant or Top. Of the women, four were Dominant/Tops, the rest submissive, or bottom, or switch.[5]

Interviews lasting between one and three hours were recorded with permission and transcribed verbatim. Most interviews were conducted individually. Twice, couples or friends wanted to speak to me together, and did so. Participants then had the opportunity to read and comment on their anonymised transcripts, and a third of them did this. These interviews were supplemented by ethnographic observations at a sex exhibition in London, UK, focusing particularly on prevailing discourses of the event: what assumptions was it making about people who would visit the event? What representation of kink was it constructing? How was the interaction between the kinky sexual practice and the mainstream space of the exhibition hall negotiated?

Clearly, people who engage in non-normative sexual practice are as diverse as can be imagined. Although the sample of interviewees is relatively diverse in terms of age, it was dominated by heterosexual, cisgender, able-bodied, white, and middle-class individuals. Despite their socially privileged positionalities (or, indeed, maybe because of it), it remains important to examine how these people interact with rape culture as part of their practice. Yet there are some troublesome omissions here. Gay men and women have been at the vanguard of BDSM practice (Rubin, 1997). The Spanner case that I discuss shortly, was about gay men's sexual practice. Pat Califia (1988, 1994) has written extensively about lesbian leather kink. And yet, in my sample, using social media specifically for the kink community as a recruitment tool, these voices were absent, despite my attempts to reach them. The dominance of heterosexuality on this platform means that the observations that I can make here are limited to a heterosexually inclined community. Again, given that heterosexual coupling is a dominant form of relationship-making, it is nonetheless useful to explore the politics that underpin, and that sustain heteronormativity within kink communities, particularly in light of the heteronormativity that saturates rape culture.

No one person or group of people can or should speak for BDSM as a whole, and my own analysis of what people told me is obviously partial. This incompleteness means that what I am talking about can only give a sense of the complexity of BDSM politics rather than provide a definitive and exhaustive picture. This is brought into sharper relief when data here about community, tolerance, or dealing with bad behaviour are compared with the findings of Margot Weiss (2011), Staci Newmahr (2011) or Meg-John Barker (2013). The somewhat divergent perspectives we uncover illustrate the heterogeneity of the ways kink is conceived of, and spoken about, by the practitioners involved. This heterogeneity is important. It will be what enables us to conceive of an alternative politics beyond rape culture.

Establishing community

Throughout this chapter I talk about the BDSM/kink *community*. And while it is problematic to conceive of the kink community as a monolith, the reason I deliberately invoke 'community' as a way of articulating the relationships between the actors that I spoke to, and about, is because of the importance that an amorphous, vernacular sense of community has to the way that participants articulate how justice operates therein.

The word 'community' is a highly charged term. To use the word 'community' is to be prepared to allow certain concepts of same-ness to pass for granted. Understanding community is complex and sometimes problematic. Yet it was a word, and a notion, that was rehearsed extensively and more or less uniformly in the discourses of the people whom I interviewed. According to Newmahr (2011: 7), following Craig Calhoun (1980), 'community is a structure of social relations that produces collective actions'. Fostering an identity as a practitioner of BDSM is part of what constitutes 'belonging' to the community (Newmahr, 2011: 98). Acquiring skills, sharing knowledge, attending workshops, developing techniques, going to munches, eating together after a night spent in the club, being on mailing lists and social media networks are all ways in which community-building is practised and evidenced by members (Weiss, 2011).

It is tempting to think of community as something that is geographically bounded – people who are proximate to each other, who share common public (or private) spaces – but as the data that

I discuss in this chapter and wide-scale responses to Star and XY's encounter demonstrate, community here is forged at local, national, and international scales and is facilitated in no small part by online groups and social networking sites. Although I interviewed men and women from across the UK and the USA, and so who were geographically disparate, many of them recounted to me the same stories of the community and of Star and Melody and XY and Orpheus. I argue, thus, that it is helpful to think about the kink community as a 'community of practice' (Lave and Wenger, 1991).

The community of practice is built through shared participation in the practice of learning something or acquiring skills: 'collective learning in a shared domain of human endeavour' (Wenger-Trayner and Wenger-Trayner, 2015: 1). According to Jean Lave and Etienne Wenger (1991), who developed the concept as a way of understanding situated learning practices, communities of practice can be informally created by groups of people working together to share an interest. A community of practice requires a shared domain, and a commitment to that domain. Here, it is kink. As Weiss and Newmahr have illustrated, a sense of belonging within kink is forged by acquiring and establishing expertise, being recognised by others as having this expertise by sharing knowledge about it in workshops or classes, or informally by participating in, or observing, play. It requires members to help each other, and share information, to interact (at munches, say) even if they 'act' alone (as some of my participants who preferred not to play in public did). It requires there to be a practice – 'what it is that we *do*' (Newmahr, 2011: 166; emphasis added), which is shared through stories, demonstrations, writings, classes and chat-rooms.

Community is experienced here a site of companionship, of safety, and is, according to Newmahr (2011: 44), built on a shared understanding among the members of the community that they are outsiders, that they do not belong to the mainstream, and that by sharing this characteristic, they belong together. Yet, as David Sibley (1998), among others, has highlighted, community is necessarily also built on exclusion. People who are in the community, with the knowledge, the tools, the expertise, and the experience, are set apart from people who are not in the community, who are variously excluded. Certain hierarchies also emerge in community, with those who are recognised to have better expertise, better equipment, or more charisma, able to acquire status in a way that those without cannot, sometimes quite apart from the status that they enjoy outside of the community, in the mainstream. The establishing and negotiating of this hierarchy is an important feature of this formation of community.

As Weiss (2011: 58) warns, it is important not to romanticise community as a place of acceptance, freedom, and safety. The vocational element of the community of practice helps us to resist this romanticisation, because it is not built on nostalgia for an imagined past (Rubin, 1997), or for an imaginary of a counter-cultural, anti-capitalist movement (Joseph, 2002). Certainly, some people to whom I spoke did romanticise community as inherently benevolent and counter-cultural, but we must not conflate this vision of community with community as I am talking about it here. Instead, a community that sees kink practice as a project – something to develop, something unfinished, something forward-looking (what can it Become-...?) – points to the potentiality of kink as a transformative practice even as it is itself transforming. It marks the political dimension of the mobilisation of 'community' as a vernacular category.

The kink community shares similar values, norms and ethics. These values centre on respect, tolerance, liberalism, inclusivity, freedom, privacy, and practices of consent, education, knowledge-sharing and performance. They incorporate status – the expert, the newbie – and an attendant hierarchy within the group; whether because of attractiveness, skill, pain threshold, edginess, or a particular kink that a person is willing to explore (especially riskier practices that might involve cutting or burning the skin, or appearing to do so, electricity or breath play). Thus, as with other social groups, some individuals enjoy more cultural capital within the group than others. But these norms are inflected with capitalistic imperatives to self-determine. Yet, community is also characterised by a commitment to the community ethic. Protecting the community, defending it from malevolent or misunderstanding outsiders, making sure that nothing harms the community, is a distinctive feature of the ethos. This helps us to understand kink as machinic; composed of molecular parts that are productive, which do something, and which harbour the potential to become a guerrilla war machine, a war machine that smooths striated space, and that resists the advance of State thought and practice (Deleuze and Guattari, 2004a [1980]).

Penetrating the mainstream

What is disruptive about kink? What happens when kink or BDSM rub up against the non-kink mainstream? As Weiss (2006: 108) notes, kink practice has become increasingly accepted within the mainstream imaginary. Once considered to be the purview of perverts, deviants and pseudo-criminals, kink desire and iconography had become more and more commonplace in film, literature, advertising and in everyday parlance. Is BDSM inherently odd, still? Or is some of it more palatable? Gayle Rubin (1984: 279) described sadomasochistic sex as 'despised'; occupying the outer limits of the 'charmed circle' of sexuality. Certainly, a judgment that condemned 16 men for their consensual participation in BDSM practices (the infamous British case of *R v Brown [1993] UKHL 19, [1994] 1 AC 212*) would seem to confirm this attitude. The well-known facts of the *Brown* case are that:

> During a raid in 1987 the police seized a videotape which showed a number of identifiable men engaging in heavy SM activities including beatings, genital abrasions and lacerations. The police claim that they immediately started a murder investigation because they were convinced that the men were being killed.... The police learned that none of the men in the video had been murdered, or even suffered injuries which required medical attention.[6]

This case involved what appeared to be genital piercing, skin laceration, beating and electrical play (White, 2006: 169). The men were tried and convicted of actual bodily harm, in spite of their claims that they had consented to the acts in question. In his judgment, Lord Templeman exclaimed that:

> 'Society is entitled and bound to protect itself against a cult of violence. Pleasure derived from the infliction of pain is an evil thing. Cruelty is uncivilised.'

'Evil', 'repugnant', 'depraved', and ultimately a danger to public health (White, 2006: 171), despite dissenting, Lord Mustill, stated in his own judgment:

> 'It is sufficient to say that whatever the outsider might feel about the subject matter of the prosecutions – perhaps horror, amazement or incomprehension, perhaps sadness – very few could read even a summary of the other activities without disgust.'

Certainly, at the time of these judgments, kink activities between consenting men and videotaped for pleasure were considered to be – in the public domain of the courts – abhorrent, beyond comprehension, and beyond the pale. Doubtless it was the homosexual nature of the activities, that they appeared to show extremely violent practices, and that they carried the risk of HIV infection in an era with heightened fear of, and stigma about, HIV/AIDS that contributed to the visceral horror of the judges (White, 2006; Ashford, 2010). Here, the men prosecuted represented nearly all of Rubin's levels of 'uncharmed' sexual practice: homosexual, casual, SM, with multiple partners, in public (that is, not in the bedroom), pornographic (videotaped), non-reproductive, using objects, sinfully. It is no wonder that presumably heterosexual, white, upper middle-class men of the bench were so disturbed by the case.

In the early 1990s, in the UK at least, kink desires and practice were underground, badly understood, and in cases like *Brown*, condemned. Even in 2018, while sentencing a sex offender who worked in a fetish club for possessing child pornography, the judge pronounced:

> You have had a longstanding interest in the fetish scene.
> It was bound to stray into criminality eventually. (Butler, 2018)

Despite the fact that since *Brown* certain visions of kink practice are increasingly becoming more and more mainstream and less and less *outré*, kink sexual practice remains stigmatised. It remains figuratively and discursively on the cusp of, in the words of Judge Lawton, "eventual criminality". Yet, as Konstantinos Tomazos and his colleagues' (2017) paper on BDSM tourism illustrates, the banalisation and incorporation of elements of kink practice into the mainstream advances in parallel to this sort of legal condemnation. This is a banalisation that has been precipitated by the popularity of films about BDSM (for a discussion, see Weiss, 2006), kinky images in advertising (see Wilkinson, 2009), and the extraordinary popularity of romance novels like the *Fifty shades of grey* trilogy released in 2012, which has generated hundreds of academic articles and thousands of newspaper reports, a film franchise, and in the UK, was reportedly the fastest-selling paperback novel of all time.[7] As a representation of BDSM, this text has been widely criticised (Barker, 2013; Downing, 2013; Tsaros, 2013), even condemned for its representation of abuse as BDSM (Bonomi et al, 2013), and it is not my intention here to rehearse these observations. The popularity of a novel like *Fifty shades of grey* serves as an indicator of a shift in attitude about kinky sexual practice in the public realm. In particular, it marks a penetration of the concept of kinky sexual practice into non-kink public space, as one research participant explained:

> 'When *Fifty shades* was out ... I'd come into work on the bus and there were a lot of girls who were sitting on the bus reading it and if appropriate, I would try and make a little comment but you know, I try and slip into normal conversation, a word like "spanking" or what have you, just to try and gauge someone's reaction and then you can see whether their eyes go "bing" or sometimes they're disgusted, sometimes they do light up, and you think "great!"' (Arlo)

Arlo, a 50-year-old, white, middle-class, single, male, bisexual, switch, used the appearance of this novel in public spaces as an opportunity to approach women and to 'test the water' about the possibility of their interest in the practices described therein, notably, 'spanking'. Indeed, the popularity of the novel, and the extent to which it was read in public space, on buses, in airports, and in trains caused consternation and teasing concern that women (for its readership targets women) were adopting the use of electronic readers in order to 'hide' that they were reading such a kinky piece of literature (Roseman, 2013). The suggestion in these reports in newspapers and blogs, and in Arlo's comment, is that reading *Fifty shades of grey* betrays a perversion in the reader which suggests that there is a coy shamefulness about being seen to be reading this text, and that readers are somehow making a spectacle of themselves by doing so in public. Indeed, according to Bonomi et al (2014), the text was banned in several public libraries in the USA. Doubtless, stories like this are not rigorous in their claims of causality between an increase in sales of e-readers and the publication of the novel, but they do point to the potential trouble that such a text in public space is perceived to cause.

Tomazos et al (2017) argue that the tourism industry should take seriously kink practitioners as a market for whom leisure services could be, and ought to be, provided. They argue that the mainstreaming of kink as a result of, for instance, *Fifty shades of grey*, demonstrates that there is a consumer market for kink tourism. They suggest that what appeals in leisure and tourism is providing a simulation of an experience; a simulacrum in which people consume a rarefied and idealised (sanitised, maybe) version of a real practice (Baudrillard, 1994 [1981]). So, for instance, not actually having your testicles nailed to a plank, but perhaps attending a club night where performance artists were doing that on stage; not actually having a shoe fetish but dressing up in elaborate footwear and costumes to attend a kinky party. The mainstreaming of BDSM, they argue, is the inevitable consequence of the 'chameleon-like quality' of capitalism that seeks to subsume human sexual desires into something that can be consumed in the service of itself. Because capitalism is propelled by (and propels) desire, there is an inherent capitalistic dimension to kink practice, which is not new. We see this also in Weiss' (2011) analysis of the consumerist culture of BDSM practice a practice forged in a community, which is in itself forged through interactions with toys, costumes, equipment, furnishings, photography, and so on. This is a far cry from Califia's (1994) writing about BDSM. There, Califia argues that BDSM is one step along a road to revolutionary practice where 'terrible penalties are no longer meted out for being sexually adventurous', because 'sado-masochists are part of the rebellion': a rebellion that will lead to gender (among others) equality (Califia, 1994: 174). This co-option into the mainstream, through consumerism and through the development of an evolving market, marks an acceptance of this deviant practice into the purview of the State that seeks to commodify it, to regulate it and to do so in part by continuing to cast the practice of kink as a marginal, if enticing and *outré*, sexual practice.

Here, acceptance of kink by the non-kink world marks the borderline of where the struggle for smooth space might occur. Yet it also marks how it is the form of heterosexual, white upper-class, young and sexy coupling that we find in *Fifty shades* that has become more acceptable in mainstream discourses and in public spaces. Part of this acceptance by the mainstream, and the development of kink tourism, is the apparatus of capture.

Capture here might be understood as recognition of kinship between State desire and sexualised practices as a way to eschew or curtail the development of an actual socio-political critique of heteronormativity and rape culture. What we see here is an evolving field that seeks to include BDSM-as-deviance into BDSM as a consumable tourist activity. Tomazos et al (2017) themselves appear to be ambivalent about the way in which BDSM can be commodified (although they seem quite satisfied that it should be). According to them, the least 'deviant' people have the most to gain from BDSM as a tourist experience. While 24/7, or 'hedonic pioneer', practitioners are less likely to find BDSM tourism thrilling because they live in a state of deviance all the time, 'mass deviants', on the other hand ('the wider public') would experience BDSM tourism as a 'feasible liminoid experience that can be packaged and sold' (Tomazos et al, 2017: 39).

In a windowless and airless exhibition hall in West London in the winter of 2015, I attended a fetish fair, which would be typical of this sort of kink tourism-as-consumption. Again, a permeable border between the grand Victorian-era exhibition hall and the fetish equipment displayed inside marks the line along which war machines might emerge or be captured. Incongruous almost among the other exhibitions that were advertised as taking place in the weeks following the event (Ideal Homes Show, Good Housekeeping Show, wedding shows, chocolate exhibitions, buy-to-let property exhibitions), this exhibition had the potential to be far more of a *risqué* event than the usual highly publicised and well-attended shows that the space usually hosted. Is this a captured kinky war machine? Recognition of the commodification of a sexual practice as something inherent to BDSM? Or does it mark the emergence of a smooth space in this otherwise non-descript part of the capital?

The entrance fee for the three days of the exhibition was £20. Therein, stalls selling jewellery, costumes, sex toys, massages, lubricants, erotic art, shoes and pornography were abuzz with men and women delighting in this cornucopia of kinky consumption. Topless models in the 'model village' in the centre of the hall promoted their 'brands' (usually their names or themselves as models), men paid to be photographed with them on their knees, in a reversed mimic of the way that children are photographed with Father Christmas at Christmas time. Alongside some dance shows (male strippers, a female burlesque troupe, some fire acrobats) and stalls selling merchandise, there was a series of seminars offered to inform attendees about different activities or sexual practices. It was attending a seminar introducing attendees to BDSM that I realised how pervasive novels like *Fifty shades* had been in popularising kink practice. Asked by the moderator how many of the hundred or so people in the room had had a 'sexual awakening' through the novel, approximately 30 people raised their hands. For them, it was through the mainstreaming of kink that they were able to find themselves at this exhibition, in order to be advised about how to incorporate power play into their sexual practice.

Tomazos and his colleagues (2017: 37) encounter participants in their research who welcome this perceived mainstreaming of kink practices. When asked if they would be as satisfied by BDSM if it were more mainstream, one participant responded that, 'I do not think I would mind, at the end of the day everyone is entitled to do what they want and if there is a market for it, I do not see why the product should not exist'. The spectre of choice, of neoliberal freedom, and of capitalism looms large here. Signalling how diverse different BDSM communities are, this is an expression that runs completely counter to the disdain that both Newmahr (2011) and Weiss (2011) encountered in their studies of BDSM communities who were, in fact, very dismissive of 'gawkers' who, new to the scene, wander around clubs like visitors at a zoo (Newmahr, 2011: 65), or who participate in what they call 'kumbaya kink' (Weiss, 2009: 67). 'Kumbaya kink', in the words of Weiss' participants, 'dilutes the SM community', who are no longer 'sexual outlaws', but who are co-opted into communities and clubs that dullen spontaneity, with rules, and protocols, and mailing lists. The community of practice is complicit with this mainstreaming. It produces and is produced by the establishment of these rules, because of the inherently capitalistic character of the practice.

As both Eleanor Wilkinson (2009) and Weiss (2006) suggest, the type of kink practice that comes into the mainstream imaginary is of a type that can be incorporated within dominant narratives of what counts as BDSM. They identify – and the same now is true of *Fifty shades* – that kink practice which occurs in a heterosexual coupling with just one man and one woman (usually Dominant/Top male and submissive/bottom female, although it can be the reverse if the presentation is supposed to be humorous, harmless or unusual – consider the dog walking vignette in Chapter One). It happens because people are 'broken', or abused, or victims, of a loveless childhood, or they are otherwise pathological. Kink is what these people desire because they are damaged.

This kind of kinky sex is not the urethral sounding of the men in the Spanner case, but the more stylised spanking or caning, or the invisible orgasm or diet control. Thus, if we were to reconfigure Rubin's (1984) charmed circle for kinky sexual practice, 'kumbaya kink' might be at the centre, along with, say, spanking, nipple clamping, using sex toys, handcuffs, reading erotic books, dressing in leather or PVC, all of which we see in *Fifty shades*, *Secretary* and in Ann Summers shops (Storr, 2003; Weiss, 2006; Wilkinson, 2009). Practices like branding, water sports, breath play, electricity play, consensual non-consent, fisting, pup play, and human ashtray might be on the outside of the circle, with kink practices like 'race' play, age play or cuckholding being among some 'despised practices'. The type of kink that is mainstream is therefore the type of kink that is acceptable to Tomazos et al's (2017) 'mass deviant': the type who is inspired by *Fifty shades* to go to sex exhibitions. Since the 2015 exhibition, the event organisers have struggled to rent exhibition space to reprise the event. Writing to former patrons for support, their literature stresses the 'mainstream nature' of the event:

> ... [the Sex Exhibition] is big business. The budget means we need to attract many tens of thousands of visitors to cover costs, and to do that, we need to be very mainstream. Our marketing and promotions are designed so as to not cause contention; we never court controversy.[8]

Indeed, the mainstream presentation of events is reflected in mainstream preferences of people attending this exhibition. One of the seminars I attended was about chemsex, in which I was one of five people in the audience (in contrast to the standing room-only crowd at the 'BDSM for beginners' talk). Chemsex is practised mostly by gay men in clubs, and has levels of risk associated with it that would place it at the outer limit of the kink charmed circle (Bourne et al, 2014). Promiscuous, non-reproductive, sometimes anonymous, sometimes dangerous, sometimes in a group, kink tourists were either much less interested in learning how to do it, suggesting that this was a predominantly heterosexual event, or that this was a predominantly risk-averse audience (or that attendees already knew all about it). What becomes mainstream, therefore, is still defined by how acceptable such a practice is in parallel with the conventional norms of the conventional charmed circle. It is therefore not enough to say that kink has become mainstream, or that it has not. Kink and non-kink are not hermeneutically sealed from other. Each composes the other. Each transforms the other. Each interacts with rape culture. They do this in the way that some practices are normalised and others condemned, even within what could be called kinky or non-normative sexual practice (as we see in the context of the sex exhibition). The way that kink can be seen to interact with, to be sustained by, and to proliferate capitalism and heteronormativity is another way in which rape culture is able to thrive (Weiss, 2011). Capitalism here, like rape culture, sustains inequalities between who is able to access these communities and these resources, and who is not.

This notwithstanding, although some of kink is mainstream and apparently 'uncontroversial', it stills harbours its rebellious, transgressive potentialities by countering what has become 'normal' even in mainstream kink. I return to the potentiality of this line of flight later, because while it is compelling, and it is necessary, it is also important not to overlook the other normalisations that are enacted through community practice and that call into question how far we can 'fuck our way to freedom' (Califia, 1988: 15).

Difficulties of belonging: establishing hierarchies

Kink is understood by practitioners to be respectful and open. On the whole, participants consent to BDSM activities, enjoy the community, and in the words of one participant, Yvette, a white lesbian Top in her twenties, find it to be a fundamental part of their lives. It is necessary, vital, and becomes a place where people feel at home. It is where they feel welcome, safe, and free to be themselves. This notwithstanding, these spaces are not Deleuzian or utopian smooth spaces of egalitarianism, cooperation and straightforwardness in a majoritarian 'vanilla' world. They are, at least in part, criss-crossed – striated – with intersectional lines of exclusion and of oppression (Weiss, 2011). In this section I examine the ways in which these lines emerge, through heteronormative constructions of gender, through exclusionary constructions of what an 'acceptable' body looks like, and through monolithic notions of status and hierarchy. I then consider the implications of this for understanding how a community deals with its own disruptive bodies, against a background of contemporary rape culture.

In the course of my fieldwork, I asked participants to talk to me about how the community holds its members to a standard of behaviour, how norms and values were established, and what happened when things went wrong. Zenobia, a working/middle-class woman in her forties, born overseas but living in the UK, told me, when asked about the different lived experiences of women and men in the scene, that "I don't think that women have access to the same levels of social approval and benefit of the doubt" when it comes to their place in the community. She elaborated:

> Zenobia: 'The stuff about appearance is one of the really striking things about becoming part of this much more straight scene than I'm used to. Like wow. Like the idea that it's a really (sorry I'm just ranting now), "it's a really body accepting scene", bullshit.'
>
> Interviewer: 'Where is this body accepting scene?'
>
> Zenobia: 'I haven't ... [laughs] ... I haven't played with a man who can look down in the shower and see his own penis in a long time and I haven't dated a man in a long time who hasn't consistently snarked about women's normal bodies.... I can't go to dinner with any of these dudes without them giving me the rundown on the ages, nationalities and stats of their latest [partner], I just kinda don't want to hear it!'

Interviewer: 'I'm smiling because I completely recognise it.'

Zenobia: 'Shall I just make you a "I'm a predator badge" already?'

Interviewer: 'In that sense, you would think that a kink scene, people are not "normal" in it and they are pleased not to be, yet there isn't the space for people to not be physically [perfect]....'

Zenobia: 'It's not a "scene", it's a marketplace, and it's a marketplace where 80 per cent of people never get what they want and 20 per cent of people do whatever they like. And I think I'm very lucky as a woman in it, that I don't want what most women in it want, so I feel protected from some of that in a way. But if I'd come here looking for a long-term partner, I'd be really fucking miserable!'

Zenobia's observations give us an insight into what counts as an acceptable body and what counts as a disruptive one and the different standards that men and women are held to. Zenobia, usually used to a less 'straight' (meaning heterosexual) scene, contests the notion that the scene to which she belongs is inclusive and 'body-accepting'. Despite men's own imperfect bodies, Zenobia demonstrates that women are held up to an unequal bodily ideal. Men of her acquaintance reduce women to their age, 'stats' and nationality in a way that both objectifies and fetishes women and echoes the sexism of mainstream appraisals of women's bodies in contemporary rape culture. Valorising youth and conventional standards of beauty and presenting these in a competitive manner to women and other men, the scene, in Zenobia's words, is a 'marketplace'. She opposes the concept of 'scene' and 'marketplace', which suggests that to her mind, they cannot be equivalent. This is a view that is echoed in the observations of many participants who posit that an ideal 'scene' does not have the instrumentalising connotations of a 'marketplace', but that rather, in this context, it is accepting of difference (something that the community recognises as an ethic, but which, as Zenobia demonstrates, does not always emerge in practice).

Newmahr's (2011: 26) own work with a BDSM community identifies a more tempered expression of imperfect bodies. She says that while it is important to be kinky or to have a particular fetish in order to be in demand with other members of the community, 'in the absence of [such] a trump card, those who conform more closely to conventional notions of sexual desirability are far more desirable as play partners.' While the community that she was involved with appear to be neutral about women's 'normal' bodies (or at least agnostic about them), the men with whom Zenobia interacts behave in a way that she thinks of as predatory and exploitative. In a marketplace of desirability, they instrumentalise their 'conquests'. The consumption of female bodies in this way makes explicit how this practice is complicit with the proliferation of rape culture. Women who do not enjoy the same leniency as men in the context of normative ideals of beauty are also set apart from men in terms of what is expected of their behaviour:

> 'Women's behaviour just gets read and policed in a different way, that means that sort of people tend to glorify male strength and male rudeness and cut it a lot of slack, where they really don't for women, so I think there are women out there who behave in ethically inappropriate and predatory ways but I think they probably have to cover for it in different ways, by making sure they keep friends around them, by making sure they're charming to the right people, by making sure they look very good, like in ways that men just don't.' (Zenobia)

> 'You do get women who do engage in abusive behaviour but because, it's almost because they stand out so much more obviously, that they kind of get noticed more quickly and also I think sometimes, because it's a very, very small segment, they can be quite an extreme segment.' (Gareth)

> 'From a male perspective ... female submissive are tending to group together, into packs, into sisters and mothers and whatever ... they're much better at communicating with each other.' (Paulo)

Whether by covering their tracks for predatory behaviour by charming people around them, remaining sexually attractive or nurturing each other in matrilineal 'packs' (Becoming-animal, again?), the way that Zenobia, Gareth and Paulo talk about women and the construction of femininity in these kink communities reflects stereotypes of femininity, where female abusive behaviour is rare and 'extreme', where women are manipulative (who make sure that they are beautiful, and keep friends around them), or where they are communicative and caring. Similarly, Zenobia's observations that masculinity and 'rudeness' is cut a lot of slack valorises a stereotypical masculine machismo. These normative constructions intersect with contemporary rape culture and inflect the ways in which bad behaviour is dealt with within the community. They do this by mobilising stereotypes of femininity and masculinity that enshrine the assumptions about gender relations which underpin rape culture; that evil women are exceptional, and that women cannot be trusted because they are wily and manipulative (that their outer beauty covers an inner deviousness; see Baker, 2010), and that men who are rude are also strong and macho:

> 'To be absolutely fair, my natural tendency is not to trust other men, I don't know their motives, I don't know the way they roll, I don't trust a horny guy anyway, you know? But I have respect for certain people, if someone has a professional background; I tend to look at the way they roll.' (Paulo)

If 'horny' hyper-sexualised men are untrustworthy, unless they command respect through their professional background, and submissive women are softer and more cooperative with each other, in this context, at least for Paulo, gender is cut along normative and hegemonic conceptualisations of masculinity and femininity. Far from being particularly revolutionary, the kink community, as it was explained to me here, reproduces prevailing gender constructs, enshrined in preconceptions about class (which runs through his account of whom Paulo expresses respect for, and whom he does not).

This sort of normativity is also mirrored in the way that gendered dynamics are expressed through the establishment of hierarchies:

> 'I think if you're seen as newer, if you're seen as smaller, if you're seen as more transient, ... and then you get your unintentional consent violations.' (Clementine)

> 'It may be coincidental, but also I don't think you can just discount that when you look at it, if you're talking about somebody who has got five friends or something, essentially a "nobody" in [kink] terms, they come out and say it [that they have had their consent violated], I'd look at it very closely and say, "I'm just an outsider but do you need any support? Is there an issue here?" If you've got somebody who's got a mob and somebody has got another mob, five Doms have a protracted long-term hate campaign against each other, I'm like "this looks a bit messy".' (Paulo)

For Clementine, service to the community develops trustworthiness, and newness is smallness in terms of influence. *Contra* this line of thought, Paulo suggests that somebody who is "essentially no one in [kink] terms" (who has few 'friends' on the online networking site used by many members of the community), and who makes a claim of consent violation against a known person, might have more credibility than someone with a 'mob' who is acting out of malice, 'hate', or to pursue a vendetta.

Salient in these different perspectives is the position that each occupies in their respective scenes, and in the community more broadly. While both Clementine and Paulo are experienced practitioners, and Clementine is a club night organiser and is therefore somewhat established within the community, she feels less secure when it comes to her right to take space – to be a disruptive body – compared to Paulo.

Paulo, dominant, heterosexual, wealthy, conventionally good-looking and charismatic, was quick to tell me in our interview that he has served time in prison for pornography-related crime. Thus, recognised both in official and unofficial discourse as a sexual outlaw, this outsider, rebellious status confirmed the influence he felt that he enjoyed and the status that he could rely on, even if he did not participate in any of the labour associated with organising club nights, or munches, and so on. His voice could hold authority and so with this authority, he could have the largesse to listen to the complaints of more isolated and vulnerable (usually) women, who had had their consent violated.

This is a privileged perspective that Clementine did not think she could afford herself. Asked what she would do if she had her consent violated by a member of the community, she replied:

> 'It would depend what happened, it would depend on who the Top was, as in who they were to me and who they were within the community. Tops with status for me would have more immunity from prosecution than Tops without status. Someone with an equal status, then I would feel more confident in, I guess, calling them out on their behaviour and saying, "when you do that, I feel like this" and if someone is new to the scene, I assume that the thing that they've done is borne of ignorance so I'm not necessarily lenient but I am much more of a "so this is the way we behave here, this is how you just behaved, this is how those two things are not the same, don't do it again".' (Clementine)

Clementine was knowledgeable about the politics of BDSM. She was a scholar herself of these issues and did have critical analytical perspectives on the dynamics of the community and the complexity of its politics. As she demonstrates here, she would rebuke and seek to educate some lower-status individuals who behaved badly, yet would tolerate and accept 'more immunity' for badly behaved higher-status people. Status, therefore, had a significant role in how consent violations are interpreted (as true, as false, as misunderstandings, as important, or not) by perpetrators, by those who are victimised, and by those who look on from the outside. This also resonates with contemporary non-kink discourses about who we listen to, who we do not, and how people with power can 'grab the pussies' of those without. Contemporary rape culture that normalises the abuse and commodification of women also sustains a *status quo* in which injustice is nurtured via the venerating of victims (or offenders) that we want to listen to and diminishing of victims (or offenders) that we don't listen to. This becomes especially pertinent when we think of different community responses to Star, Melody, XY, Orpheus, and sexual violence more broadly.

The ban

In a community of practice that values autonomy, risk-taking, self-determination, freedom, privacy and tolerance, any transgression of taboos around safety and consent are taken very seriously and become forms of 'bad behaviour'. This is not to say that BDSM practice is inherently safe, or even that safety is the object of desire; much of the pleasure of BDSM, and much of what renders it transgressive, is that it is not always 'safe'. Consent, too, is understood as a phenomenon that is not black and white. I have argued elsewhere against simply using 'yes means yes/no means no' models of consent (Fanghanel and Lim, 2017). Consensual non-consent (that is, play with forced themes; see Weiss, 2011) has evolved into an increasingly common practice within BDSM. And while not everyone might do it, it is recognised as a legitimate way of playing.

This said, even risky, kinky play, and even consensual non-consent takes place in frameworks that distinguish BDSM from violence (Weiss, 2011; Pitagora, 2013). It is important for the practice, and for the community, that this is always the case, in order to avoid the stigma we saw in the *Brown* case and which can circulate in debates around BDSM practice (see Lee et al, 2015). What is possible within kink is vast but is also composed within this community of practice along striated lines of permissibility:

> 'I think the worst thing that can happen to you is to be labelled, dangerous or an unsafe player or whatever and the bogie man that everyone's been taught to fear, which is "There are predators out there, there are people [do] all these bad things, yeah, they're the ones who are bringing down the scene, they're the ones who are serial violators and they're evil and they're hiding behind this very charismatic, charming exterior, with friends who defend them", and all this kind of stuff. And this idea that a group is capable of assessing the truth because group dynamics come into play and I very much question that; ... the more people there are, the smarter the conclusion? I'm not sure about that.' (Paulo)

While it can be seen to harbour vast potentiality, playfulness, and lines of flight, kink is also blighted by the curtailment of these. Because it occupies a somewhat 'uncharmed' position despite its nascent mainstreaming (Rubin, 1984), because it operates within a vernacular sense of community, and because its practice involves the mastery of specific techniques and norms (how to flog someone safely, how to suspend someone with rope, how to use knives), kink practice does not ostensibly accommodate aleatory, smooth lines of flight, particularly when these lines of flight are lines that 'bring down the scene' such as non-consensual or unsafe play. Paulo's comments above explain this. The worst thing that you can suffer is to be 'labelled' an 'unsafe' player. Insistently flogging the body in the wrong places (kidneys, throat, neck) makes one an unsafe or dangerous player; tying someone up badly so that their nerves in their arms are damaged makes one an unsafe or dangerous player; becoming known as a consent violator makes one an unsafe or dangerous player. In the first two cases, participants may simply not consent to play with a perpetrator. In the latter case, because of how consent violations emerge (usually when participants are already somehow engaged with each other), prevention is not always possible. The sanction for this is often exclusion, or the ban.

Paulo's comments are very evocative. Consent violators are positioned as "bogie men" and "predators out there". From the proto-germanic *bannan*, a ban is a proclamation or edict of a ruler. The act of banishment is to 'summon, outlaw and forbid'. A ban is a pronouncement of exclusion from a group, community, or state.

A bandit is someone who is living in a state of exception without formal recourse to the *polis*. In the course of my research, it was banishment which, more than anything else, was named by members of the community as a habitual way of dealing with transgression. For Giorgio Agamben (1998), a bandit is stripped of legal status by the sovereign. Excluded from the *polis* (and so, 'out there'), he must exist in a state of exception, designated by the State, beyond the beneficence of state protection and recognition as a legal person. In the context of kink, consent violations can be punished with such a ban.

> Gareth: 'You did occasionally come across dodgy people who turn up to a club and do something and would be, you know, thrown out … and that would seem to be quite effective, so we came across people who would turn up on the scene, maybe come to a few events, then do something, they would start pushing boundaries and engaging in non-consensual stuff and they would be asked not to come again or people just wouldn't talk to them and would ask them to leave and so that would be….'
>
> Interviewer: 'That would work, they wouldn't come again?'
>
> Gareth: 'That would work quite well.'

The bandit who is excluded in Gareth's example is one who is new on the scene, which, as Clementine has suggested, means that they have fewer 'rights' than more established members:

> 'The way I understand it, if you organise an event and you take control of the venue as you organise your event, then you are able to ban somebody from that event, so they can actually say to people, "no you're not welcome, we won't let you in", and if people organise munches in public spaces, they can't actually say to people, "you're not allowed in", but again, from my very simplistic point of view, we're spending £15,000 in a pub every month, we know the bar staff and we know the manager and we're familiar with the bouncers and stuff like that, if we said to somebody, "this guy is making a nuisance of himself, can we get rid of him?", the chances are they probably would do.' (Alan)

Who is the sovereign? Who can make these pronouncements? A community of practice has no leader or figurehead, necessarily. And here we begin to see how distinctions are made based on hierarchies of status and reputation, which, when they emerge in a context of unacknowledged rape culture (vernacular rape culture) exacerbate gendered injustice. What happens to 'unsafe' players – transformed into grotesque 'bogie men' – is down to a collective notion of a group decision, according to Paulo. For Alan, his status as an event organiser, as a good customer in the pub where his event meets, entitles him to have a say in who is welcome and who can come in. Perhaps the assumption in what Gareth and Alan say is that more experienced members of the community are less likely to violate consent and are better arbiters of abusive and non-abusive behaviour. This assumption is one that echoes narratives of 'stranger danger', which posits that sex offenders are strangers 'out there' and not our kin. This imaginary of the ideal perpetrator is also composed by a pervasive rape culture, because it is accompanies an unwillingness to hear things that make us uncomfortable. It assumes that we know the difference between the bogie men and the good guys. Yet, as the stories of Star, Melody, XY, and Orpheus demonstrate, this is not at all the case:

> 'Here's a very good example, so this guy, the organiser himself [Orpheus], could end up being excluded [from his own event] because he's already being boycotted in terms of a lot of people who are on those munches are saying "you're not welcome", now you could obviously ask the same question which is what gives you the right to physically prevent this guy from turning up? If he has a friend who's going and he comes along to have a drink with his friend, happens to be at your munch, are you the landlord? Do you have a security force around you? How can you stop this guy from being there anyway? But at least you can make him feel not welcome, that seems to be the sanction. There are people I think who are not welcome, they're made to feel not welcome. I think the first thing is basically ... they're mocked in public and there's a lot of kind of talking around that person, you can't mention them by name but everybody knows who you're talking about, it's like classroom stuff and I think that is one form of indicating that person is not, he doesn't have the social credibility, doesn't have the social validation, that's been withdrawn.' (Paulo)

Paulo is talking about a high-status dominant male – Orpheus – who was accused by a number of women of being a consent violator at the time in which I was doing my research. And he highlights some of the issues with issuing a ban. How do you effectively ban people? For Paulo, it is by making them feel 'not welcome' that a sanction might be meted.

When belonging to a community is a fundamental part of your selfhood, when you are 'home' when you are in the community, or in the words of Alan, "realised you fitted in" on finding the community, being shunned as well as being banned has the potentiality to become an effective punishment for transgression. Jeremy Bentham (1838) articulated this as a 'presence banishment', that an 'offender immediately leave the place in which he meets with the offended party'. Here Paulo describes, as Gareth does above, that banned people are made to not feel welcome. People do not speak to them. In the case of online discussions, they are actually erased ("you can't mention them by name"). This erasure accompanies a loss of personhood. If 'everybody knows who you are talking about', but their name is not mentioned, they come to exist in contemporary discourse only through this lacuna. For Agamben (1998: 105):

> The life of the bandit … is a threshold of indistinction and of passage between man and animal … the life of the bandit is the life of the werewolf who is precisely neither man nor beast and who dwells paradoxically within both whilst belonging to neither.

The consent violator, simultaneously named and unnamed, occupies this bandit position. Notwithstanding the speciesist undertones of Agamben's formulation, understanding this punishment as a placing of a perpetrator within a state of exception is helpful. As Paolo states, a banned man does not have "the social credibility, doesn't have the social validation, that's been withdrawn". That a right has been withdrawn presupposed actors – sovereigns – who are in the position to do the withdrawing. Given that being "labelled an unsafe player" is the "worst thing that can happen to you", according to Paulo, it is not surprising that to be punished for this transgression amounts to the 'withdrawal' of 'social validation': a social death that recalls the similar effects of the naked curse. A social death here does not produce a precarious life as a position to mobilise from because the social death of the bandit is in a state of *zoê*, shunned from the protection of the *polis* of the kink community.

Banned from events, not spoken to, erased from discussions, these shunning practices were retributions that were informally recognised by all people I spoke to as the habitual mechanism they would use to deal with infringements of community norms or values. More serious, obviously criminal acts might be reported to the police, but informally, in-group policing would, according to the people to whom I spoke, take this form. Of course, banishment is not as easy as all that. Bentham (1838) was dubious about its efficacy as a punishment. Described as 'preventing an individual from enjoying a … right which he possessed before', a restrictive punishment requires a withdrawal of the right, but is, according to Bentham, difficult to supervise, difficult to ensure it has an impact (is it too severe? Is it enough of a punishment?), and risks negatively impacting a group wider than the person intended to be punished (for instance, the people intended to supervise that the prohibition is upheld). These are concerns that resonate with Paulo above, but also with others:

> Zenobia: 'So there are a lot of people like self-selecting and self-excluding, who no one will miss, like I'm thinking, I'm supposed to go to a party in about a week and I just think I'm not going to because it just … what am I going to do? Stand there and like sort of frown while everyone says, "ha! So glad that bitch [Melody] isn't here" – probably not that openly – but where that's hanging in the air? Then people more comfortable in the scene than me, will I think, line up to say "Well, she should have known he's [Orpheus] edgy and I don't think she's like all that great herself and she's friends with so-and-so who's a total bitch". So my problem is, in a sense, not really with [what happened], there are guys like that everywhere, they do their thing, the only thing that stops them is being denied victims or ageing out of it. The problem is with the façade of "Oh no, this is cool and we're not going to say anything to anyone and if anything happens, which we know will happen, we will blame them and close ranks".'
> Interviewer: 'And is what's happened with this girl [Melody]?'
> Zenobia: 'That's what I can see happening.'

The question of who is banned is a fraught one. Ordinarily, participants agreed, it should be the perpetrator. Yet Zenobia's account of community responses to Melody's encounter with Orpheus here explains how in practice victims of abuse can exclude themselves from a community where, even if the perpetrator is also banned, his behaviour is condoned by other members of the community and victim-blaming and misogyny prevails, against a background of contemporary rape culture. "Closing ranks", as Zenobia puts it, is something that only becomes possible in a community with a strong sense of *a priori* identity. An idiom originating from the 18th century, it describes military ranks standing together to close gaps between them and to ward off oncoming attacks. Thus, to close ranks in this way discursively suggests that the calling out of bad behaviour – dangerous behaviour or calling out Orpheus' consent violations – can be perceived as an attack on the community *itself*. All of which recalls Douglas' (1992) analysis of blame, when an individual suffers a mishap, an accident or another trauma, they must in some way be responsible for it. The community must protect itself from this bad luck or curse by expelling the individual or punishing them for their probable transgressions. Again, that this 'hangs in the air', rather than being actually articulated, has the effect of obfuscating these issues. Echoing the way that rape culture is manifest outside of the kink world, the act of excluding people, not-naming them and talking around them also silences acts of violence committed within this community (usually against women):

'There was a thread [online] I was writing on and somebody listed or put on there that they knew of a guy who had been convicted [of a sexual assault], who was back on the scene but they didn't name him and I asked the question that's never been answered, I asked "Why do you not name him?" and then someone else said, "it's the terms and conditions of the website" and I read through the terms and conditions of website and it talks about you're not allowed to "out" anybody, you're not allowed to accuse anybody, but this guy had been accused and convicted and so it was public knowledge. I thought to myself, I wonder if he's not saying anything because we're indoctrinated into not saying anything, not saying anything and when they're arrested, we still don't say anything or when they're convicted, we still don't say anything and that worries me really because if we're as a society being told to keep our mouths shut, then I think that's a bad thing, but within the context of the kink world, I think people are more predisposed to opening their mouth and saying stuff and I think that's a good thing, but also obviously the rhetoric happens as well and that's not quite such a good thing.' (Alan)

Clearly, once an offender has served a sentence related to any abuse or sexual assault that they have committed, and even if it may be relevant to their place in the kink community, it is important to let them get on with their lives, so maybe it is right that the website that Alan mentions prohibits any naming and shaming. At the same time, formal registers of sex offenders do exist in both the UK and USA, and these crimes are a matter of public document, so the reticence around naming is worth thinking about, even if the penal populism that supports naming and shaming campaigns in official discourse is not something I am at all interested in advocating (and it becomes another striating form of micro-fascism).

Alan's broader point that "we are so indoctrinated into not saying anything" is pertinent to this analysis of rape culture within kink communities. Cultures of silence and of secrecy have widespread impacts on how rape culture is perpetuated. As we saw in Chapter Two in the context of pregnancy, a secret, like 'sacred', from the Latin *secretus*, 'sets apart' what is being concealed from what is known. Even in a community in which people are 'predisposed' to talking about experience of abuse or consent violations, this silencing reinforces and protects the boundary around which information about potential abusers can be obscured. Whether by silencing women who call out instances of sexualised violence in these contexts, erasing the oppressors by speaking about them as if they were not there, and banning known abusers from the community, this exclusionary, emetic approach to dealing with bad behaviour does nothing but further entrench a rigid framework for kink to operate through.

The pillory

The opposite of ejecting people from the community is to hold them under the full glare of community scrutiny in a sort of public pillory. Paulo hinted at such a thing, above: "the first thing is basically they're mocked in public". Although not usually mentioned as a way in which bad behaviour is dealt with in the community, a recurrent image of the pillory emerged in my discussions.

To pillory someone is to ridicule them in public. The *Statute of Labourers* (passed in 1351, in order to prevent labourers from demanding higher wages in the wake of the scarcity of workers after the Black Death in England) decreed that 'stocks be made in every town', to punish dissenters or rebellious workers. Stocks, or a pillory, are a wooden frame with holes, through which were placed heads, arms or legs in order to immobilise the offender and to expose them to the humiliation of their peers. Pillories were positioned in the centre of the town or village, on a raised platform so that the offender could better be seen in public.

Pillorying was a public punishment. It was a spectacular punishment. The purpose of the pillory was to humiliate and to educate: 'this man is an adulterer', 'this other one a sodomite', 'this woman procures abortions', and so on. Therefore, the relationship with the crowd – with the audience – was important. They would jeer and torment convicts in the stocks. They would use 'dead cats, rotten eggs, potatoes, and buckets filled with blood, offal, and dung' as missiles with which to pelt the perpetrator, in order to add to the humiliation (White, 2007: 405). Such a thing – embarrassing people, covering them with rotten food, jeering at them – might on the face of it look like quite a bizarre, carnivalesque, if unpleasant and cruel punishment. The pillory was, however, also potentially life-threatening. Depending on how long somebody was pilloried for, or what their crime was, their treatment at the pillory could vary greatly. The difference in treatment that pilloried men and women received became part of the problem of justice with this sort of punishment. It was unpredictable and had the potential to be capricious. Some individuals were blinded by the missiles thrown at them, some had their ears ripped off either by the objects thrown at them or because their heads struggled so much in the stocks, some were killed, others, like satirist Daniel Defoe, were pelted with flowers by sympathetic crowds (Greene, 2003: 212).

Although the parallels between these pre-modern punishments (which continued in England until the 19th century) and the pillorying that appears within kink is figurative rather than literal, what is evidenced in the examples that follow is that women and sometimes men who are considered to be disruptive and who break norms and values of the community can be lambasted online by a baying crowd: humiliating them and castigating them, and in some ways, expressing violence that might be very harmful indeed.

'It works both ways, though. If you get your story out first as "me, the horrific consent violator", whatever it was that I did when we were on stage doing that rope demo or when you were very reasonable and sent me an email privately to discuss the thing that had happened, I, then, as the consent violator, having to correct your narrative, which means that my truth is very difficult to be heard. Two camps rock up online and one's on your side, one's in my side and then you get a third and a fourth camp, third camp is going "let's just think this through" and the fourth camp going, "oi, shut up, you're siding with people" and "I didn't think I was siding with anyone, I was just thinking maybe we could be nice", "no, what you're saying be nice, you're like all the rapists!" and then all of a sudden, 600 posts later and the two original people are going, "what on earth did we do?"...

'But we all have so much of our own stuff when we rock up to that conversation, that says whatever I say, if I say something positive or if I say something negative, I'm going to be construed as supporting consent violators, being a consent violator, someone who's going to crawl out of my past and say I violated their consent. There are so many reasons why we cannot have that adult conversation, as individuals or as a small micro-community or as the whole community.' (Clementine)

The pillory – ironically not be out of place as a piece of dungeon equipment in BDSM play spaces – is online, here. At the time when I was conducting my research, a series of consent violations in public spaces by significant people within the community emerged. Some of these are outlined at the outset of this chapter between Star who was abused by XY and Orpheus who abused Melody. Clementine demonstrates how vigorous these discussions are. And sometimes, they are very heated, and sometimes they are very aggressive.

A response to events like the consent violations perpetrated by XY and Orpheus prompted the creation of an online support forum in which women were invited to voice any abuse they had suffered and, in a private message to the moderators of the group (all young women), name their abuser. His name would then be placed on a private list that they would keep. The intention appears to have been to use this database as a resource for women seeking information about people they were encountering for play (heteronormative understandings of perpetrator and victim run through this, of course; women were reporting male abusers: not vice versa and not same-sex abuse).

These tactics are controversial. While the pursuit of safe spaces to play without violation of consent is a more or less universal concern within kinky spaces (at least discursively), the naming of offenders without giving them the right to reply and the keeping of information on a database is an anathema to a community that privileges tolerance, freedom, and privacy. Moreover, given that "the worst thing that can happen to you is to be labelled", the creation of such a database must have been a grave concern for men who might have feared being named on such a document. And because the document was privately held, they would not have been able to respond to it, or to even know about it. The short-lived group organised a public meeting to discuss these issues, and invited various community leaders in London to join them. They were ejected from their own meeting, such was the vitriol their actions provoked. Afterwards, the group disappeared from online space without warning.

While I was able to see all of this unfold online, the evidence I draw on in this section stems only from discussions that participants had with me, which demonstrates how prevalent it was in their minds at the time of my research. The forum that the women had created was an example of policing bad behaviour of sexual predators in the scene. However, with a procedure that sinisterly recalls Orwellian information-gathering or the keeping of an unaccountable sex offender register, it was also no wonder that it was considered to be so infuriating. Although there exist other (also fiercely criticised) online databases of male and female abusers from across the world (usually USA-centric) warning people in the BDSM community about their behaviour, this attempt to police bad behaviour was violently curtailed. Both before and after it disappeared, the creators of the list were pilloried online with extraordinary fury. Esme, a lesbian sub in her early twenties, who was enthusiastically supportive of this group, was struck by this abuse and read me the following extract from a discussion board:

> 'Let me show you this discussion [READS]:
> "A: I personally found it most odd that the magic circle consists entirely of rope femsubs!
> B: One has only twelve months in the scene!
> C: Straight out of university and into [kink]. *Fifty shades* or what?
> B: What the fuck can any of us really do about arseholes and sociopaths? We do what we can, when we can. Beyond that, I'm fucked if I'm going to police people's desires."
>
> And later:
> "D: What galls me most is their claim that they are too busy with their jobs to respond promptly to questions

and yet a slightly contentious comment can be deleted within minutes.

A: Perhaps their typing fingers are busy elsewhere! Or full mouths. It's rude to speak with your mouth full.

E: I think they are just looking for a different sexuality. These kinds of people hate being straight so end up kissing a girl and calling themselves bi, or own a strap-on and call themselves trans. It isn't a great leap to own rope and call themselves kinky.

B: I don't think the experience level of this group of blinkered, young, self-promoting, idealistic girlies is enough to take on a monumental project such as this

F: Considering the range or lack of range of kinks this lot adhere to. An ulterior motive must be considered.

B: Not so sure about a 'lack of range of kinks', in fact perusing the profiles and fetish lists of the team is quite, quite, illuminating! Have a look yourself, and see the hypocrisy, hubris, and contradictions inherent in some of their professed fets [fetishes] and their beliefs...

A: What a bunch of cunts.

C: Please don't call them cunts... cunts are useful.'" (Esme)

These women are lambasted using misogynistic slurs, ageist language and, extraordinarily perhaps for a kink community, slut- and kink-shaming. Some of the women are new to the scene ("straight out of university" – which is also a classed positionality), which, as we have established, means they have a lower status than longer-serving members. Simultaneously too perverse and not perverse enough, the women are dismissed as "blinkered ... girlies", too busy to respond to comments online because, it is suggested, their fingers are figuratively in their vaginas while their mouths are filled with penises. Within a sex-positive community, this sort of language used to shame women illustrates the back-drop of rape culture against which these things play out. It is only because of broader rape culture that a comment like this has any currency. Thus, the women are criticised for not being authentically kinky ("just looking for a different sexuality", "*Fifty shades* or what?"), having a "lack of range of kinks", and for having so many kinks, or such awful kinks, that they display 'hypocrisy and hubris' by also making claims for consent in sexual practice. Here, this group of what appears to be six different people have scrutinised the profiles of the organisers of the forum looking for evidence to use to ridicule them. Scouring a personal profile with this intention is an attempt to belittle and humiliate the women, even if, marginally at least, one of the writers appears to accept that there is a problem that needs to be solved:

> 'What the fuck can any of us really do about arseholes and sociopaths? We do what we can, when we can. Beyond that, I'm fucked if I'm going to police people's desires…. I don't think the experience level of this group of blinkered, young, self-promoting, idealistic girlies is enough to take on a monumental project such as this.'

As I have argued elsewhere, designating perpetrators of sexual violence as 'arseholes' or 'sociopaths' or 'bogie men' has the discursive effect of casting them 'out there' (Fanghanel and Lim, 2017). You and I are not arseholes, arseholes are other people – people we do not care about, people we do not love, people we do not know – the figure of the arsehole is not fully formed but is mobilised to stand in as an excuse for bad behaviour. Even Zenobia allowed this distinction between guys who "are like that", who "do their thing" and everyone else; we do not need to deal with him because cannot deal with him. He is always-already arsehole.

The author of this comment does not want to police desire even, apparently, if desire is consent violation, which resonates with the deeply neoliberal principles of non-interference, of self-determination, and of tolerance that structure the community. Notably, this is a tolerance that extends only towards people's kinks and not to women's calls for consent violations to be taken seriously. A token gesture of addressing the problem of the arsehole is possible, but not for these inexperienced 'girlies'. As we have come to see, the silencing of victims of sexual violence, here manifesting as a dismissal of their right to speak against consent violations, is a technique used to maintain unequal power relations and to sustain rape culture.

Therefore, although they may accept that there is a 'monumental project' that does need to be addressed within the kink community (and indeed, addressing rape culture *is* a monumental project), the way in which these women approached the problem (the creation of a 'register') and the characteristics of these women – that they lacked the clout or status to undertake such a project – outraged many members of the community who were active online. Part of the punishment of the pillory was the stain of shame on the pilloried that would serve for a while as a means of policing bad behaviour beyond the pillory (Greene, 2003: 214). And indeed, denigrating these women and this support forum in public is a shaming tactic that not only pushed the women into 'hiding' on the internet, but also discouraged other people from aligning themselves with their views. Not all critics used violence to express their anger, but those who did, as evidenced here, ensured that the women were brought down via this public pillorying.

These women were disruptive because they were speaking out-of-turn, given their status. They were breaking the norms of the community, centred on confidentiality, trust and tolerance. They were taking up space that did not belong to them, and which they were made to realise did not belong to them. This pillorying is their punishment for this disruption. Not only does it seek to violently recapture the offenders into a machinic kink community and into their 'correct' place, but also as a punishment that the community is implicated in administering, and this works to further entrench or bolster the 'social and moral boundaries' of the community (Greene, 2003: 207).

Yet, their disruption within the striated politics of kink might also appear as a counter-striation rather than a line of flight. After all, keeping a database of abusers and asking women to denounce consent violators resembles a fascistic policing tactic (Guattari, 1984). Of course, it was a *potential* line of flight. And as Alan says, it could have proved an alternative way of dealing with consent violations if it had been accompanied by a different way of thinking on the part of the community, including those who might have been on the register:

> 'From my point of view, I would welcome a list and people say to me, "What happens if you're on that list?".... In some ways it would irk me because somebody would have had to have said something bad about me, but in other ways, if I'm on a list and somebody emails in and they say, yes, I'm there, then people aren't going to get into a situation with me and that's fine, it doesn't really worry me and if I have to take that on the chin and it stops someone else from being abused somewhere else, then I'm almost more than happy to take that, I don't see a problem with it and again it worries me that lots of people who think they'd be mature enough and adult enough and if they're Dom especially, you would think that they would be controlled enough to do what they have to do, when they want to do it and not step over the lines, you would think most people would be happy for that kind of thing to happen.' (Alan)

Alan deterritorialises what it means to be a Dom in order to accommodate the potentiality of the list. In a community where being labelled an unsafe player does serious reputational damage, being on a list of people who are unsafe for reasons of consent violations risks a form of social death. It is therefore not surprising that so many dissident voices abjure the concept of a list so violently. It represents a grave potential danger to them. Alan, here, is willing to figuratively place his neck on the line in the service of preventing sexual abuse and consent violations. As such, although he appears to have submitted to official discourses about the importance of being 'registered', he also creates the potential of a smooth space, deterritorialised from State-like imperative within the community, to always be perceived as being 'safe'. This is not the same as micro-fascistic thought that if you have nothing to hide, you have nothing to fear. Alan describes a scenario where he would be on the list as one that would 'irk' him, even if he would accept it. For him, it is okay to not always be well thought of, or to sometimes be in the wrong. He attributes his willingness to be judged by these standards as a constituent part of his identity as a Dom: controlled, able to do what is needed. These are standard Dom characteristics, but by reframing them in line with acknowledging a perceived need for this 'list' to protect other people, Alan puts them to work differently in the service of gendered justice and against rape culture.

Of course what Alan does not allow for here is that group of individuals (male and female) who *want to* violate consent – whose kink is other people's fear – who are what Zenobia calls "missing stairs":

> 'If a bunch of people hang out in a house, like an old crappy house and one of the stairs is broken, no one gets hurt because everyone knows, everyone's learned, you go up the stairs, and you miss the third one, and when you're coming down, you make sure the light is on, no one even thinks about it. But when new people come to the house for a party, they get hurt because no one thinks to tell them because everyone will say "It's obvious that that stair is broken".' (Zenobia)

This database, or list, might be a way of signalling where the 'missing stairs' are, and so it has the potential to take away the risk that people may fall through the gap. It also prevents them from acting on their kink (however problematic). Tolerance for other people's kinks is a central tenet of the kink community. For Alan's perspective to gain more momentum, there would need to be agreement about what stepping over the line looks like, which, as we have seen from the complex debates around the rules, and around consent, is easier said than done.

Kink as revolution?

Melody and Star both experienced consent violations in public spaces. Yet whereas Melody was pilloried alongside the women who set up the support forum discussed above, Star was – for the most part – widely supported. Instead, it was the perpetrator, XY, who was vilified online:

> 'Then every time he..., I'm one of the people saying, "I think it's important to understand, what was he thinking?", it seems so crazy, what he did, it seems so unprofessional, it's like really, what was he thinking? Was he intending to take advantage of the situation? Or was it really a mistake? Or is it something more sinister? Every time the guy posted, he was totally annihilated, totally shut down.' (Paulo)

Both XY and Star are professional performers in the kink scene with international reputations. As with professional pornography, women in the professional kink scene usually command more of a fee than men (Rich, 2001), and their roles in professional scenes are more valued than men's. Indeed, here, the different reactions of the community to the consent violations suffered by Star and Melody can be attributed to their commercialised status within the community. Even though the outcome was different for each woman – Melody was pilloried and ostracised whereas for Star it was her abuser who was 'totally annihilated' – it is the background noise of rape culture that mobilised these outcomes. Melody was abused by a 'missing stair' event organiser, who had a reputation for being edgy, but also for being charismatic and for throwing great parties. Star was abused by someone with status, but not with a status that exceeded hers. Thus, what we can see is that that the emphasis on the hierarchical within kink, once again, attributes different levels of legitimacy to different actors based on their worth – what they mean to the community, what they bring, whether they matter – and this is based here on their currency as women to be consumed.

What does this tell us about kink as a counter-cultural site? Sexual practice is 'a symbol of freedom, rebellion, or intimacy unbound', yet it is also this belief which sustains capitalist modes of relation which exploit people along 'raced', classed, sexed, and gendered lines (Weiss, 2011: 7). For a community that expressly values inclusivity, tolerance, freedom and autonomy, it appears that the community's attachment to status, hierarchy and self-sufficiency and the way that it is utterly complicit with capitalist desire, has the effect of striating and atrophying the liberatory potential of the practice.

Yet, although it is somewhat mainstreamed, kink practice can, and does, push the edges of normative sexual practice and of what the body can do. More extreme kink practices such as water sports, piercing the skin with needles, branding, or even something non-pain-orientated like pup play can be difficult for people not involved in the subculture to understand as sexual practices (Wignall and McCormack, 2017). Gareth, among others, has suggested that kink might also be at the vanguard of sexual practice for its espoused commitment to consent, tolerance and acceptance. For Califia (1994: 168), 'SM relationships are egalitarian', with both the 'Top' and the 'bottom' sharing the same project and having responsibility for its success. However, although this is true during a consensual scene, as we have seen, power plays out differently when these dynamics break down and one accuses the other of bad behaviour.

What we see instead are heteropatriarchal and hierarchical ways of dealing with disruptive bodies in the community. Notwithstanding the desire for it to be doing something different – deterritorialising from normative expressions of sexual desire, practice and politics – when challenged by the bad behaviour of its members, it resorts to almost pre-modern forms of policing based on punitive punishment rather than what we might call restorative, dialectic sanctions, such as those hinted at by Clementine above. This maintains the *status quo*, and it is a *status quo* that relies on the existence of rape culture to gain traction. Thus, normative discourses about women's bodies (in particular), desirability, and heterosexuality trickle through how BDSM is striated. The right to speak, the right to banish, the right to contest the *status quo* are dominated by hegemonic ideas about gender and heteronormativity.

Additionally, a community that privileges self-sufficiency and self-determination above other forms of organising is necessarily one that is laced by an unacknowledged class, gender and 'race' privilege. To think that experiences of abuse, oppression, rejection or desire are experienced sufficiently uniformly that all participants are on an equal playing field when encountering them and dealing with them erases the material conditions of people's lived experience of social and spatial injustice. Relying on self-realisation as a shared norm through which to police bad behaviour betrays the quintessential neoliberalism at the root of these dynamics and erases the path that people have trodden to get there. Sure, as Newmahr (2011) suggests, they may be united by their outsider status, but there are different ways of being outside or being Other(ed). This is not incorporated into any of the debates or discussions community members have about how to address bad behaviour, and is a lacuna that sustains the influence of rape culture on this practice that seeks to exceed, or operate without, rape or non-consensual violence. Kink is currently complicit in rape culture because it relies on the fact of rape culture to punish dissident women and men, both in the ways in which they are punished, and in deciding on whether they should be punished in the first place.

Where does this leave the transgressive potential of kink? In a contemporary context where sexuality is relegated to the private sphere (a relegation that sustains rape culture), the practice of kink is a crucible that illuminates the social dimension of much other sexual practice. Kink does interrupt dominant striations of sexual desire. In the words of Califia (1994: 170), it parodies fascism, sexual abuse and sexual violence. Power, in a BDSM encounter, does not operate monolithically. Although the 'Top' or 'Dom/me' performs strength, control, and domination, and although the bottom or submissive appears to be more passive, subject to, rather than agent of, what happens between the players, the exchange of power is not simply often only temporary, it is also only possible because the submissive, or the bottom, *has given over their own power* to the 'Top' (Deleuze, 2006 [1971]). And this, in itself, is powerful and takes great strength. Circuits of power within BDSM play are, therefore, nuanced. They incorporate a delicate interplay between actors in a consensual scene.

Although it has somewhat been accepted into the mainstream, kink is held in place there because it is still at odds with the norm. Even in the widely read *Fifty shades of grey*, the BDSM that happens is presented as a pathology. It is thus not so mainstream that it can be taken at face value as simply an alternative sexual practice. It appears in the mainstream accompanied by a discursive apology or explanation (Stephanie Corneliussen's character in the TV series, *Mr Robot*, directed by Esmail 2015), or punch line (consider graffiti in London of British Prime Minister May spanking a male politician over her knee, or elsewhere, of her in her underwear wielding a whip). In this way, it still harbours the capacity to disrupt by not being totally co-opted into the mainstream and eluding these attempts at capture.

Yet, within kink communities themselves, the influence of normative discourses is rife. Although kink might represent a smooth space of potentiality within a broader construct of sexuality, within itself, it is nonetheless heavily striated. Norms and values are strongly coded. Vernacular language describes phenomena specific to kink itself. Rules of what will and will not pass, what can and cannot happen here or there, are, in many instances, enshrined in the dynamic of how the community interacts with itself and creates itself. Its dealings with justice also fall along these striated lines of thought and action. In this respect, kink could be said to be a tightly territorialised deterritorialising force. In order to more readily nurture the revolutionary potentials of kink, we need to interrogate how what makes kink, kink, comes together – what its molecular components are – and to explore what they can do differently.

Perhaps by losing the attachment to hierarchy that pervades nearly all discussions I have had about kink during my research, this might become possible. It might be about refusing to shun, or ban, people who are perceived to have behaved badly, and instead trying to hear what they are saying and where they come from, and where they are trying to go with their bad behaviour. It might be by refusing to lambast somebody on the internet for a perceived wrong they have committed, and again, figuratively travelling to the position from which they speak to strive for a different outcome (Lugones, 1987). If a superstar performer is sexually molested at the same time that a non-superstar participant is also sexually molested, it might be by attending to the differences in the treatment they receive and in reflecting on it that an alternate response emerges. It might be that the community does not pat itself on the back for supporting this Star when it knows that it possibly only does so because her performances are a commodity that they also consume. It might be something different altogether. It will be a changing of what the body of kink can do that revolution might become possible again:

> It is only by gradually modifying the constraints upon desire that a working team can set up analytic and revolutionary machines of a new kind. Illusory as I believe it to be to count on an approaching transformation of society, I am equally sure that projects on a small scale … can play a crucial role. Better ten successive failures or insignificant achievements than a gormless passivity in face of processes of co-option

and the bureaucratic manipulation of professional militants.
(Guattari, 1984: 260-1)

Félix Guattari's thought here resonates with Samuel Beckett's (1983) 'fail again, fail better...' incitement. It urges us to try, to take risks, to experiment with 'ten successive failures' rather than a capitulation to co-option into a regime that here, nurtures rape culture. It brings us back to the importance of interrogating the world at a molecular level, and of recognising the role of desire within that. Subversion, refusals, radical vulnerabilities, like those espoused by Alan above, or by Zenobia, all work to compose alternative ways of becoming, thinking, acting, outside of, or notwithstanding the striations of, the kink community itself. By nurturing more fluid or dynamic or smooth lines of flight as ways of interacting with BDSM sexual practice within the community, the subversiveness of this practice will remain latent, potential, and exciting.

This chapter has explored how far kinky practice can become a disruptive body. We have examined how this non-normative expression of sexual desire rubs up against mainstream organisation and expression of sexual desire, including examination of how elements of this kinky desire have been co-opted into elements of this mainstream. We have also examined how mainstream, non-kinky ethics might permeate the kink communities where I conducted my research, especially in their dealings with bad behaviour. We have been able to use this practice as a lens through which to analyse the role that rape culture plays in its composition.

Drawing on analyses of how kink politics, practices, and ethics are represented in the non-kink, majoritarian world and on analyses of how practitioners of kink talk about negotiating the complex terrain of kink politics and practices, this chapter demonstrates how this minoritarian practices oscillates – sometimes with grace and favour, sometimes with disgust and horror – in and out of a non-kink world, always against a background of contemporary rape culture. I concluded this chapter by building on discussions started in the context of the sexualised pregnancy and the sexualised protest, by thinking about how they sustain rape culture and yet might be imagined as ways to make a guerrilla war machine. The next, and final, chapter brings these debates together to envision different Becomings-, to articulate different war machines, to imagine different ways of fostering a world without rape culture.

FIVE

Disruptive bodies

> But there are no new ideas still waiting in the wings to save
> us as women, as human. There are only old and forgotten
> ones, new combinations, extrapolations, and recognitions
> from within ourselves, along with the renewed courage to
> try them out. And we must constantly encourage ourselves
> and each other to attempt the heretical actions our dreams
> imply and some of our old ideas disparage. (Lorde, 1984: 38)

From the human dog-walking performance that we encountered
at the beginning of this book, via the ambiguous positioning of
sexualised pregnancy, and the disruptive potentiality of the protesting
body, through to the confrontation of the body of kink within the
mainstream and the confronting kinky body within the subculture, this
book examines what happens at the boundaries along which everyday
space is penetrated with disruption. With contemporary rape culture as
the object of analysis – articulated, in this book, as a normative setting
against which these case studies have played out – these chapters have
considered the extent to which the disobedient, transgressive, and
troubling body has the capacity to disturb the way that public space –
in all its guises – is striated. The ethics and politics of how social and
spatial justice are played out therein is becoming uncovered.

Throughout, I have posited that public and semi-public space – the
City of London, the street, the shopping mall, Trafalgar Square, the
centre of Kiev, public transport, Kensington Olympia, bars, shops,
munches, parks, even online spaces – are striated spaces. Striates, as we
have seen, are capitalistic devices of the State to make space productive:
to have progress (Deleuze and Guattari, 2004a [1980]: 543). What we
mean when we talk about the State is not simply the 'nation-state'; it
is not about that sort of concentrated, totalitarian expression of power.
Following Guy Debord (1990 [1988]), what we call State power is

integrated, and variously embodied, into the neoliberal subject. This is reflected at the individual, group, community, national and global level, in all aspects of life. Discourses of family, religion, ecology, of climate change deniers; which are pro-vegan, anti-obesity, pro-drugs legalisation, militant left-wing/right-wing ideologies; which are patriotic, or anti-royalist, or pro- and anti-Brexit, are all *potential* expressions of striated (State) thought. Stockpiling, surplus, work – all belong to striated space. Striated spaces also seek to conquer smooth spaces that emerge among, within, or about the striates. For, as we began to see in Chapter One, striated and smooth spaces compose each other (Deleuze and Guattari, 2004a [1980]: 524). Whereas smooth spaces are whence deterritorialisation, or Becomings-, emerge, they are always-already in a dialectical tension of mutual composition with striated space. It is this multifaceted dimension of domination that needs to be challenged. And this is not an easy task. We all participate in sustaining and reproducing it somehow; your husband, my wife, the health visitor, the gas engineer, the telesales agent, the entrepreneur, the student, the academic, the queer, the heterosexual, the porn addict, the President: all are complicit in this rendering. Discourses of the State exert power, organise and discipline, of course, but they also mediate and humanise the neoliberal encroachment into issues of social and spatial justice. This encourages us to pay no heed to the way that things have turned: 'the lights musts never go out, the music must always play' (Auden, 1940; Foucault, 1994). This chapter excavates some of the ways in which war machines might be composed to challenge contemporary rape culture, while attending to the problems that emerge when trying to do so, in the service of establishing a praxis that might disrupt rape culture.

The guerrilla war machine, Becoming-, and the margin

Building on Nirmal Puwar's (2004) analysis of the way that the 'consecrated somatic norm' is constructed through the discourses that compose public space, this book demonstrates how striated space is forged along ethnocentric, heteropatriarchal, capitalistic lines of desire, and that these both sustain and are sustained by contemporary rape culture. Smooth space, deterritorialisations and lines of desiring-otherwise offer the potentiality of becoming-something/one/how-else. Part of this potentiality emerges through the war machine. As outlined in Chapter One, a guerrilla war machine is composed of unlimited flows of desire. It is guerrilla precisely because it is irregular, resistant and outside the immediate reach of the State. A guerrilla war machine deterritorialises the striates of space – the normative ways in which public space is organised, conceptualised or politicised – to co-produce smooth spaces and to foster Becomings-. A war machine has the capacity to become a line of flight, or a line of destruction, or to be co-opted within the mainstream, through the apparatus of capture (Deleuze and Guattari 2004a [1980]: 466). The carnivalesque penetration of the human dog-walking into the streets of London; the spectacularised tortured human-as-animal protest; the bare breasts of Femen, or at SlutWalk, or of heavily pregnant women; the infiltration of kinky sexual practice into the morning commute to work; or the infiltration of a disobedient community member at a kinky club night – all present lines of flight of sorts. As each chapter has shown, where these interjections into public space have contested some of the ways in which it is constructed, and some of the politics that compose it, they are also susceptible to capture by the apparatus of the State. Indeed, as with many of the tools that Félix Deleuze and Gilles Guattari articulate, and as we have seen in forms of Becoming- that emerge in kink communities, or in pregnancy photoshoots, or in naked protests, there is nothing that is *inherently transgressive* about the forging of smooth spaces. We must 'never believe that a smooth space will suffice to save us', they warn (2004a [1980]: 551):

> Smooth space[s] ... do not have an irresistible revolutionary calling but change meaning drastically depending on the interactions they are a part of and the concrete conditions of their exercise. (Deleuze and Guattari, 2004a [1980]: 427)

This means that when considering the disruptions to rape culture, we need to examine how disruptive practices connect with other bodies, the affects they produce, and the bodies that compose it, before more fully understanding their disruptive capacities, and imagining other ones. Given this, how can we sustain smooth space? How can we mobilise a guerrilla war machine that might forge alternate Becomings- outside of rape culture?

We know that a war machine is composed of flows that foster different forms of Becomings-. Becoming- is something that happens in the continuous present. It is an ongoing composition of flows, and through this conceptualisation, becomes politically potent (Rockefeller, 2011). The notion of flow, which Deleuze and Guattari borrow from Henri Bergson (1984 [1944/1907]), describes the eventfulness of bodies, ideas, practices, language, thought, and politics. Following Bergson, these concepts, or issues, or things, cannot simply *be*; rather they are flows driven by desire, which have durations that we take to be static (molar, in the language of Deleuze and Guattari) events as opposed to decentred eventfulnesses. Flow, composed in part of molecular parts that come together to compose a certain body, opens up this body to the potentiality of connecting with other bodies to forge a milieu of deterritorialisations that might contest the striation of space.

State thought, doing and politics prioritise molarity or models, and habits of thought. Thence, 'common sense' and taken-for-grantedness emerged (Deleuze and Guattari, 2004a [1980]: 390). Understanding the war machine as one that is guerrilla means understanding it as one that is capable of producing affects that contest the integration of State power. It pitches itself against the State, and importantly, does so in unexpected ways. In this context, the proliferation of rape culture is a State instrument. Rape culture, as I have outlined throughout this book, is a term used to describe the normalisation of sexualised violence in the socio-cultural, post-industrialist contexts in which the debates in this book are situated. This is a violence that manifests itself explicitly through crimes like rape or sexual assault, stalking, or harassment. It is a violence that manifests itself implicitly through representations of idealised femininity and masculinity in advertising. It also appears in contemporary popular culture, or through the under-representation of women in positions of influence in public life, or through fat-shaming, or slut-shaming, or kink-shaming. It is a violence that manifests itself as benevolence. It is in the proliferation of crime prevention advice that urges women not to walk about in the street at night alone, which curtails women's expressions of sexual desire, or which positions idealised masculinity as one which, within a heteronormative dynamic, emphasises women as vulnerable, demure, chaste, and in need of protection (by men) that it manifests. It is one that stigmatises the rape of men and fosters so-called toxic masculinity.[1] Rape culture oppresses everyone. Part of its potency lies in the fact that like capitalism, homo-nationalism, or racism, some people are advantaged by it in some areas of life, even if they are disadvantaged by it in others. It is sometimes hidden in plain sight, and thus is difficult to discern. Moreover, we are led to believe it is this way because of the *types of choices* people have made (Douglas, 1992). The guerrilla war machine is a force of metamorphosis or transformation, but it certainly has its work cut out (Deleuze and Guattari, 2004a [1980]: 483).

The war machine holds a contentious place in the politics of transformation. It creates smooth spaces of deterritorialisation, but as

Deleuze and Guattari are the first to recognise, we must not assume that the war machine will bring about a benevolent or emancipatory metamorphosis. And even if a benevolent or emancipatory metamorphosis did emerge, benevolent or emancipatory according to whom? The politics of positionality and situatedness are crucial when analysing how it is that we say we have made a war machine (Rich, 1984; Crenshaw, 1991). Part of the work of analysing the work of the war machine in this book, and in this life, will involve attending to this precarious element of what the war machine can do.

Deleuze and Guattari's political project is one of justice. Certainly, the object of their analysis is not gender politics, rape culture, or even specifically gendered questions, but it is dynamic, anti-capitalist, and pursues a notion of justice through the possibility of what the body can do, or can Become- (Deleuze and Guattari, 1983). For many reasons, there is no end point, or target, or moment when we will know whether Becoming- and deterritorialising has 'worked' or has made us free. Instead, it is a politics put into play in the service of fostering molecular revolutions: small-scale disruption or usurpations, or disruptions that are vast but that take effect at a molecular level. They forge a Becoming- – a guerrilla war machine – out of whatever it is that is the object of molecular revolutionary politics (Guattari, 1984). We saw some of these at play in Chapter Four in the context of kink and in Chapter Three in what becoming-animal does within naked protests, but we could just as easily have perceived them in the context of herethical pregnancies, in Chapter Two.

Herethical politics posit a radical vision of motherhood as a creative, rather than subjugated, practice. Yet the herethical ethics of love are not simply about mothers or about women; rather, they offer a political ethic through which to live, and to challenge the violence of the *status quo*. Motherhood, in Julia Kristeva's demonstration, becomes a synecdoche for this sort of political work. Through herethics, Kristeva (1985, 1995) offers the figure of the 'irrecuperable foreigner', who embodies a 'sort of vigilance, a strangeness, as always to be on guard and contestatory' (Kristeva, quoted in Guberman, 1996: 45). The herethical actor is strategically on the margin; subverting, transgressing, and 'deriding' the majoritarian centre (McAfee, 2004: 980). Such a positioning reminds us of Carol Adams' (2016 [1990]) observations about what is revealed about majoritarian politics (in her case, non-vegetarianism) when one occupies a marginal position. The new violence, antagonism, exclusion and suffering that is perceived from this outsider's vantage reveals something else about a mainstream that was perhaps taken for granted (Cresswell; 1996; Sibley, 1988).

Yet the margin is not inherently subversive. And not everyone who is on the margin wants to be there. And not everyone who is on the margin has any choice but to be there. The perspective that Adams acquired from her minoritarian perspective of majoritarian politics was only new to her, because as a white, educated woman she occupied majoritarian positionality in other areas of life. But the perspective of the outsider, of the vigilant derider, can also be thought of as a place to muster transformation. We have seen this potentiality in the context of precarious life of the protest (Butler, 2004), and we see this in the ethics of *autre-mondialisation* that Donna Haraway (2008) invites us to strive for. While, unlike David Sibley (1995), I do not suggest that being outside the boundary is simply to be more free, less constrained, and unlike Tim Cresswell (1996), I do not think that being cast as an abject rejection necessarily means that what is abject should be or could be transformed (some of the power of being cast as abject might be in refusing to be otherwise), I am curious about the possibilities of contestation, subversion, and becoming-otherwise that a suspicion of majoritarian politics and ethics – a disinvestment from them – might afford. I am curious about this, while remaining attentive to the privilege positionality that this positioning might suggest. This fact of this tension will also be what composes the sorts of guerrilla war machines we need in order to undo a thriving contemporary rape culture.

Sex -negative/positive- machines

I started writing this book soon after a self-confessed sexual assaulter was elected to the office of President of the United States in 2016. As I finish writing this book, the #MeToo feminist movement that emerged several months ago has yet to abate. #MeToo gained momentum in direct response to the revelation that (mostly) men[2] in positions of power in the creative industries (film, TV, and theatre) had been able to sexually harass women and other men with impunity because of their status.[3] Unlike other instances of hashtag feminism, the #MeToo tag proliferated enthusiastically in countries around the world, both on and off social media. Women who had ever been 'sexually harassed or assaulted' or who had experienced other forms of sexualised violence were invited to post #MeToo on their social networking profiles to demonstrate the scale of the problem. The original idea behind speaking about this sexualised harassment was to promote 'empowerment through empathy' (Burke, quoted in Ohlheiser, 2017), and to contest a culture of silence and denigration about sexualised gender violence. According to these social media platforms, #MeToo tags appeared several million times in the days, weeks, and months that followed its original appearance in mainstream discourses.[4] Clearly, this movement, and its widespread manifestation, suggests an emerging, vociferous rejection of a rape culture that normalises sexualised violence. Given that it has become such an important movement within issues of gendered social justice, and given that it has engaged so directly with rape culture, I do think it is worth thinking about its potentiality as a war machine, even if I am not suggesting that social media in general offers lines of flight from the problem of rape culture that this book targets (and as we have seen in discussion of the kink community in Chapter Four, although see Mendes et al, 2018).

The #MeToo movement, not unlike the SlutWalk in 2011, captured attention from across the globe. It moved beyond the sphere of social media, to be widely discussed on news platforms, in parliaments, in courtrooms, in classrooms, to name just a few places. It spawned parallel hashtags in many different languages,[5] and appears to continue to influence the denouncing of known sex offenders, particularly those within specific professional communities: the arts, athletics, the church, the military, politics, and humanitarian aid organisations. It signals an intolerance for those taken-for-granted abuses that, for instance, Carol Gardner (1995) identifies as everyday harassments, and that we saw were reported by pregnant women in Chapter Two. Certainly, in giving voice to abuses of all forms, including those which are, at first glance, hard to identify as acts of violence (strange comments, unwanted compliments, not-necessarily-sexual touching), #MeToo reflects some sort of deterritorialisation from a majoritarian status quo that silences and diminishes women's (and men's) experiences of sexual violence.

#MeToo might be a line of flight from heteropatriarchal notions of the sorts of violence that can be spoken about; it ruptures the striates of who can speak and about what. It offers a way of articulating a multiplicity of instances of sexual violence without creating explicit hierarchies of what counts and what does not count as a #MeToo moment (Mendes et al, 2018). The speaking of #MeToo, for women and men who proclaim it, gives voice to the array of experiences. Whether the #MeToo indicates a rape, an incidence of intimate partner violence, a cat-call, sexual discrimination in the workplace, being flashed at, or anything else, whether it happened, once, or twice, or every day, whether it happened 50 years ago, or 50 minutes ago, the five letters of the #MeToo hashtag cover it. The universalism, of course, gives everyone who wants it a home for their story. It serves to demonstrate simply how vast is the proliferation of rape culture. Yet this multiplicity might also be what curtails the potentiality of the movement as a deterritorialising war machine. Multiplicity offers breadth, but it also effaces differences. By collapsing all acts of sexual violence under the same umbrella, #MeToo shows us sexual violence without showing us it. It continues to fold into the illusion that sexual violence is an unknowable and generalised vernacular backdrop to everyday life. Or something that women who experience sexual harassment know, rather than something that anyone can do anything about.

The #MeToo movement has, at times, become associated with specific industries. Some, I have already mentioned, others – musicians, models, scientists, publishers – have denounced their industries for sustaining, supporting, or enabling sexual violence and rape culture to thrive within them. When these are reported in the media they appear as heterotopic entities against an undifferentiated background that we might call rape culture, but that we do not pay attention to. Attention paid to these specific cases, however, become points of crystallised momentum against this background. Treating these cases as if they are distinct has the effect of obliterating the actual, common pervasiveness of this violence. Moreover, the stories of film stars or politicians are the stories of people who are already elite, in some way (see Zarkov and Davis, 2018). Women and men with more prosaic professions, or without the platforms, voice or audience that these elites already enjoy, are still silenced. When will shopkeepers, or asylum-seekers, or traffic wardens, or NEETs[6] have their #MeToo moment?

So I have suggested that #MeToo is both too generalised or universal to give voice to abuse while also being dominated by specific experiences of elites. Ouroboros-like, it finishes by devouring itself. In this sense #MeToo could be understood as something like a war machine that is captured by the State; so focused on destruction that it risks obliterating itself into a fascist, molecular revolution. We see this in some of the backlash against #MeToo as a feminist protest which, according to its critics, has 'gone too far', or has become a 'witch-hunt', or that espouses a moral authoritarianism of State politics.

Once again, the backlash against #MeToo is led most vocally by elites: journalists, actors, and media personalities as well by amorphous multitudes emerging from social media. Maladroit attempts to seduce, or unwanted flirtations, particularly by men in public life (scholars, politicians, activists), are not the same as deliberate acts of sexual harassment, it is argued by some feminists (*Le Monde*, 2018). And even if it were, should we not at least listen to what the accused have to say before summarily sacking them from their jobs, boycotting their work, or denigrating them on social media, ask others. If #MeToo has been a line of flight, it has also been accompanied by a vehement apparatus of capture that striates sanctioned ways of claiming it, and violently abjures those who speak outside of these sanctions. The shutting-down of thinking differently about #MeToo is accompanied by the same sort of misogynistic violence that the #MeToo movement tried to contest. Said one female journalist about another who had criticised her public lambasting of a comedian who had been accused of sexual violence:

> 'I hope the 500 retweets on the single news write-up made that burgundy-lipstick, bad-highlights, second-wave feminist has-been feel really relevant for a little while … I'm 22 and so far, not too shabby … I will laugh the day you fold.' (Way, cited in Butter, 2018)

Crone, harridan, hag: the old woman is frightening, even to other feminists (Ussher, 2008). Elsewhere, feminist critics of #MeToo (and so, women who publicly identify with feminist ideas about gender equality and the eradication of gender violence) are dismissed as old, ugly, unaware of their cisgender, or white, or class privilege, and irrelevant. Unawareness of privilege is something that blights almost everybody at some point and needs to be taken seriously. Yet dismissing women because of their age or appearance, as Katie Way does here, is firmly part of the machine of rape culture that valorises some bodies over others, even if part of that valorisation is also about the desire to consume those bodies.

Thus, dissenting voices that support the ethic of #MeToo but that propose a more agonistic, dialectical approach to encountering it – seen by some as collaborative rape-apologia – are violently pilloried in the same way that we saw dissenting voices shut down in the context of kink communities in Chapter Four. The State apparatus that attends this silencing, shouting-down and shaming is marked by an ascetic striation in which acts, people, thoughts, or words are either good or bad, with us or against us. Thus, rigorous analytical understanding of the complexity and the nuances that compose these problems – the acts that #MeToo is capable of condemning – is obliterated. As novelist Margaret Attwood writes:

> In times of extremes, extremists win. Their ideology becomes a religion, anyone who doesn't puppet their views

> is seen as an apostate, a heretic, or a traitor, and moderates
> in the middle are annihilated.... The aim of ideology is to
> eliminate ambiguity. (Attwood, 2018)

In a socio-cultural context where the lowest common denominator often prevails, and egalitarianism becomes even more illusory, holding on to the fact of nuance and ambiguity will form an important part of the praxis of forging a war machine that will smash rape culture.

Another charge levelled at #MeToo is that it has become ascetic and disinvests women of their sexual agency:

> It is typical of puritanical approaches to adopt, in the name
> of their so-called general wellbeing, the argument that it is
> for the protection of women and for the protection of their
> emancipation [that we need #MeToo], in order actually
> better to bind women to the status of eternal victim; of
> "poor little things". (*Le Monde*, 2018; author's translation)

This famous letter published in a major left-leaning French newspaper posits that women should not decry every single 'clumsy pass' or awkward flirtation as a #MeToo moment because to do so risks veering towards a puritanism. Men are accused without the right to respond, they say. Women who are reluctant to jump on this moral bandwagon are accused of collaborating with abusers. Yet this letter seems to make a claim for the sexual freedom of women outside of these chastisements. Is the claim for sexual agency that the authors of the note published in *Le Monde*, and reproduced in part here, another form of war machine? Is this form of sex-positivity a Becoming-? Or is it another form of tyranny?

Sex-positivity – contemporaneously understood to describe an acceptance or tolerance of an array of sexual practices, enthusiasm about sexual practice, a refusal of slut-shaming, a celebration of the expression of sexual desire – has its roots in what we might approximately call some strands of second-wave feminism. Sex-positive scholars including Gayle Rubin (1984), Catherine Millet (2001) and Pat Califia (1988, 1994), some of whose influence we analysed in the context of kink in Chapter Four, challenge dominant constructions of sexual desire as something that can only be expressed along specific heteronormative or homonormative lines of practice. Preferring desire and sexual practice over sexually desired partners, former leather dyke Califia (1994: 158) writes:

If I had a choice between being shipwrecked on a desert island with a vanilla lesbian and a hot male masochist, I'd pick the boy.

Countering the anti-pornography, anti-sex work, anti-kink perspectives of scholars such as Catherine MacKinnon (1987), Andrea Dworkin (1989), and Sheila Jeffreys (1993), to name just a few, Califia's writing is a celebration of sexual desire, in all its manifestations.

Critics of sex-positivism broadly argue that women are inherently exploited by pornography, and by sex work, and by BDSM, and that even if they say they are participating in these acts voluntarily, this impression of agency is a patriarchal ruse, to give the illusion of choice. This false consciousness argument – hugely unpopular with sex-positive feminists – has been reworked more recently into a more nuanced framing. Ariel Levy (2005) suggests that contemporary hypersexualisation of social life (in now-obsolete so-called 'Lad's mags', or pole-dancing classes at gyms, for instance) betrays a 'raunch culture', in which to be socially, sexually accepted, young women internalise the obligation to be hetero-sexy, open-minded about sexual practices, 'up for it', 'game', and 'cool', and a failure to do this 'frigid'. What Levy (2005) describes as 'raunch culture', we can understand as a manifestation of rape culture: sexual objectification and denigration, sold back to women as compulsory sexually positive freedom (Powell, 2008).

Given this, how does sex-positivity have the potentiality to transform how sexual practice is imagined? Deterritorialised from shame or stigma, desires might be articulated and heard with curiosity and 'loving perception' (Lugones, 1987). It is sex-positivity that sustains the politics of movements like SlutWalk and Femen: the right to take pleasure in show the naked body, the right to reclaim the word 'slut' as an empowering position from which to speak. We see sex-positivity in the way that men and women who practise kink talk about accommodating difference inclusively in their community. We see sex-positivity in the way that some women claim sexual agency and the contested space of sexual desirability while pregnant. Yet, as Anastasia Powell (2008) has shown, sex-positivity can also be mobilised as an alibi for pressuring or procuring certain sexual practices from a reluctant partner(s), or for stigmatising sexual refusals or decisions to abstain from sex as prudish, puritanical or joyless.

A Becoming- that might emerge from a war machine which deterritorialises the striates of rape culture would be one through which sexual desire and sexual practice, in any of its forms, is no longer stigmatised as particularly negative, shocking, interesting or, indeed, positive. Deterritorialising sexual desire or practice from its position as a fetish object[7] would be one way of contesting rape culture. Slut-shaming is no longer possible in a context where it means nothing to be a 'slut', where the word 'slut' is not understood as having a pejorative meaning because people can express sexual desire, engage in sexual practice with as many or as few people as they want, whenever and however they want to, or not, and where these sexual practices are not stigmatised. The sex-positive or -negative machine only does some of this work.

Not only can this sex-positivity be used as an excuse for 'bad behaviour', but it is also vulnerable to the same exclusions and spectacularisations about the desirability of the body and the type of body that might be allowed to be properly sex-positive (usually white, usually thin, usually able-bodied, usually young, usually not poor, or uneducated, or otherwise excluded). My discussion of pregnancy, where women are constructed as both hyper-sexual and sexless, and their contestations of these positionalities, demonstrates some of the difficulties with interacting with sex-positivity.

If the war machine of sex-positivity can only get us so far, might sex-negativity, or radical refusals of desirability, offer a more convincing deterritorialisation? Sex-negativity has been cast as the opposite of sexy, agentic and adventurous sexual practice. Anti-pornography feminists have, for instance, been charged with promoting censorship, preventing freedom of speech, being killjoys, being patronising, and not recognising their own privilege. Is there something to be recuperated from a refusal to participate in the hypersexualised mainstream as a political act to undo rape culture?

Becoming-ugly, or: how to break a rape culture

When I was studying for my Master's, I took a class on the gendered politics of embodiment. As part of our discussions, one of my classmates suggested that to truly break patriarchy, we should invent 'uglifying' make-up that gave us wrinkles and spots and marks. We should invent a cream which, rather than giving skin an anti-ageing tightened appearance, we use on our upper arms to make them flabby and saggy; that to refuse to be beautiful, to refuse to be sexy, to valorise ugliness could become a radical refusal of rape culture that sustains the imperative to follow beauty norms. Women enrolled on this class were mostly white, mostly from wealthy backgrounds – the fees were very high for this degree and with a majority of the class coming from overseas, for them it was even higher – and mostly young, able-bodied individuals. I remember the outrage that tittered around the room at this suggestion of 'uglification'. I remember, myself, finding such a proposition absolutely abhorrent. We were so shocked by the suggestion, as a collective, that we completely shut down the discussion. When I reflect on it now, as I have done in the 15 or so years since I took that class, the collective dismay that was voiced was one which saw, perhaps, the potentialities of refusal as a guerrilla war machine (even though I did not know what one was then), and was terrified by its implications. We were privileged women, studying at an elite institution, and enjoying a level of what Pierre Bourdieu (1984 [1979]) would call cultural capital that we were not ready to give up, even if it kept us complicit in contemporary rape culture.

Before it meant 'unpleasant to look at', the word 'ugly', from the old Norse, meant 'dreadful' or 'fearful'. Would it not be potent to be fearful and dreadful as we set about eradicating rape culture? As Naomi Baker (2010) and Sara Halprin (1996) have suggested, and as the comments at the beginning of Chapter Two showed us, ugliness can be thought to bring freedom, freedom from the desiring male gaze, freedom from the exercise of heteropatriarchy, even if it is still rape culture that designates something or someone as ugly or not. Yet looking ugly is not the only way to mobilise resistance through uglification. As Karina Eileraas (1997) has suggested, speaking ugly and doing ugly can also be mobilised as resistances. Saying things that people do not want to hear and in ways that people do not want to hear them is a reality that is experienced by women (we saw some attempts at this in the context of consent violations in kink), especially women of colour speaking about racism, or trans people speaking about transphobia within feminist politics, for instance (Loza, 2014). While they are difficult positions to occupy because they are accompanied by tone-policing vitriol, denials, and attempts to silence, they are also resistances. Ugly voices are refusals to cohere, or to step in line, or to 'make nice'. They are strident challenges to majoritarian politics that make speaking out shameful, frightening, or otherwise impossible.

Recall the 'sex bomb' that we encountered in Chapter Three: an overweight, nearly-naked, Femen protestor who, as a 'sex bomb', flirted with onlookers and passers-by who were trying to access the metro station outside which she was protesting. Sure, in the context of the protest, it was the fact of her supposed unattractiveness that was part of the protest: beware of the bomb. But what of her non-conforming body occupying the public space in this disruptive fashion beyond this stigmatisation? What about this body as a refusal to be sexy in the way that sexy bodies are conventionally imagined? What about this body also refusing to be ugly, and rather claiming sexiness for herself, on her own terms?

We might reframe the body of the 'sex bomb' into a setting that seeks not to exploit her, but to see her as a protester rejecting norms of sexual desirability. We might open ourselves up to the dangerous potentiality of refusing to invest in norms of sexiness, not just through physical uglification, but also through becoming somewhat of a grinch[8] when it comes to sexual ethics. Maybe interrogating these ethics, this agency (what is vested in it? In what is it invested?), becoming able to move from the security of acceptance (exclusions of what is accepted notwithstanding) towards the uncertainty of rejecting what assimilates us, will form part of how we might make a guerrilla war machine, how we might start a molecular revolution. In the words of #MeToo founder Tarana Burke, 'you have to use your privilege to serve other people'. Beginning with these refusals that are based on disinvesting the self from its privilege, starts that work.

As we have seen in the context of challenging norms in kink, or the practice of Becoming-animal in non-human animal rights protest, or the tensions between a sexy and unsexy public pregnancy, the Becoming- that a war machine produces is always susceptible to the apparatus of capture that seeks to curtail the line of flight and to put it back in the service of State politics. For a war machine that breaks rape culture to evade this capture it must retain the elements of the flow, of the eventfulness through which Becomings- emerge. And this entails, to a certain extent, establishing a relationship with exteriority in order to cultivate and nurture this momentum. Recall the herethical approach to mobilising transformative politics that we explored in Chapter Two (Kristeva, 1977; 1985; 2005). This was about vigilant scrutiny of the politics of the centre; of the State.

Of course, making a claim for operating a political position of outsider has different implications for different women, and different lives. Women of colour, queer women, women with disabilities, poor women, stateless women have been forced – are forced – to occupy marginal and excluded positions, and it is important not to erase this fact. Yet, what Kristeva (2005) suggests, and as Audre Lorde (1984) and bell hooks (1984) demonstrate, the margin, the outside, *can become a place of subversive power*. It harbours the potentiality for transformation; even it can be obliterated through assimilation into the majoritarian desires and organisation of the State. It is important not to overlook that the path taken to this margin varies from person to person; whether you have always-already been marginal, or have chosen to travel there, or have *had* to travel there, your impressions of, feelings about, and experience on, the margin will always be different (Rich, 1984).

And it is important not to overlook the fact that being on the margin can be painful, even if it also harbours the potentiality to alter the centre. Who is speaking? Who am I, speaking? Where am I speaking from? What does it mean for you, or for us, that we speak from different places? Part of what will assist in this work of recognising the impact that difference has on experiences of operating politics from the margin will be by attending to this painfulness. It will be by constantly considering the positionality from which people articulate their desire, politics, and anticipations for a world without rape culture (Crenshaw, 1991).

As I have said throughout this book, breaking a rape culture is no humble project: changing any culture is hard. War machines that might break rape culture pose thorny problems. Many women and men are invested in rape culture in some areas of their lives, even if they are subjugated by it in other. In many instances, what rape culture is understood to be is so amorphous as to be unidentifiable, and this is part of its power. In other instances, we are still trying to prove that rape culture exists in order to take it down, so successful the majoritarian machine has been to occlude it or to make us take it for granted. And yet it is still possible for us to act.

Part of the work of the guerrilla war machine, in this respect, will be of 'making (Becoming-) strange' all that seems natural about vernacular contemporary rape culture, which enables it to encroach even in areas where it seems that it might have been disrupted such as #MeToo. The revolutionary playwright and theatre practitioner, Bertolt Brecht (2014 [1964/1935]), wrote about this as a fostering of a form of alienation. Although inspired by Marxian ethics, the way that Brecht talks about alienation is not the same as the way that alienation – *Entfremdung* – is understood by Karl Marx. For Brecht, the alienation effect – *Verfremdungseffekt* – does not describe the disenfranchisement between the labourer and the product of her labour, it is not simply understood as estrangement or isolation from society, but describes a productive process of making the familiar strange:

The dramatic [classical] theatre's spectator says:
Yes, I have felt like that too. – Just like me. – It's only natural – It'll never change – This person's suffering

shocks me, because there is no way out. – That's great art; everything is self-evident – I weep when they weep, I laugh when they laugh.

The epic [alienated] theatre's spectator says:

I'd never have thought so – That's not the way – That's extraordinary, hardly believable – It's got to stop – This person's suffering shocks me, because there might be a way out. – That's great art: nothing is self-evident – I laugh when they weep, I weep when they laugh. (Brecht, 1986 [1964/1935]): 71)

Alienated from the action on stage (the majoritarian centre), the on-looking audience is actively implicated in what unfolds in front of them through the critical distance they adopt from the action. Unlike with classical theatre, they are not sucked into the narrative 'laugh[ing] when they [the characters] laugh'. They are sufficiently exterior to the narrative to see it and *think for themselves*. An alienated (minoritarian) audience sees analytically, perhaps sometimes for the first time, the exploitation, the injustice, the way that some characters consider their fates to be inevitable when in fact they are not, the constrained choices, the types of problems that they had not thought about as problems before. Translate this into the sorts of Becomings-that a guerrilla war machine can foster: if a guerrilla war machine marks a breaking away from the striates of rape culture, then it is both propelled by, and fosters, the sort of 'making strange' that enables us to see with new eyes how rape culture operates, the forces that sustain it, which it sustains, *and then to act*.

Towards a praxis of disruption

Paulo Freire (2017[1970]: 25) defines praxis as 'reflection and action upon the world in order to transform it'. More than ideology or activism, praxis is conscious, thoughtful action against oppression in the service of freedom, and of acquiring a 'fuller humanity' (2017 [1970]: 21). In this book, we have explored different ways in which the female body penetrates public spaces and causes disruption against a background of contemporary rape culture. Sometimes the rupture has been deliberate – in the case of semi-naked protest, for instance, or when contesting consent violations in kink communities – sometimes the simple fact of her penetration has become a disruption, as in the case of the sexless/hyper-sexualised pregnancy, or the *Fifty shades of grey* reader. In each case, the disruptive body has penetrated the mainstream causing a rupture in the flows that compose public space. These disruptions begin, and continue, the work of this praxis.

I have argued throughout this book that rape culture saturates and sustains all elements of social life in the socio-cultural, geographic context from which the examples in this book are drawn (predominantly the USA and UK). I have argued that rape culture forms part of majoritarian, mainstream thinking and designates which bodies might legitimately occupy public space, or move in public life, how, and how they may not. Rape culture casts the pregnant body as one that is demure, beatific, sacred and sexless. It is also rape culture that casts the pregnant body as unruly, unreliable, abject and possessed by another. It is rape culture that casts the sexy pregnant body as problematic. The sexiness of pregnancy is either erased (in nude pregnancy portraiture), or only for certain elites (in supposedly transgressive lingerie advertising), or rendered grotesque and ridiculous (by encounters with sexual harassment). In each case the sexuality of pregnancy is disruptive. This fosters contemporary rape culture, and also rape culture makes it so. Recognising the emergence of this antagonism and understanding the dialectical relationship between sexual practice and pregnancy begins to undo this, by making visible the way in which this relationship is occluded by rape culture.

I have demonstrated that naked public protests are disruptive, but that this nakedness is only disruptive because of how the naked female body is figured, through rape culture, as something to be consumed and objectified. At the same time, we have explored how naked protests of this sort might forge a sort-of Becoming-animal, or Becoming-minoritarian, or Becoming-smith that can penetrate the socio-cultural injustices that sustain inequalities and forge a line of flight from them. Indeed, the very uglification that protesters partake in – screaming, branding, shaving hair, the wearing of flayed flesh suits – might begin to become legible outside of rape culture if they more actively unsettled rape culture in the bodies that we can see. For this, the vernacular rape culture that they rely on – the allure of the violated young naked woman – needs to become made-strange, rather than naturalistic (Brecht, 1986 [1964/1935]).

We have seen how kink sexual practice posits itself as an alternative to mainstream, hetero/homo-normative ways of engaging in sexual practice. Yet, when this alternative penetrates mainstream, non-kinky spaces (Kensington Olympia, the streets of Farringdon, public buses, courts of law) it causes a disruption only insofar as it is permitted to by a dominant and pervasive rape culture that striates the kinky and the non-kinky. When disruptions happen within the kink community – through consent violation, breaking ranks, violating the norms and ethics of the community – it is rape culture that is mobilised to recoup a *status quo*. We saw this in the different responses to Melody's and to Star's experience of consent violation, and we saw this in response to the 'register' of consent violators that some members of the community tried to create, including the slut-shaming that they were subjected to. The potentialities of revolution at a molecular scale were offered to the would-be smith. The potentialities of not taking knowledge for granted, of interrogating what composes the community of practice, of refusing the molarisation – ossification/stagnation – of hierarchies, were explored as possible ways through these striations.

Although separate cases, the stories told in these chapters demonstrate how rape culture functions in all sorts of different ways to sustain a dynamic where the exploitation of women is normalised and heteropatriarchy consolidated. These chapters have explored some of how resistances might be – have been – mounted in each case. All of which brings me back to the guerrilla war machine. Rape culture is vast. It is ingrained in my body, it sustains the history that we know, and the politics that you live with. No single war machine can undo it in its entirety. Instead, as Guattari (1984) advanced, as Lorde (1985) invites us, as Freire incites us (2017 [1970/1968]), it will be through a plethora of minor and molecular revolutionary acts, and thoughts, and speech, and praxis, that what rape culture can do is undone. By making-strange the taken-for-granted, by being and doing ugly, by being ambivalent about expressions of State apparatus, and outside of the thrall of dominant ways of thinking, we might build this disruptive praxis.

Given the eventfulness of the war machine, and the pervasiveness of the apparatus of capture, given that whatever a war machine which breaks rape culture is, it will be always-already in a state of Becoming-, the ways in which to make a guerrilla war machine are legion. The immanence of the war machine also makes it impossible to prescribe, or to suggest, or even to imagine *a definitive way* of fostering one that will break rape culture, and that will not be captured. Indeed, to do so would be already to imagine the limit of such a war machine. What we can do instead is to learn to forge war machines, and learn to recognise them when we do, and to allow ourselves to pursue their lines of flight. Some will work, some will not, and all will do something to disrupt the *status quo*.

At the outset of this book, I explained that one way to disrupt rape culture and foster this critical praxis would be to work to recognise the vernacular of rape culture, to critique it analytically, without the analysis itself becoming vernacular. As Freire (2017 [1970/1968]: 31, 33) reminds us, groups that have been oppressed by how things are will have trouble conceiving of things differently. Moreover, the power held by those who benefit from the *status quo* will not be given over with acquiescence. Becoming agile, open, critical; holding the centre to account; being able to see what has hitherto been taken for granted; interrogating the assumptions, oppressions and objectification that make up this common sense through an active praxis of alienation or 'making the familiar strange'; knowing where you are speaking from and listening to where others speak from (Rich, 1984; Crenshaw; 1991); knowing your privilege and working hard not to use it to exploit others; and working hard to put it in the service of others – these are ways in which to do this work. All of this must be accompanied by a praxis of contesting, and denouncing, the encroachment of the State into these lines of flight.

These interventions accommodate the emergence of a war machine and encourage us to pursue the trouble it might cause. Yes, it will be through slow incremental molecular revolution that we will start to break rape culture's grasp on everyday life and to promote social and spatial justice (Guattari, 1984). By listening, through what Maria Lugones (1987) termed 'loving perception', and through 'world travelling' we will continue to understand the differences that have brought us all here to this project. Furiously wary of recapture, we need to continue to produce flows of this sort by politicising the disruptions bodies make in public space, by nurturing a critical praxis of refusing to 'make nice', for those to whom that is available and to support those for whom it is not, or who are always-already nasty.

I have finished this book by talking about different ways in which guerrilla war machines might have emerged: #MeToo, uglification, sex-positivity, sex-negativity – all of which disrupt rape culture in some way. It will be by cultivating an active Brechtian alienation, by acting and trying to act, by refusing to silence the heteroglossia or to be silenced by it, that the effect of rape culture can be seen, and ideas, and ethics to undo this, might make themselves felt.

Over and again we have seen how contesting rape culture is a path fraught with trouble. We could harness this trouble; we might Become-trouble, and become attentive, aware, awake and wild, in order to forge a critical praxis of revolt against rape culture.

Endnotes

Chapter One

[1] ArchantLondon, 11 April 2014, www.youtube.com/watch?v= RoTL7zGSNtI

[2] For Deleuze and Guattari (2004a [1980]), the State describes not just the nation, but also other institutions of power, including the family, the military and the law, among others.

[3] The 'Greek system' here refers to the fraternities and sororities common on university campuses in the USA that bear letters from the Greek alphabet as their names.

[4] Here, I am talking about cisgender and cisgender passing women's bodies. Trans, male, non-binary and gender-non-conforming bodies can all also be subject to sexualised violence in public space and sexualided harassment, and this violence will also be an expression of heteropatriarchy or be laced with heteropatriarchal dynamics of power (see, for instance, Day, 2001; Lombardi et al, 2002; Stotzer, 2009; Moore and Breeze, 2012). It is not within the scope of this study to explore all the different meanings that this form of sexual harassment has, or the many implications it has for spatial and social justice. Instead, I restrict my focus to the more commonplace, and in some senses, more taken-for-granted harassment of women.

[5] This is not limited to cisgender women, but extends also to women whose bodies are legible as cisgender.

[6] The word 'Becoming-' appears in this form to remind us of the fluid, contingent, imminent qualities of 'Becoming-'; it is unfinished, it is in flux – running into the next idea, or body, or concept – the hyphen marks the incompleteness of 'Becoming-' and the energy with which 'Becomings-' flow.

Chapter Two

1   This is, of course, a revisionist imagining of childbirth in pre-modern times. Certainly, as Drglin (2015) and Epstein (1995) demonstrate, pregnancy and childbirth have become increasingly medicalised over the past century, even if discourses about less interventionist birth and pregnancy (which, for instance, promote breast-feeding and water or unassisted births) are now more common in the some parts of the Global North. However, pregnancy, especially of 'important' babies, has always been political, and therefore of the public realm. Pregnancy was a reprieve for many women throughout history (as well as a potential death sentence, given its dangers); French feminist revolutionary Olympe de Gouges feigned pregnancy in 1793 in order to escape the guillotine. The confinement that we imagine common in the pre-modern era was only imposed on, and undertaken by, wealthy women, so it was not a reality for many women. The word 'confine', used in reference to childbirth, only became common usage in the 1770s. The relevance of this revisionism is that it reminds us of the problem of pregnancy in public: we are asked to think that it is private, but it is always-already a social, public problem.

2   www.motherandbaby.co.uk/pregnancy-and-birth/pregnancy/your-relationship-and-sex-during-pregnancy/your-pregnancy-sex-drive-what-a-rollercoaster

3   www.motherandbaby.co.uk/pregnancy-and-birth/pregnancy/your-relationship-and-sex-during-pregnancy/how-to-get-it-on-with-a-bump

4   Google Trends statistics offer relative figures as a proportion of peak interest in a topic: 'Numbers represent search interest relative to the highest point on the chart for the given region and time. A value of 100 is the peak popularity for the term. A value of 50 means that the term is half as popular. Likewise a score of 0 means the term was less than 1% as popular as the peak' (trends.google.co.uk, 'Help' definition).

5   Consider the traditional wedding image of the bride being carried over the threshold; although not 'created' as an idea by wedding photographers, its reiteration in wedding photos enshrines it as an icon within the heteronormative wedding imagery, and confirms the image of sacredness of the feminine that we find echoed in the sacredness of pregnancy.

6   www.candyfieldsphotography.com/pregnancy-posing-guide-nude.html

7   www.motherandbaby.co.uk/pregnancy-and-birth/pregnancy/your-relationship-and-sex-during-pregnancy/how-to-get-it-on-with-a-bump

8   http://jenniferwilliams.com/2016/07/18/jennifer-williams-maternity-boudoir

9   https://uk.hotmilklingerie.com/pages/our-story

10 https://youtu.be/TMNLIgp_rIE

11 https://youtu.be/QeTnP95EuKs

12 https://youtu.be/XDY7ILgE0Ag

13 www.motherandbaby.co.uk/pregnancy-and-birth/pregnancy/your-relationship-and-sex-during-pregnancy/your-pregnancy-sex-worries-sorted

14 www.motherandbaby.co.uk/pregnancy-and-birth/pregnancy/your-relationship-and-sex-during-pregnancy/how-to-get-it-on-with-a-bump

15 www.motherandbaby.co.uk/pregnancy-and-birth/pregnancy/your-relationship-and-sex-during-pregnancy/bringing-on-labour-the-sex-factor

16 Two sites were used to try to even out the number of responses from women not in the USA.

17 Particularly in the Global North, where fertility has decreased since from 2.7 births per woman in 1960 to 1.8 in 2015 in the UK and 3.7 to 1.8 births per woman over the same time frame in the USA; see https://data.worldbank.org/indicator/SP.DYN.TFRT.IN

18 Note that the participants were able to select more than one behaviour in response to the question, 'What type of sexual harassment have you experienced while you have been pregnant?' Percentages are given to indicate scale and propensity, and do not add up to 100.

Chapter Three

1 Evidence of this curse is mobilised in many different parts of Africa (including Uganda, Côte d'Ivoire, Nigeria and Kenya), so I use the language of African curse because this is the language used by women who talk about it, and also because its use is not limited to one country or one region in Africa.

2 Turner refers to these 'modern' spaces as 'liminoid' as opposed to 'liminal', 'as if' they are liminal while remaining unlike liminal space, which Turner associated with 'pre-modern' societies (see Deflem, 1991: 16).

3 It is interesting to note, recalling the power of the 'naked curse' above, that the dirty body, which has the capacity to pollute, is also a cause of anxiety here (Douglas, 1966). To call a woman a slut is insulting, and to elide sexual practice with 'low standards of cleanliness' lays bare the tension between the female body, propriety and politics.

4   SlutWalks have taken place in France, India, Israel, South Africa, South Korea and Switzerland, to name only a few. Reports suggest they have taken place in as many as 200 countries around the world (http://amberroseslutwalk.com/the-history).

5   http://femen.org/about-us

6   According to Theresa O'Keefe (2014: 15), SlutWalk Toronto actually refuses the label of 'feminist', so it could be problematic to suggest that this is even a feminist protest. There is little doubt, however, that the issue of sexual violence is one that disproportionately affects women and trans people, that it is an issue of gendered social justice, and in my own research in London, UK, participants have expressed feminist sentiment to account for their participation in the protest. Even if organisers do not recognise SlutWalk as feminist, it is certainly interpreted this way by people who participate in it, and those who watch it.

7   www.slutwalktoronto.com/about/why (now defunct).

8   Indeed, the daubing of supposedly humiliating words such as 'slut' on to the flesh of the female body evokes not only the ownership of branding within Bondage Domination/Discipline Sadism Masochosm (BDSM) practice, but is also part of BDSM iconography for 'submissive' participants.

9   In response, Putin reportedly said: 'if someone wants to debate political questions, then it's better to do it clothed rather than getting undressed. You should undress in other places, such as on nudist beaches', which reminds of how nakedness and political action are spatialised (see Vasagar and Parfitt, 2013).

10 For example, Breasts not Bombs, an anti-war movement that mobilised in California in the USA in 2005, three years before Femen was founded; and Free the Nipple, which fights for women's rights to appear topless in public spaces in the same way that men's naked torsos are acceptable in many public spaces. Arguably so-called lactivists who protest for women's rights to breastfeed their children in public might also fall into this category; see Brett Lunceford (2012) for more discussion of these.

11 https://femen.org/about-us

12 www.peta.org/about-peta/faq/why-does-peta-sometimes-use-nudity-in-its-campaigns

13 Hooters restaurant chain was created when 'six businessmen with no restaurant experience whatsoever got together to open a place they couldn't get kicked out of'. It is a sports bar/restaurant where servers ('Hooters Girls') wear skimpy shorts and tight t-shirts as part of their uniform.

They are described in recruitment literature as being 'entertaining, goal oriented, glamorous, and charismatic. In the restaurant she is identified by her glamorous styled hair, camera ready make-up, and her fit body which all contribute to her confidence and poise' (https://hgcareers-hooters. icims.com/jobs/5055/hooters-girls/job?hub=6).

[14] https://uk.lush.com/tag/our-policies

[15] An exception is a point where Donna Haraway (2008: 10-11) describes a rape threat that she receives at a conference from 'ecology anarchist activists' who, mobilising a discourse of human exceptionalism, objected to Haraway's (1991) well-known work on hybrids and cyborgs. Elsewhere, she describes a man espousing a so-called 'ecofeminist' position that 'rape seems a legitimate instrument against those who rape the earth'. This exception inadvertently reveals that we cannot yet too easily move too far away from the spectre of rape culture, no matter the scenario.

[16] 'Old Bill' is vernacular/slang word used to describe the police.

Chapter Four

[1] Here, I am using the word 'kink' to describe non-normative sexual practice more broadly. When I am talking specifically about BDSM (bondage, discipline, domination, submission, sadism, masochism) I use this acronym. I use the word 'kink' more than 'BDSM' as this is mostly what participants called it (if they named it anything at all), and it refers to practices beyond the traditional power play implied by BDSM.

[2] All names here are 'scene' pseudonyms chosen by the author.

[3] I use the words 'bad behaviour' to designate that range of behaviours that violate the norms and values of the community and which are broadly agreed to be problematic practices. They include (non-exhaustively) consent violations, employing unsafe techniques in play, interrupting a scene, and so on. Although I use the word 'bad', this is simply to indicate that they are practices that in general the community agrees is not acceptable. Use of the word 'bad' here should not be taken to always imply a particular moral position.

[4] A low-key social gathering in a bar, for instance, where people interested in BDSM get together to socialise, and usually to eat, but not to participate in any overtly sexualised practice.

[5] Dominant/Top players enjoy ostensibly taking charge of an encounter, enjoy dominating their partner and enjoy a partner being submissive. A submissive or bottom player enjoys having power ostensibly removed in an

encounter, submitting to experiences. A switch enjoys moving between these positions. Dominant positions are usually written with a capital first letter, while submissive positions tend not to be.

6   See www.spannertrust.org/documents/spannerhistory.asp

7   See www.booksnreview.com/articles/1428/20121017/hilary-mantel-j-k-rowling-bash-fifty-shades-of-grey-e-l-james-erotica-casual-vacancy-man-booker-prize.htm

8   See www.change.org/p/james-campion-head-of-exhibition-sales-at-the-london-excel-venue-help-bring-sexpouk-back-to-london-excellondon

Chapter Five

1   'Toxic masculinity' is a term used to describe forms of masculinity that foster violence and aggression as part of idealised constructions of masculinity, and that also abjures sensitivity, vulnerability or other 'feminine' constructions of self. Of course, idealised masculinity is as harmful for men and women as idealised femininity. Its prevalence evidences the heteropatriarchal construction of social life against a background of contemporary rape culture (see Segal, 1990; Connell and Messerschmidt, 2005).

2   There have been at least one or two high-profile cases of women harassing men or other women. Although these are cases that are in the minority they are, of course, also expressions of rape culture.

3   This pertinently mirrors the experiences examined in Chapter 4 about rape culture in BDSM/kink. When I looked for evidence of discussions that #MeToo might have generated within the community – given that kink struggles with its own consent problems – I found four events/seminars planned about this topic and two discussion groups (one with 17 members and one with two members). Many millions of people have accounts on this social networking site, so it is telling that these numbers talking about #MeToo are so paltry.

4   Here, I am distinguishing this period from #MeToo's original conceptualisation in 2006 by activist Tarana Burke, which was prolific on Twitter among Black women whose experiences of sexual violence and assault are disproportionately silenced and belittled. Clearly, Burke's campaign is the origin of contemporary #MeToo, but the global appeal of the hashtag and these statistics date from its usage in 2017 (Ohlheiser, 2017). This disparity reflects, of course, the problematic and racialised politics of recognition.

5   For instance. #BalanceTonPorc in French, #ונהנאמסג, in Hebrew, #QuellaVoltaChe in Italian and #YoTambien in Spanish.

6   'Not in education, employment or training', designates (in UK policy) a category of unemployed, inactive people aged 16-24.

7   Fetish, from the Latin, *facticius*, meaning 'made by art, artificial', and related to the Portuguese *feiticeria*, meaning 'sorcery' or 'witchcraft'. Originally meaning a 'material object, or a class of material objects, plants, or animals, which is regarded by man with superstitious respect, and between whom and man there is supposed to exist an invisible but effective force'. Sexual practice as a fetish object, therefore, suggests it occupies a revered and sacred place within a popular imaginary. A Marxist understanding of fetish, not unlike a Debordian analysis of spectacle, described a commodification of an object that has been divorced from the labour that has produced it.

8   Rudyard Kipling used the word grinching (1892) to describe a harsh, grating noise.

References

Adams, C.J. (2016 [1990]) *The sexual politics of meat*, London: Bloomsbury

Agamben, G. (1998) *Homo sacer: Sovereign power and bare life*, Stanford, CA: Stanford University Press

Ainley, A. (1990) 'The ethics of sexual difference', in J. Fletcher and A. Benjamin (eds) *Abjection, melancholia and love: The work of Julia Kristeva*, London: Routledge, 53-62

Ardener, S. (1981) *Women and space: Ground rules and social maps*, London: Croom Helm

Aronczyk, M. (2013) 'Market(ing) activism: Lush cosmetics, ethical oil and the self-mediation of protest', *JOMEC Journal*, 1-20

Ashford, C. (2010) 'Bare-backing and the "cult of violence": Queering the Criminal Law', *The Journal of the Criminal Law* 74: 339-57

Atkinson, R. and Willis, P. (2007) 'Charting the Ludodrome: The mediation of urban and simulated space and rise of the *flâneur electronique*', *Information, Communication & Society* 10: 818-45

Attwood, M. (2018) 'Am I a bad feminist?', *The Globe and the Mail*, 13 January, www.theglobeandmail.com/opinion/am-i-a-bad-feminist/article37591823

Auden, W.H. (1940) 'September 1, 1939', *Another Time*, West Chester: Aralia Press

Baker, N. (2010) *Plain ugly: The unattractive body in early modern culture*, Manchester: Manchester University Press

Bailey, L. (2001) 'Gender shows: First time mothers and embodied selves', *Gender and Society* 15(1): 110-29

Bakhtin, M. (1984) *Rabelais and his world*, Bloomington, IN: Indiana University Press

Baraitser, L. (2009) 'Mothers who make thing public', *Feminist Review* 93: 8-26

Barker, M.J. (2013) 'Consent is a grey area? A comparison of understandings of consent in *Fifty shades of grey* and on the BDSM blogosphere', *Sexualities* 16(8): 896-914

Baudelaire, C. (2010 [1863]) *The painter of modern life*, London: Penguin

Baudrillard, J. (1994 [1981]) *Simulacra and simulation*, translated by S.F. Glaser, Michigan, MI: University of Michigan Press

Beckett, K. and Herbert, S. (2008) 'Dealing with disorder: Social control in the post-industrial city', *Theoretical Criminology* 12(1): 5-30

Beckett, S. (1983) *Worstwood ho*, London: John Calder Publishers

Benjamin, W. (1999 [1972]) *The Arcades Project*, Cambridge, MA: Harvard University Press

Bentham, J. (1838) 'Of simply restrictive punishments', in *The Works of Jeremy Bentham, Now first collected: Under the superintendence of John Bowring*, University College Collections Box 36, lxviii, 350, 352, 354

Bergson, H. (1984 [1944/1907]) *Creative evolution*, Lanham, MD: University Press of America

Bird-David, N. (1990) 'The giving environment: Another perspective on the economic system of gatherer-hunters', *Current Anthropology* 31(2): 189-96

Bongiorno, R., Bain, P. and Hasalm, N. (2013) 'When sex doesn't sell: Using sexualised images of women reduces support for ethical campaigns', *PLOS One* 8(12): e83311

Bonomi, A.E., Altenburger, L.E. and Walton, N.L. (2013) '"Double crap!" Abuse and harmed identity in *Fifty shades of grey*', *Journal of Women's Health* September: 733-44

Bonomi, A.E., Nemeth, J.M., Altenburger, L.E., Anderson, M.L., Snyder, A. and Dotto, I. (2014) 'Fiction or not? *Fifty shades* is associated with health risks in adolescent and young adult females', *Journal of Women's Health* September: 720-8

Bourdieu, P. (1984 [1979]) *Distinction: A social critique of the judgement of taste*, Cambridge, MA: Harvard University Press

Bourne, A., Reid, D., Hickson, F., Torres Rueda, S. and Weatherburn, P. (2014) *The Chemsex study: Drug use in sexual settings among gay and bisexual men in Lambeth, Southwark & Lewisham*, London: Sigma Research, London School of Hygiene & Tropical Medicine, www.sigmaresearch.org.uk/chemsex

Braidotti, R. (1994) *Nomadic subjects: Embodiment and sexual difference in contemporary feminist theory*, New York: Columbia University Press

Brecht, B. (1986 [1964/1935]) 'Theatre for pleasure, or theatre for instruction', in J. Willets (ed and translator) *Brecht on theatre*, London and New York: Methuen, 69-77

Brooks, O. (2011) '"Guys! Stop doing it!" Young women's adoption and rejection of safety advice when socializing in bars, pubs and clubs', *The British Journal of Criminology* 51(4): 635-51

Bruner, M.L. (2005) 'Carnivalesque protest and the humorless state', *Text and Performance Quarterly* 25, 2

Buchanan, I. (1997) 'The problem of the body in Deleuze and Guattari, Or, What can the body do?', *Body & Society* 3(3): 73-91

Butler, J. (1990) *Gender trouble and the subversion of identity*, New York and London: Routledge

Butler, J. (2004) *Precarious life: The powers of mourning and violence*, New York: Verso

Butler, J. (2011) 'Bodies in alliance and the politics of the street', Lecture, Venice, 7 September, in the framework of the series *The State of Things*, organised by the Office for Contemporary Art (OCA) Norway

Butler, K. (2018) 'Fetish club DJ who collected animal porn and indecent images of children was caught when he left images on USB stick', *Manchester Evening News*, 25 January, www.manchestereveningnews.co.uk/news/greater-manchester-news/fetish-club-dj-who-collected-14204707

Butter, S. (2018) 'The rise of the #MeToo backlash: How the mood of the movement changed', *The Evening Standard*, 18 January, www.standard.co.uk/lifestyle/london-life/metoo-backlash-aziz-ansari-margaret-atwood-a3743616.html

Calhoun, C. (1980) 'Community: Toward a variable conceptualisation for comparative research', *Social History* 5: 105-29

Califia, P. (1988) *Macho sluts: A little sister's classic*, Vancouver, BC: Arsenal Pulp Press

Califia, P. (1994) *Public sex: The culture of radical sex*, Pittsburgh, PA: Penn Cleis Press

Campbell, A. (2005) 'Keeping the "lady" safe: The regulation of femininity through crime prevention literature', *Critical Criminology* 13: 119-40

Carr-Gomm, P. (2010) *A brief history of nakedness*, London: Reaktion Books

Césaire, A. (1983) *Aimé Césaire: The collected poetry*, Berkeley, CA: University of California Press

Clifford, J. (1988) *The predicament of culture: Twentieth-century ethnography, literature and art*, Cambridge, MA: Harvard University Press

Connell, R.W. and Messerschmidt, J.W. (2005) 'Hegemonic masculinity: Rethinking the concept', *Gender & Society* 19(6): 829-59

Côté-Arsenault, D., Brody, D. and Dombeck, M. (2009) 'Pregnancy as a rite of passage: Liminality, rituals and communitas', *Journal of Prenatal and Peri-natal Psychology and Health* 24(2): 69-88

Coverley, M. (2010) *Psychogeography*, Harpenden: Pocket Essentials

Crenshaw, K. (1991) 'Mapping the margins: Identity politics, intersectionality, and violence against women', *Stanford Law Review* 43(6): 1241-99

Cresswell, T. (1996) *In place/Out of place: Geography, ideology and transgression*, Minneapolis, MN: University of Minnesota Press

Cresswell, T. (1997) 'Weeds, plagues and bodily secretions: A geographical interpretation of metaphors of displacement', *Annals of the Association of American Geographers* 87(2): 330-45

Day, K. (2001) 'Constructing masculinity and women's fear in public space in Irvine, California', *Gender, Place and Culture* 8(2): 109-27

de Beauvoir, S. (1953 [1949]) *The second sex*, translated by H.M. Parshley, London: Jonathan Cape

Debord, G. (1994 [1967]) *The society of the spectacle*, New York: Zone Books

Debord, G. (1990 [1988]) *Comments on the society of the spectacle*, London: Verso

Deckha, M. (2008) 'Disturbing images: PETA and the feminist ethics of animal advocacy', *Ethics and the Environment* 13(2): 35-67

Deflem, M. (1991) 'Ritual, anti-structure, and religion: A discussion of Victor Turner's processual symbolic analysis', *Journal for the Scientific Study of Religion* 30(1): 1-25

Deleuze, G. (2006 [1971]) *Masochism: Coldness and cruelty*, New York: Zone Books

Deleuze, G. (2006 [1977]) *Dialogues II*, London and New York: Continuum

Deleuze, G. and Guattari, F. (1983) *On the line*, Semiotext(e)/Foreign Agents series, Cambridge, MI: The MIT Press

Deleuze, G. and Guattari, F. (1994 [1991]) *What is philosophy?*, London: Verso

Deleuze, G. and Guattari, F. (2004a [1980]) *A thousand plateaus: Capitalism and schizophrenia*, London: Continuum

Deleuze, G. and Guattari, F. (2004b [1972]) *Anti-Oedipus: Capitalism and schizophrenia*, Minneapolis, MN: University of Minneapolis Press

Dörk, M., Carpendale, S. and Williamson, C. (2011) 'The information *flâneur*: A fresh look at information seeking', *Proceedings of the SIGCHI Conference on Human Factors in Computing Systems* 1215-24

Douglas, M. (1966) *Purity and danger*, Abingdon: Routledge

Douglas, M. (1992) *Risk and blame: Essays in cultural theory*, London: Routledge

Downing, L. (2013) 'Safewording! Kinkphobia and gender normativity in *Fifty shades of grey*', *Psychology and Sexuality* 4(1): 92-101

Drglin, Z. (2015) 'Female sexuality and medicine – Sexualisation of everyday life, desexualisation of childbirth', in A.P. Mivsek (ed) *Sexology and midwifery*, London: IntechOpen Limited, 143-63

Dugan, E. (2008) 'Mothers detained in immigration centre hold "naked" protest', *The Independent*, 10 April, www.independent.co.uk/news/uk/home-news/mothers-detained-in-immigration-centre-hold-naked-protest-807802.html

Dworkin, A. (1987) 'Pornography is a civil rights issue for women', *University of Michigan Journal of Law Reform* 21, 55

Eileraas, K. (1997) 'Witches, bitches, and fluids: Girl bands performing ugliness as resistance', *The Drama Review* 41(3): 122-39

Eileraas, K. (2014) 'Sex(t)ing revolution, femen-izing the public square: Aliaa Magda Elmahdy, nude protest and transnational body politics', *Signs: Journal of Women in Culture and Society* 40(1): 40-52

Ekine, S. (2001) *Blood and oil: Testimonies of violence from women of the Niger Delta*, London: Centre for Democracy and Development, Unit, 6

Elkin, L. (2016) *Flâneuse: Women walk the city in Paris*, New York, Tokyo, Venice and London, London: Chatto & Windus

Epstein, J. (1995) 'The pregnant imagination, fetal rights, and women's bodies: A historical inquiry', *Yale Journal of Law and the Humanities* 7: 139-62

Fanghanel, A. (2014) 'Approaching/departure: Effacement, erasure and "undoing" the fear of crime', *Cultural Geography* 21(3): 343-61

Fanghanel, A. (2015) 'The trouble with safety: Subjectification, safety and of fear of crime in public space', *Theoretical Criminology* 20(1): 57-74

Fanghanel, A. (2018) 'How to break a rape culture: Gendered fear of crime and the myth of the stranger-rapist', in M. Lee and G. Mythen, *The Routledge international handbook on fear of crime*, Abingdon: Routledge, 149-61

Fanghanel, A. and Lim, J. (2017) 'Of "sluts" and "arseholes": Antagonistic desire and the production of sexual vigilance', *Feminist Criminologies*, doi: 10.1177/1557085115613431

Foucault, M. (1998 [1976]) *The history of sexuality, Part one: The will to knowledge*, London: Penguin

Foucault, M. (1994) *Michel Foucault: Essential works of Foucault 1954-1984, Vol 3: Power*, edited by J. Faubion, London: Penguin

Fox, R., Heffernan, K. and Nicolson, P. (2009) '"I don't think it was such an issue back then": Changing experienced of pregnancy across two generations of women in South-East England', *Gender, Place and Culture* 16(5): 553-68

Freire, P. (2017 [1970/1968]) *Pedagogy of the oppressed*, London: Penguin, Random House

Frug, M.J. (1992) 'A postmodern feminist legal manifesto (An unfinished draft)', *Harvard Law Review* 105(5): 1045-75

Gardner, C.B. (1995) *Passing by: Gender and public harassment*, Berkeley and Los Angeles, CA: University of California Press

Gilroy, P. (1993) *Small acts: Thoughts on the politics of black cultures*, London: Serpent's Tail

Gittos, L. (2015) *Why rape culture is a dangerous myth: From Steubenville to Ched Evans* (Vol 23), Luton: Andrews UK Limited

Glasser, C.L. (2011) 'Tied oppressions: An analysis of how sexist imagery reinforces speciesist sentiment', *The Brock Review* 12(1): 51-68

Green, K. (director) *Ukraine is not a brothel* [film], USA: Magnolia Pictures

Greene, J. (2003) 'Public secrets: Sodomy and the pillory on the eighteenth century and beyond', *The Eighteenth Century* 44(2-3): 203-32

Grosz, E.A. (1994) *Volatile bodies: Toward a corporeal feminism*, Bloomington and Indianapolis, IN: Indiana University Press

Guattari, F. (1984) *Molecular revolution: Psychiatry and politics*, New York: Penguin Group USA

Guberman, R. (ed) (1996) *Julia Kristeva interviews*, New York: Columbia University Press

Halprin, S. (1996) *Look at my ugly face: Myths and musings on beauty and other perilous obsessions with women's appearance*, London: Penguin

Haraway, D. (1991) 'A cyborg manifesto', in S. Stryker and S. Whittle (eds) *The transgender studies reader*, New York: Routledge and Taylor & Francis, 103-18

Haraway, D. (2008) *When species meet*, Minneapolis, MN: University of Minnesota Press

hooks, b. (1984) *Ain't I a woman? Black women and feminism*, New York: Pluto Press

Hooton, C. (2014) 'A businessman is being walked on a leash in Farringdon', *The Independent*, 11 April, www.independent.co.uk/news/weird-news/a-businessman-is-being-walked-on-a-leash-in-farringdon-9254188.html

Hubert, H. and Mauss, M. (1981 [1964]) *Sacrifice: Its nature and functions*, Chicago, IL: University of Chicago Press

Huntley, R. (2000) 'Sexing the belly: An exploration of sex and the pregnant body', *Sexualities* 3(3): 347-62

James, S. (2011) 'My placard read "Pensioner Slut" and I was proud of it', *The Guardian*, Opinion', 19 June, www.theguardian.com/commentisfree/2011/jun/19/slutwalk-new-womens-movement

Jeffreys, S. (1993) *The lesbian heresy: A feminist perspective on the lesbian sexual revolution*, London: The Woman's Press

Jenks, C. (2003) *Transgression*, London: Routledge

Johnstone, L. and Longhurst, R. (2009) *Space, place and sex: Geographies of sexualities*, Lanham, MD: Rowman & Littlefield Publishers

Joseph, M. (2002) *Against the romance of community*, Minneapolis, MN: University of Minnesota Press

Kapur, R. (2012) 'Pink chaddis and SlutWalk couture: The postcolonial politics of feminism lite', *Feminist Legal Studies* 20(1): 1-20

Kelly, L. (1987) 'The continuum of sexual violence', in J. Hanmer and M. Maynard (eds) *Women, violence and social control*, Explorations in Sociology (British Sociological Association Conference, Volume series), London: Palgrave Macmillan, 46-61

Kelly, L. and Radford, J. (1990) '"Nothing really happened": The invalidation of women's experiences of sexual violence', *Critical Social Policy* 10(39): 39-53

Kingsolver, B. (2018) '#MeToo isn't enough. Now women need to get ugly', *The Guardian*, 16 January, www.theguardian.com/commentisfree/2018/jan/16/metoo-women-daughters-harassment-powerful-men?CMP=share_btn_fb

Kissling, E.A. (1991) 'Street harassment: The language of sexual terrorism', *Discourse and Society* 2(4): 451-60

Koskela, H. (1997) '"Bold walk and breakings": Women's spatial confidence versus fear of violence', *Gender, Place and Culture* 4(3): 301-19

Koskela, H. and Pain, R. (2000) 'Revisiting fear and place: Women's fear of attack and the built environment', *Geoforum* 31(2): 269-80

Kristeva, J. (1977) 'Hérétique de l'amour', *Tel Quel* 74, Winter: 30-49

Kristeva, J. (1982 [1980]) *Powers of horror: An essay on abjection*, translated by L. Roudiez, New York: Columbia University Press

Kristeva, J. (1981) 'Woman's time', *Signs* 7(1): 13-35

Kristeva, J. (1985) 'Stabat mater', *Poetics Today, 6 1-2 The Female Body in Western Culture: Semiotic Perspectives*, 133-52

Kristeva, J. (1995) *New maladies of the soul*, New York: Columbia University Press

Kristeva, J. (2005) 'Motherhood today', *Colloques Gypsy V*, 22 October, Museum National d'histoire naturelle, Paris

Lave, J. and Wenger, E. (1991) *Situated learning: Legitimate peripheral participation*, Cambridge: Cambridge University Press

Lee, E.M., Klement, K.R. and Sagarin, B.J. (2015) 'Double hanging during consensual sexual asphyxia: A response to Roma, Pazzelli, Pompili, Girardi, and Ferracuti (2013)', *Archives of Sexual Behavior* October, 44(7): 1751-3

Lee, M. (2007) *Inventing fear of crime: Criminology and the politics of anxiety*, Collumpton: Willan

Lefebvre, H. (1996 [1968]) *Writing on cities*, Oxford: Blackwell

Le Monde (2018) 'Nous défendons une liberté d'importuner, indispensable à la liberté sexuelle', LeMonde.fr, 13 January, www.lemonde.fr/idees/article/2018/01/09/nous-defendons-une-liberte-d-importuner-indispensable-a-la-liberte-sexuelle_5239134_3232.html#iVw0e1AbKsTVD0rH.99

Lévi-Strauss, C. (1963) *Structural anthropology*, New York: Basic Books

Levy, A. (2005) *Female chauvinist pigs: Women and the rise of raunch culture*, New York: Simon & Schuster

Lim, J. and Fanghanel, A. (2013) '"Hijabs, hoodies and hotpants": Negotiating the "slut" in SlutWalk', *Geoforum* 48: 207-15

Lombardi, E.L., Wilchins, R.A. Priesing Esq, D. and Malouf, D. (2002) 'Gender violence: Transgender experiences with violence and discrimination', *Journal of Homosexuality* 42(1): 89-101

Longhurst, R. (1997) '"Going nuts": Representing pregnant women', *New Zealand Geographer* 53(2): 34-8

Longhurst, R. (1999) 'Pregnant bodies, public scrutiny: "Giving" advice to pregnant women', in E. Teather (ed) *Embodied geographies: Spaces, bodies and rites of passage*, Abingdon: Routledge, 78-91

Longhurst, R. (2000) '"Corporeographies" of pregnancy: "Bikini babes"', *Environment and Planning D: Society and Space* 18: 453-72

Longhurst, R. (2001) 'Breaking corporeal boundaries: Pregnant bodies in public places', in R. Holliday and J. Hassad (ed) *Contested bodies*, Abingdon: Routledge, 81-94

Longhurst, R. (2006) 'A pornography of birth: Crossing moral boundaries', *ACME: An International e-Journal for Critical Geographies* 5(2): 209-29

Lorde, A. (1984) 'Poetry is not a luxury', in A. Lorde, *Sister outsider: Essays and speeches*, Berkeley, CA: California, Crossing Press, 36-40

Loza, S. (2014) 'Hashtag feminism #SolidarityIsForWhiteWomen, and the other#FemFuture', *Ada: A Journal of Gender, New Media, and Technology* 5

Lugones, M. (1987) 'Playfulness, "world"-travelling, and loving perception', *Hypatia* 2(2): 3-19

Lunceford, B.L. (2012) *Naked politics: Nudity, political action, and the rhetoric of the body*, Lanham, MD: Lexington Books

Lundquist, C. (2008) 'Being torn: Towards a phenomenology of unwanted pregnancy', *Hypatia* 23(3): 136-55

Lupton, D. (2012a) *Configuring maternal, preborn and infant embodiment*, Sydney Health and Society Group Working Paper No 2, Sydney, NSW: Sydney Health and Society Group

Lupton, D. (2012b) '"Precious cargo": Foetal subjects, risk and reproductive citizenship', *Critical Public Health* 22(3): 329-40

Lush (2012) 'Lush fighting animal testing: Live demonstration at Regents Street', 25 April, www.youtube.com/watch?v=f4K9iSyj_lk

MacKinnon, C.A. (1987) *Feminism unmodified: Discourses on life and law*, Cambridge, MA: Harvard University Press

Mason, C. (2000) 'Cracked babies and the partial birth of.a nation: Millennialism and fetal citizenship', *Cultural Studies* 14(1): 35-60

McAfee, N. (2004) *Julia Kristeva*, Abingdon: Routledge

Mendes, K. (2015) *SlutWalk: Feminism, activism and media*, New York: Springer

Mendes, K., Ringrose, J. and Keeler, J. (2018) '#MeToo and the promise and pitfalls of challenging rape culture through digital feminism activism', *European Journal of Women's Studies* 25(2): 236-46

Mika, M. (2006) 'Framing the issue: Religion, secular ethics and the case of animal rights mobilization', *Social Forces* 85(2): 915-41

Millet, C (2001) *The sexual life of Catherine M*, New York: Grove Press

Miriam, K. (2012) 'Feminism, neoliberalism, and SlutWalk', *Feminist Studies* 38(1): 262-6

Moore, S. and Breeze, S. (2012) 'Spaces of male fear: The sexual politics of being watched', *British Journal of Criminology* 52: 1172-91

Morse, F. (2014) 'Man on a leash in Farringdon, London: Mystery of "walkies" solved: BDSM or a PR stunt? Neither, actually', *The Independent*, 15 April, www.independent.co.uk/news/uk/man-on-a-leash-in-farringdon-london-mystery-of-walkies-solved-9261062.html

Mort, F. (1995) 'Archaeologies of city life: Commercial culture, masculinity, and spatial relations in 1980s London', *Environment and Planning D: Society and Space* 13(5): 573-90

Munt, S. (1995) 'The lesbian *flâneur*', in D. Bell and G. Valentine (eds) *Mapping desire: Geographies of sexuality*, Abingdon: Routledge, 114-26

Musial, J. (2014) 'From "Madonna" to "whore": Sexuality, pregnancy and popular culture', *Sexualities* 17(4): 394-411

Newmahr, S. (2011) *Playing on the edge: Sadomasochism, risk, and intimacy*, Bloomington, IN: Indiana University Press

Noyes, J.K. (2004) 'Nomadism, nomadology and post-colonialism: By way of introduction', *Interventions* 6(2): 159-68

Ohlheiser, A. (2017) 'The woman behind "Me Too" knew the power of the phrase when she created it – 10 years ago', *The Washington Post*, 19 October, www.washingtonpost.com/news/the-intersect/wp/2017/10/19/the-woman-behind-me-too-knew-the-power-of-the-phrase-when-she-created-it-10-years-ago/?utm_term=.accc6093e5ad

O'Keefe, T. (2006) 'Menstrual blood as a weapon of resistance', *International Feminist Journal of Politics* 8(4): 535–56

O'Keefe, T. (2011) 'Flaunting our way to freedom? SlutWalks, gendered protest and feminist futures', in *New Agendas in Social Movement Studies*, November 2011, National University of Ireland Maynooth

O'Keefe,.T. (2014) 'My body is my manifesto! SlutWalk, FEMEN and femmenist protest', *Feminist Review* 107(1): 1–19

Okin, S.M. (1999) *Is multiculturalism bad for women?*, Princeton, NJ: Princeton University Press.

Oliver, K. (1993) 'Julia Kristeva's feminist revolutions', *Hypatia* 8(3): 94–114

Oliver, K. (2008–10) 'Julia Kristeva's maternal passions', *Journal of French and Francophone Philosophy* 18(1): 1–8

Oliver, K. (2010) 'Motherhood, sexuality, and pregnant embodiment: Twenty-five years of gestation', *Hypatia* 25(4): 760–76

Olney, M. (2015) 'Towards a socially responsible application of the criminal law to the problem of street harassment', *William and Mary Journal of Women and the Law* 22(1): 129–64

Omond, T. (2012) 'Lush's human performance art was about animal cruelty not titillation', *The Guardian*, 27 April, www.theguardian.com/commentisfree/2012/apr/27/lush-animal-cruelty-performance-art

Oriola, T. (2012) 'The Delta creeks, women's engagement and Nigeria's oil insurgency', *British Journal of Criminology* 52: 534–55

Owens, P. (2009) 'Reclaiming "bare life"? Against Agamben on refugees', *International Relations* 23(4): 567–82

Pace, L. (2005) 'Image events and PETA's Anti-Fur Campaign', *Women and Language* 28(2): 33–41

Pain, R. (1991) 'Space, sexual violence and social control: Integrating geographical and feminist analyses of women's fear of crime', *Progress in Human Geography* 15(4): 415–31

Pateman, C. (1995) *The disorder of women: Democracy, feminism and political theory*, Cambridge: Polity

Patton, P. (2000) *Deleuze and the political*, London and New York: Routledge

PETA (People for the Ethical Treatment of Animals) (no date) 'Why does PETA sometimes use nudity in its campaigns?', www.peta. org/about-peta/faq/why-does-peta-sometimes-use-nudity-in-its-campaigns

Pitagora, D. (2013) 'Consent vs coercion: BDSM interactions highlight a fine but immutable line', *The New School Psychology Bulletin* 10(1): 27-36

Poe, E.A. (2017 [1840] *The complete short stories of Edgar Allan Poe*, Musaicum Books

Pollock, G. (1988) *Vision and difference: Femininity, feminism and histories of art*, London: Routledge

Powell, A. (2008) 'Amor fati? Gender habitus and young people's negotiation of (hetero)sexual consent', *Journal of Sociology* 44(2): 167-84

Purcell, M. (2002) 'Excavating Lefebvre: The right to the city and its urban politics of the Inhabitant', *GeoJournal* 58: 99-108

Puwar, N. (2004) *Space invaders: Race, gender and bodies out of place*, Oxford: Berg

RAINN (Rape Abuse Incest National Network) (2014) 'Letter to White House Task Force to protect students from sexual assault', 28 February, https://rainn.org/images/03-2014/WH-Task-Force-RAINN-Recommendations.pdf

Reed, T.V. (2005) *The art of protest: Culture and activism from the Civil Rights movement to the streets of Seattle*, Minneapolis, MN: Minnesota University Press

Reestorff, C.M. (2014) 'Mediatised affective activism: The activist imaginary and the topless body in the Femen movement', *Convergence: The International Journal of Research into New Media Technologies* 20(4): 478-95

Rich, A. (1980) 'Compulsory heterosexuality and lesbian existence', *Signs: Journal of Women in Culture and Society* 5: 631-60

Rich, A. (1984) 'Notes towards a politics of location', in *Feminist postcolonial theory: A reader*, 29-42, http://people.unica.it/ fiorenzoiuliano/files/2014/10/Adrienne-Rich-Notes-Toward-a-Politics-of-Location.pdf

Rich, F. (2001) 'Naked capitalists', *New York Times*, 20 May, www. nytimes.com/2001/05/20/magazine/naked-capitalists.html

Robinson, A. (2010) 'In theory. Why Deleuze (still) matters: States, war-machines and radical transformations', *Ceasefire Magazine*, 10 September, https://ceasefiremagazine.co.uk/in-theory-deleuze-war-machine

Robson, S. (2014) 'Video: Bizarre scene as woman spotted taking man for walkies on dog lead in London street', *The Mirror*, 11 April, www.mirror.co.uk/news/woman-spotted-walking-man-dog-3400243

Rockefeller, S.A. (2011) 'Flow', *Current Anthropology* August, 52(4): 557-78

Root, R. and Browner, C.H. (2001) 'Practices of the resistant self: Compliance with and resistance to pre-natal norms', *Culture, Medicine and Society* 25: 195-223

Rosario, C. (2015) 'Animals and angels', *Performance Research* 20(2): 96-101

Roseman, E. (2013) '50 Shades of grey puts ebooks in the black', *The Star*, 1 January, www.thestar.com/business/2013/01/01/50_shades_of_grey_puts_ebooks_in_the_black.html

Rosenburg, O. (2012) 'Dozens of Israeli "SlutWalk" protesters hit streets of Jerusalem', *Haaretz*, 4 May, www.haaretz.com/israel-news/dozens-of-israeli-8216-slutwalk-protesters-hit-streets-of-jerusalem-1.428276

Rubin, G. (1984) 'Thinking sex: Notes for a radical theory of the politics of sexuality', in C. Vance (ed) *Pleasure and danger: Exploring female sexuality*, Boston, MA and London: Routledge & Keegan Paul, 143-78

Rubin, G. (1997) 'Elegy for the Valley of the Kings: AIDS and the Leather Community in San Francisco, 1981-1996', in J.H. Gangon, M.P. Levine and P.M. Nardi (eds) *In changing times: Gay men and lesbians encounter HIV/AIDS*, Chicago, IL: University of Chicago Press, 101-44

Russo, M. (1995) *The female grotesque: Risk, excess and modernity*, New York and London: Routledge

Segal, L. (1990) *Slow motion: Changing masculinities, changing men*, London: Virago

Sibley, D. (1988) 'Purification of space', *Environment and Planning D: Society and Space* 6: 409-21

Sibley, D. (1995) *Geographies of exclusion*, London: Routledge

Sibley, D. (1998) 'The problematic nature of exclusion', *Geoforum* 29(2): 119-21

Smith, M. (1994) 'Enhancing the quality of survey data on violence against women: A feminist approach', *Gender and Society* 8(1): 109-27

Soja, E. (2009) 'The city and spatial justice', *Spatial Justice*, 1 September, www.jssj.org/wp-content/uploads/2012/12/JSSJ1-1en4.pdf

Solnit, R. (2000) *Wanderlust: A history of walking*, London: Granta

Stanescu, J. (2012) 'Species trouble: Judith Butler, mourning and the precarious life of animals', *Hypatia* 27(3): 567-81

Stanko, E. (1990) *Everyday violence: How women and men experience sexual and physical danger*, London: Pandora

Stanko, E. (1996) 'Warnings to women: Police advice and women's safety in Britain', *Violence Against Women* 2: 5-24

Staples, B. (1986) 'Just walk on by: A black man ponders his power to alter public space', *Ms Magazine* 15(3): 1-2

Stevens Jr, P. (2006) 'Women's aggressive use of genital power in Africa', *Transcultural Psychiatry* 43(4): 592-9

Storr, M. (2003) *Latex and lingerie: Shopping for pleasure at Ann Summers parties*, London: Bloomsbury Academic

Stotzer, R.L. (2009) 'Violence against transgender people: A review of United States data', *Aggression and Violent Behavior* 14(3): 170-9

Tester, K. (1994) 'Introduction: The *flâneur*', *Social Theory* 23: 1-22

Thrift, N. (2004) 'Driving in the city', *Theory, Culture & Society* 21(4-5): 41-5

Tomazos, K., O'Gorman, K. and MacLaren, A. (2017) 'From leisure to tourism: How BDSM demonstrates the transition of deviant pursuits to mainstream products', *Tourism Management* 1-23

Tsaros, A. (2013) 'Consensual non-consent: Comparing E.L. James's *Fifty shades of grey* and Pauline Réage's *Story of O*', *Sexualities* 16(8): 864-79

Tuerkheimer, D. (1997) 'Street harassment as sexual subordination: The phenomenology of gender-specific harm', *Wisconsin Women's Law Journal* 12: 167-8

Turner, T.E. and Brownhill, L.S. (2004) 'Why women are at war with Chevron: Nigerian subsistence struggles against the international oil industry', *Journal of Asian and African Studies* 39(1/2): 63-93

Turner, V.W. (1967) *The forest of symbols: Aspects of Ndembu ritual*, Ithaca, NY: Cornell University Press

Tuzin, D.F. (1978) 'Sex and meat-eating in Ilhata', *Canberra Anthropology* 1(3): 82-93

Tyler, I. (2000) 'Reframing pregnant embodiment', in S. Ahmed (ed) *Transformations: Thinking through feminism*, London: Psychology Press, 288-303

Tyler, I. (2008) '"Chav mum, chav scum": Class, disgust in contemporary Britain', *Feminist Media Studies* 89(1): 17-34

Tyler, I. (2011) 'Pregnant beauty: Maternal femininities under neoliberalism', in R. Gill and C. Schaffer (eds) *New femininities: Postfeminism, neoliberalism and subjectivity*, London: Palgrave Macmillan, 21-36

Tyler, I. (2013) 'Naked protest: the maternal politics of citizenship and revolt', *Citizenship Studies* 17(2): 211-26

Ussher, J.M. (2006) *Managing the monstrous feminine: Regulating the reproductive body*, Hove: Routledge

Vasagar, J. and Parfitt, T. (2013) 'Bemused Vladimir Putin and Angela Merkel confronted by topless Femen protester in Hanover', *The Telegraph*, 8 April, www.telegraph.co.uk/news/worldnews/vladimir-putin/9978447/Bemused-Vladimir-Putin-and-Angela-Merkel-confronted-by-topless-Femen-protester-in-Hanover.html

Volpp, L. (2000) 'Blaming culture for bad behaviour', *Yale Journal of Law and the Humanities* 12: 89

Wallace, A. (2007) 'Public humiliation that was all too familiar during Troubles', *Belfast Telegraph*, 28 August, www.belfasttelegraph.co.uk/news/public-humiliation-that-was-all-too-familiar-during-troubles-28397271.html

Wearing, B. and Wearing, S. (1996) 'Refocussing the tourist experience: The *flâneur* and the choraster', *Leisure Studies* 15(4): 229-43

Weiss, M. (2006) 'Mainstreaming kink: The politics of BDSM representation in US popular culture', in P.J. Kleinplatz and C. Moser (eds) *Sadomasochism: Powerful pleasures*, New York: Harrington Park Press, 103-32

Weiss, M. (2009) '"Rumsfeld!" Consensual BDSM and "sadomasochistic" torture at Abu Ghraib', in E. Lewin and W. Leap (eds) *Out in public: Reinventing lesbian/gay anthropology in a globalizing world*, Malden, MA: Blackwell, 180-201

Weiss, M. (2011) *Techniques of pleasure: BDSM and the circuits of sexuality*, Durham, NC and London: Duke University Press

Weizman, E. (2006) 'The art of war: Deleuze, Guattari, Debord and the Israeli defense force', *InterActivist Info Exchange*, 3 August, www.metamute.org/editorial/articles/art-war-deleuze-guattari-debord-and-israeli-defence-force

Wenger-Trayner, E. and Wenger-Trayner, B. (2015) 'Communities of practice: A brief introduction', http://wenger-trayner.com/wp-content/uploads/2015/04/07-Brief-introduction-to-communities-of-practice.pdf

Werner, J.V. (2001) 'The detective gaze: Edgar A. Poe, the *flâneur*, and the physiognomy of crime', *American Transcendental Quarterly* 15(1): 5-21

White, C. (2006) 'The Spanner trials and the changing law on sadomasochism in the UK', *Journal of Homosexuality* 50(2-3): 167-87

White, J. (2007) *London in the 19th century*, London: Vintage

Wignall, L. and McCormack, M. (2017) 'An exploratory study of a new kink activity: "Pup play"', *Archives of Sexual Behaviour* 46(3): 801-11

Wilkinson, E. (2009) 'Perverting visual pleasure: Representing sadomasochism', *Sexualities* 12(2): 181-98

Wilson, E. (1991) *The sphinx in the city: Urban life, the control of disorder, and women*, London: University of California

Wood, F. (2005) '"What happens [in Vegas]": Performing the post-tourist *flâneur* in "New York" and "Paris"', *Text and Performance Quarterly* 25(4): 315-33

Wrenn, C.L. (2015) 'The role of professionalization regarding female exploitation in the nonhuman animal rights movement', *Journal of Gender Studies* 24(2): 131-46

Wuthnow, J. (2002) 'Deleuze in the postcolonial: On nomads and indigenous politics', *Feminist Theory* 3(2): 183-200

Wyckoff, J. (2014) 'Linking sexism and speciesism', *Hypatia* 29(4): 721-37

Young, I.M. (1980) 'Throwing like a girl: A phenomenology of feminine body comportment, motility, and spatiality', *Human Studies* 3 (2): 137-56

Young, I.M. (1984) 'Pregnant embodiment: Subjectivity and alienation', *The Journal of Medicine and Philosophy* 9: 45-61

Young, I.M. (2005) *On female body experience: Throwing like a girl and other essays*, Oxford: Oxford University Press

Zarkov, D. and Davis, K. (2018) 'Ambiguities and dilemmas around #MeToo: #ForHow Long and #WhereTo?', *European Journal of Women's Studies* 25(1): 3-9

Zychowicz, J. (2011) 'Two bad words: Femen and feminism in Independent Ukraine', *Anthropology of East Europe Review* 29(2): 215-27

Zychowicz, J. (2015) 'Performing protest: Femen, nation and the marketing of resistance', *Journal of Ukrainian Politics and Society* 1(1): 74-104

Index

Page references for notes are followed by n

and rape culture 123, 124, 125, 141, 144, 146
and status 115, 124, 128-9, 131, 138-40, 141
and stigma 118, 122, 146
and the criminal justice system 117-18
and the mainstream 6, 26, 111, 113, 116-17, 118, 121-3, 145, 165
and transgression 123, 134, 137, 138-40, 146
and violence 96, 111, 129, 137, 139
as community 26, 112, 114-16, 124, 134, 139, 143, 144
as political 112
as subculture 26, 141-5
body-shaming 124-5, 140
diversity in 113, 114, 121-2
edgework 96
ethics of 116, 124, 129, 138-9, 141, 143, 144, 145
hierarchy 115, 124, 128, 131-2, 138-40, 144
munches 113, 115, 131, 173n
power dynamics 96, 138-40
punishment *see also* the ban, the pillory, 134, 139-40, 142, 145
register of abusers 138-9, 141-4, 166
representations of 113
kink tourism 119-22, 121
commodification 120, 121
simulacra 119-20
Koskela, Hille 65
Kristeva, Julia 15, 23, 44-8, 153
and psychoanalysis 46
essentialism 46
symbolic and semiotic 45-6
Woman's Time 45-6, 47

L

Las Vegas 111
laughter 7, 28, 57-8, 95, 136
Lave, Jean and Wenger, Etienne 115
Lefebvre, Henri 3
liminality 22, 74
Lolita 78
London 1, 2, 80-1, 104-5, 111, 121, 139, 149, 151
Farringdon 1, 4, 28, 165
Kensington Olympia 165
Trafalgar Square 71, 81, 87, 106, 107, 108, 149
Lorde, Audre 149, 162, 166
Lugones , Maria 91, 147
Lush 25, 91, 99, 100, 103, 108
and violence 106
brand 91
campaigns 92-3, 97-8

magazines 33, 37
see also social media

M

machinism 19-20
of kink 115, 142
male gaze 37-8
masturbation 49, 63, 140
meat 88-9, 91
and capitalism 89
cross-cultural meaning of 89-90
micro-aggressions 53, 55, 56
molecular revolution 23, 25, 153, 156, 162, 166, 167
Moore, Demi 33
mothering 67, 73-4

N

nakedness 34, 72, 86, 97, 108
as compared to nudity 34, 39
in protest 72, 97
naked curse, the 74-5, 83-4, 108, 133, 171n
and Chevron 74-5
nation 76, 108
neoliberalism 20, 26, 81, 149
Newmahr, Staci 122, 125, 146
nomadism 21, 101
critiques of 21
non-human animal rights protests 25, 71, 73, 85, 92, 95, 102
and rape culture 97
commercialisation of 91
gendering of 98
role of men 87, 98
use of humiliation 94, 96-7, 98
use of violence 94, 108
normalisation 6, 14, 47-8, 56, 65, 80, 142, 145
and masculinity 108
and striation 7, 12, 45, 51, 83, 145
beauty norms 34, 42, 77, 80, 125, 160
common sense 66, 152, 153, 167
of social injustice 4, 56
of uses of space 2, 8, 12, 87
propriety 23
nudity 39
see also nakedness

O

obscenity 58
outsider 68, 90, 146, 153, 162-4

P

pain 97
patriarchy 64, 82, 88, 90, 99